Preparing Teachers for the Early Childhood Classroom

Preparing Teachers for the Early Childhood Classroom

Proven Models and Key Principles

edited by

Susan B. Neuman, Ed.D.
University of Michigan
Ann Arbor, Michigan

and

Michael L. Kamil, Ph.D.
Stanford University
Stanford, California

·P·A·U·L·H·
BROOKES
PUBLISHING CO.®

Baltimore • London • Sydney

Paul H. Brookes Publishing Co.
Post Office Box 10624
Baltimore, Maryland 21285-0624
USA
www.brookespublishing.com

"Paul H. Brookes Publishing Co." is a registered trademark
of Paul H. Brookes Publishing Co., Inc.

Typeset by Broad Books, Baltimore, Maryland.
Manufactured in the United States of America by
Versa Press, Inc., East Peoria, Illinois.

The individuals described in this book are composites based on the authors' actual experiences.
In all instances, names and identifying details have been changed to protect confidentiality.

Library of Congress Cataloging-in-Publication Data

Preparing teachers for the early childhood classroom : proven models and key principles / edited by
    Susan B. Neuman and Michael L. Kamil.
        p.   cm.
    Includes bibliographical references and index.
    ISBN-13: 978-1-59857-081-6 (pbk.)
    ISBN-10: 1-59857-081-1 (pbk.)
    1. Early childhood teachers—Training of—United States.   2. Early childhood educators—United
    States. I. Neuman, Susan B.   II. Kamil, Michael L.   III. Title.

LB1732.3.P73 2010
370.71'1—dc22   2010018869

British Library Cataloguing in Publication data are available from the British Library.

2014   2013   2012   2011   2010

10   9   8   7   6   5   4   3   2   1

Contents

About the Editors vii
Contributors ix
Foreword   *Dorothy S. Strickland* xv
Preface xix
Acknowledgments xxi

1   A Comprehensive Perspective on Early Childhood:
    Educator Professional Development
    Michael L. Kamil 1

**I   Who Are Early Childhood Educators: Understanding the
    Needs, Challenges, and Opportunities** 17

2   Emerging Research on Early Childhood
    Professional Development
    *Martha Zaslow, Kathryn Tout, Tamara Halle, Jessica E. Vick
    Whittaker, and Bridget Lavelle* 19

3   Beyond Babysitting: Challenges and Opportunities in
    Early Childhood Education
    Shira M. Peterson and Constance Valk 49

II   What Practices Are Promising **65**

4   Choosing Content
    Richard G. Lambert, Annette Sibley, Robert Lawrence 67

5   Coaching: It's Not Just for Little League
    *Sarah Jo Sandefur, Amye R. Warren, Anne B. Gamble,
    Jenny M. Holcombe, and Heather K. Hicks* 87

6   Mentoring: More Than a Promising Strategy
    Annette Sibley, Robert Lawrence, and Richard G. Lambert 105

7   Participatory Action Research: An Effective Methodology
    for Promoting Community-Based Professional Development
    Amy C. Baker and Shira M. Peterson 123

III   Where Does Professional Development Occur? **135**

8   Professional Development in the Community College Setting
      Susan M. Doescher and Jennifer Knapp Beudert 137

9   Professional Development in Training Programs
      *Jacqueline Hawkins, Courtney Crim, Jenifer Thornton,
      and Amye R. Warren* 151

10 Professional Development in Culturally Diverse Settings
      Renee Rubin, John A. Sutterby, and James V. Hoffman 163

IV   When to Do It and How to Know It's Working **173**

11 Beyond How Much: What We Are
      Learning About Structuring Effective Early
      Childhood Professional Development
      *Tamara Halle, Martha Zaslow, Kathryn Tout, Rebecca Starr,
      Julia Wessel, and Meagan McSwiggan* 175

12 Measuring Early Childhood Educators' Instructional
      Practices and Interactions
      *Amye R. Warren, Jenny M. Holcombe, Sarah Jo Sandefur, Anne B.
      Gamble, and Heather K. Hicks* 189

13 Online Logs: A Tool to Monitor Fidelity of Implementation
      in Large-Scale Interventions
      Tanya S. Wright 207

14 The Research We Have; The Research We Need
      Susan B. Neuman 221

Glossary 237
Index 243

About the Editors

Susan B. Neuman, Ed.D., Professor of Educational Studies, School of Education, University of Michigan, 610 East University Avenue, Ann Arbor, Michigan 48109

Dr. Neuman is a professor in educational studies, specializing in early literacy development. Previously, she served as the U.S. Assistant Secretary of Elementary and Secondary Education. She is especially proud of her work in establishing the Early Reading First program and the Early Childhood Professional Development Education Program and enhancing accountability efforts to improve children's achievement. At the University of Michigan, she has directed the Center for the Improvement of Early Reading Achievement, focusing on early childhood policy, curriculum, and early reading instruction in prekindergarten through Grade 3. Dr. Neuman is Director of the Michigan Research Program on Ready to Learn, which includes projects working to change the odds for children in poverty.

Michael L. Kamil, Ph.D., Consulting Professor of Psychological Studies in Education, Stanford University School of Education, 123 Cubberley Hall, 485 Lasuen Mall, Stanford, California 94305

Dr. Kamil conducts research in literacy and the effects of technology on literacy and the acquisition of literacy. He has been a member of the National Reading Panel and the National Literacy Panel, reflecting his interest in both first and second language learners. He is currently an advisor to the Early Childhood Educator Professional Development Program for the U.S. Department of Education.

Contributors

Amy C. Baker, M.A., Clinical Associate, Children's Institute, Inc., University of Rochester, 274 North Goodman Street, Suite D103, Rochester, New York 14607. Ms. Baker's research explores the quality of caregiver–parent–child relationships in child care settings, with an emphasis on the emotional well-being of infants and toddlers. She is coauthor (with Lynn A. Manfredi-Petitt) of two books for practitioners: *Circle of Love: Relationships between Parents, Providers and Children in Family Child Ca*re (Redleaf Press, 2002) and *Relationships, the Heart of Quality Care: Creating Community Among Adults in Early Care Settings* (National Association for the Education of Young Children, 2004).

Jennifer Knapp Beudert, M.S., Manager, University of Notre Dame's Robinson Community Learning Center, 921 North Eddy Street, South Bend, Indiana 46617. Ms. Beudert served as Associate Coordinator of the Early Education Partnership program (a Linn-Benton Community College program) from the earliest planning stages through completion. She taught classes in early literacy, early childhood curriculum, and child development and coordinated the early childhood lab school for the Education/Child and Family Studies Department. Ms. Beudert holds two master's degrees from Bank Street College of Education in early childhood and elementary education and in early childhood educational leadership.

Courtney Crim, Ed.D., Education Department, Trinity University, 1 Trinity Place, San Antonio, Texas 78212. Dr. Crim's research interests focus on differentiated instruction and how it relates to the classroom as well as professional development design for both preservice and in-service teachers. This line of research explores how the practice of differentiated instruction links to programmatic changes and the development of transformative leadership in the field of education.

Susan M. Doescher, Ph.D., Department Chair, Education/Child and Family Studies Department, Linn-Benton Community College (LBCC), 6500 Pacific Boulevard SW, Albany, Oregon 97321. Dr. Doescher served as the director of the LBCC Early Education Partnership program, an Early Childhood Educator Professional Development project that provided professional development to early childhood educators in two counties. She earned her doctorate in child development from Oregon State University, and her 25 years of teaching and research has encompassed the areas of children's social-emotional development and early childhood professional development. She is the coauthor of *Case Studies in Early Childhood Education: Implementing Developmentally Appropriate Practices* (with Rachel Ozretich, Linda Burt, & Martha Foster; Merrill, 2009).

Anne B. Gamble, M.Ed., Director, Project Ready for School, University of Tennessee at Chattanooga, Department 4254, 615 McCallie Avenue, Chattanooga, Tennessee 37403. Ms. Gamble, an early childhood educator for more than 35 years, has served as Co-director of two Early Childhood Educator Professional Development grants (Early SUCCESS and Project REEL) at the University of Tennessee at Chattanooga. Currently director of a United Way–led community initiative, Project Ready for School, she has directed a university child development center and taught at the preschool, elementary, and college level.

Tamara Halle, Ph.D., Co-director of Early Childhood Research, Child Trends, 4301 Connecticut Avenue NW, Suite 350, Washington, DC 20008. Dr. Halle's research interests include children's early cognitive and social development, early care and education, family and community supports for school readiness, and school characteristics associated with ongoing achievement and positive development. Her recent work focuses especially on early literacy development among English language learning children and evaluations of early childhood curricula, programs, and professional development aimed at supporting children's school readiness.

Jacqueline Hawkins, Ed.D., Associate Dean, Institutional Effectiveness and Outreach, University of Houston, 160 Farish Hall, 2400 Calhoun Road, Houston, Texas 77204. Dr. Hawkins's professional efforts focus on developing appropriate instruction and social skills development for all children in public schools. Her primary goal is to prepare educators with the skills and dispositions to respond to the unique needs of the variety of children who will enter their classrooms.

Heather K. Hicks, M.Ed., Strengthening Families Network Coordinator, Signal Centers, Tennessee Child Care Resources and Referral Network, 109 North Germantown Road, Chattanooga, Tennessee 37411. Ms. Hicks served as Project Manager for an Early Childhood Educator Professional Development Department of Education grant for Project REEL (Resources for Early Childhood Educators).

James V. Hoffman, Ph.D., Professor of Language and Literacy Studies, The University of Texas at Austin, SZB 406 College of Education, Austin, Texas

78712. Dr. Hoffman directs the reading specialization program at The University of Texas at Austin. This program was featured as part of the International Reading Association's "Prepared to Make a Difference" study. Dr. Hoffman's research interests focus on teaching and teacher education in the area of literacy.

Jenny M. Holcombe, M.S., Adjunct Faculty Member, Department of Psychology # 2803, University of Tennessee at Chattanooga, 615 McCallie Avenue, Chattanooga, Tennessee 37403. Ms. Hallcombe is a doctoral student in the Research Evaluation and Measurement Program at the University of Tennessee in Knoxville and an adjunct faculty member at the University of Tennessee at Chattanooga. She was Evaluation Coordinator and Data Manager for two Early Childhood Educator Professional Development projects (Early SUCCESS and Project REEL), focusing her efforts on the development and analysis of measures of teacher practice. Her research interests include instrument development and evaluation of training programs.

Richard G. Lambert, Ph.D., Professor, University of North Carolina, Charlotte, 280 College of Education Building, Charlotte, North Carolina 28223. Dr. Lambert teaches statistics and research methods to graduate students in the College of Education at the University of North Carolina, Charlotte. His research interests include evaluating the quality of programs for young children, teacher stress and coping, and applied statistics.

Bridget Lavelle, M.S., Ph.D. Precandidate in Public Policy and Sociology, Department of Sociology, University of Michigan, 3001 LSA Building, Ann Arbor, Michigan 48109. Ms. Lavelle is a doctoral student in Public Policy and Sociology at the University of Michigan and a trainee at the University of Michigan's Population Studies Center. Her research focuses on economic insecurity and its effects on the well-being of American families.

Robert Lawrence, Ph.D., Assistant Professor, Mercer University, 3001 Mercer University Drive, Atlanta, Georgia 30341. Dr. Lawrence is a member of the graduate faculty in the Tift College of Education at Mercer University, where he teaches courses in research methods, teacher leadership, and school philosophy. Prior to joining the Mercer faculty in 2008, Dr. Lawrence was Director of Special Projects, Research, and Accountability for the Georgia Department of Early Care and Learning and Director of the Georgia Head Start State Collaboration Office. His primary research interests are in the area of evaluating the characteristics of "teacher effectiveness" in elementary school teachers.

Meagan McSwiggan, Research Assistant, Child Trends, 4301 Connecticut Avenue NW, Suite 350, Washington, DC 20008. Ms. McSwiggan is a research assistant in the early childhood development area at Child Trends, a nonprofit children's research organization in Washington, D.C. She is interested in mother–infant attachment relationships and early social and emotional development. She plans to pursue a Ph.D. in clinical psychology.

Shira M. Peterson, Ph.D., Research Associate, Children's Institute, Inc., University of Rochester, 274 North Goodman Street, Suite D103, Rochester, New York 14607. Dr. Peterson conducts research on early educator professional development, with a focus on creating emotionally supportive language and literacy environments for young children. She has published articles on preschool classroom discourse and on science as a means of promoting early literacy. Her recent work investigates the readiness to change of early educators enrolled in professional development programs.

Renee Rubin, Ed.D., Associate Professor of Literacy, University of Texas at Brownsville, 80 Fort Brown, Brownsville, Texas 78520. Dr. Rubin served as Co-principal Investigator for an Early Childhood Educator Professional Development Program grant along the Texas–Mexico border. Her major research interests are literacy and English language learners.

Sarah Jo Sandefur, Ph.D., UC Foundation Associate Professor of Literacy Education, Teacher Preparation Academy, The University of Tennessee at Chattanooga, 651 McCallie Avenue, Department 4154, Chattanooga, Tennessee 37403. Dr. Sandefur codirected two Early Childhood Educator Professional Development Program grants: Early SUCCESS in 2002 and Project REEL in 2005. Her current research includes examining the role of professional development in integrating literacy and science content in early childhood environments.

Annette Sibley, Ph.D., President, Quality Assist, Inc., 17 Executive Park Drive, Suite 150, Atlanta, Georgia 30329. Dr. Sibley has extensive experience in research and program evaluation, training, and technical assistance. Dr. Sibley is coauthor of the *Assessment Profile for Early Childhood Programs* and the *Assessment Profile for Family Child Care Homes* (both with Martha Abbott-Shim; Quality Assist, 1987). She developed a professional designation system for technical assistance consultants and has established numerous intensive professional development programs for a variety of early childhood education settings, including the Partners in Quality Mentor Course, Art of Technical Assistance, and the Challenging Teachers Institute.

Rebecca Starr, Ph.D., Research Scientist, Child Trends, 615 First Avenue NE, Suite 225, Minneapolis, Minnesota 55413. Dr. Starr earned her doctorate in child psychology from the University of Minnesota in 2004. She has been a research scientist at Child Trends since 2007; she works on projects examining the quality of early care and education settings and the effects on children's developmental outcomes.

John A. Sutterby, Ph.D., Associate Professor, University of Texas at Brownsville (UTB), 80 Fort Brown, Brownsville, Texas 78520. Dr. Sutterby's scholarly research interests include outdoor play environments, bilingual education, and early childhood education. Dr. Sutterby served as Project Director of the UTB Early Childhood Educator Professional Development Program grant. He is currently editor of *Advances in Early Education and Day Care.*

Jenifer Thornton, Ed.D., Assistant Professor, University of Texas at San Antonio (UTSA), 1 UTSA Circle, San Antonio, Texas 78249. Dr. Thornton is a former early childhood and elementary classroom teacher who has taught in both general education and inclusive classroom settings. Her interest areas focus on differentiated instructional practices and effective professional development models for in-service and preservice early childhood and elementary educators, particularly in the area of mathematics and differentiated instruction.

Kathryn Tout, Ph.D., Codirector of Early Childhood Research, Child Trends, 615 First Avenue NE, Suite 225, Minneapolis, Minnesota 55413. Dr. Tout oversees projects in Child Trends's Minnesota office. Her research focuses on policies and programs to improve the quality of early care and education and families' access to quality settings. She also conducts research on programs to improve the quality and effectiveness of the early childhood work force.

Constance Valk, M.S.Ed., Clinical Associate for Psychology, Children's Institute, 274 North Goodman Street, Suite D103, Rochester, New York 14607. Formerly the Director of Early Childhood for the Rochester City School District, Ms. Valk was Children's Institute's Lead Mentor for the Early Childhood Educator Professional Development Program grant. She is presently the coordinator of Pathways: National Early Education and Care Accreditation.

Jessica E. Vick Whittaker, Ph.D., Research Associate, University of Virginia, Post Office Box 400878, Charlottesville, Virginia 22904. Dr. Vick Whittaker is a developmental psychologist whose research focuses on the measurement of quality in early childhood settings and the development and evaluation of early childhood interventions aimed at improving teacher practices and child outcomes. She is currently overseeing the My Teaching Partner—Math/Science project, designed to examine the effects of a math and science intervention on children's learning.

Amye R. Warren, Ph.D., Patricia Draper Obear Distinguished Teaching Professor, University of Tennessee at Chattanooga, Department of Psychology #2803, 615 McCallie Avenue, Chattanooga, Tennessee 37403. Dr. Warren served as a co-principal investigator for two Early Childhood Educator Professional Development Program grants (Early SUCCESS and Project REEL), providing expertise in language development and program evaluation. She has published work on many topics under the broad heading of language development, including the relation between phonological awareness and early reading achievement, the effects of various forms of speech to children, the development of pragmatic skills, and theories of language acquisition.

Julia Wessel, Research Assistant, Early Childhood Development, Child Trends, 4301 Connecticut Avenue NW, Suite 350, Washington, DC 20008. Ms. Wessel graduated from Kenyon College in 2008 with a B.A. in psychology and anthropology. Currently, she is a research assistant at Child Trends, a nonprofit children's research organization in Washington, D.C., where she focuses on early childhood education and education policy. She hopes to pursue a degree in social work or public policy.

Tanya S. Wright, M.A., Doctoral Student, School of Education, University of Michigan, 610 East University Avenue, Room 3117B, Ann Arbor, Michigan 48109. Ms. Wright received her master of arts degree as a reading specialist from Teachers College, Columbia University, and her bachelor of arts degree from Columbia College, Columbia University. She is a former kindergarten teacher whose research interests include instruction and professional development in early childhood language and literacy.

Martha Zaslow, Ph.D., Director, Office for Policy and Communications, Society for Research in Child Development, and Senior Scholar, Child Trends, 4301 Connecticut Avenue NW, Washington, DC 20008. Dr. Zaslow is a developmental psychologist whose work focuses on quality in early care and education and the evaluation of approaches to improve quality, with a particular focus on approaches to improving quality through professional development.

Foreword

WHY PROFESSIONAL DEVELOPMENT FOR EARLY CHILDHOOD TEACHERS IS SO IMPORTANT

The need for highly capable teachers is a constant theme in the literature on early childhood education. National reports and government mandates have raised expectations for the formal education and training of early childhood teachers, especially in Head Start and in state-funded prekindergarten programs (U.S. Department of Health and Human Services, 2003). Rising expectations coupled with an expanding number of early childhood programs have led to serious challenges in staffing, both in terms of the number of early childhood teachers needed and in the quality of their preparation. Ironically, the research that supports increased attention to early childhood education (Barnett, 2002) is based on high-quality programmatic efforts that are often hard to duplicate when there is pressure to engage in large-scale implementation.

While increased expectations apply to all aspects of early education, it is particularly true in the area of early literacy. Today's early childhood teachers are expected to implement more challenging and effective curricula in language and literacy and to assess and document progress in increasingly complex ways (National Research Council, 2001). Teachers of young children need to know the importance of oral language competencies, early literacy experiences, and family literacy in learning to read. They need to demonstrate their ability to foster a wide range of language- and literacy-related dispositions and competencies, including a love of literacy and the development of vocabulary, oral language abilities, phonological awareness, and print-related knowledge. They must show competence in the use of a variety of instructional methods that are age and developmentally appropriate and in the ability to adjust those methods to the specific needs of individuals. They must be skilled in the ability to use multiple methods of monitoring children's literacy development and interpreting assessments in order to make sound instructional decisions (Strickland & Riley-Ayers, 2007).

In order to develop these competencies, schools of education must provide preservice programs that are grounded in current scientific knowledge about young children's overall development, how they learn to read and write, and the best instructional practices to help them learn. Obviously, it is not possible to offer prospective teachers all the knowledge they need in even the most rigorous preservice programs. The need for ongoing professional development is critical. Like other professional fields, the knowledge base for learning and teaching is strengthened on the job, as new knowledge is gained and meshed with old. In today's world, teacher education is viewed as an ongoing process involving rigorous preservice training with meaningful experiential opportunities that are supported and strengthened with continued professional development.

WHY THIS BOOK IS SO IMPORTANT

Coupled with the recognition of the importance of high-quality professional development programs is the need for research to inform and guide the decision making required to plan, implement, and sustain them. Neuman and Kamil have assembled the work of an outstanding group of researchers who have done just that. The wide range of topics explored are those that policy makers and practitioners must address as they design credible and successful long-term teacher education.

The book starts with a close examination of key areas of interest and challenges to the early childhood profession. Challenges related to the human and social capital of early educators, the effectiveness of institutions in providing professional development, outcomes in key domains of development, and the overall quality of children's experiences are described, along with the research evidence on how they have been addressed successfully. Specific models for developing teacher expertise and providing sources of teacher support are the basis of several research efforts included in this book. Models of coaching and mentoring are carefully examined to provide information about evidence-based approaches.

Of great importance to practitioners and researchers is an examination of strategies designed to monitor progress in field-based interventions. Designing methods of assessment that truly measure desired outcomes is important both for the participants involved in the models described, as well as those who use the results of these studies to design future research. Another critical aspect of much of the research included is the attention paid to adapting models and strategies to diverse teacher populations and to different cultural, linguistic, and geographic contexts.

Without question, this book is an invaluable resource for those charged with planning, implementing, and monitoring evidence-based early childhood programs. While the focus is largely on the work of early childhood teachers, it is clear that the findings have implications for all those who work in early childhood settings, whether they work as administrators, supervisors, teachers, or education support personnel. Early childhood directors in state departments of education, who are required to plan large-scale professional development efforts, will also find the material invaluable. At a time when early childhood education is gaining increased recognition and respect as a critical part of the nation's educational infrastructure, this book provides much needed information to move the field forward.

Dorothy S. Strickland, Ph.D.
Samuel DeWitt Proctor Professor of Education Emerita
Rutgers, The State University of New Jersey

REFERENCES

Barnett, W.S. (2002). Preschool education for economically disadvantaged children: Effects on reading achievement and related outcomes. In S. Neuman & D.K. Dickinson (Eds.), *Handbook of early literacy research* (pp. 421–443). New York: Guilford.

National Research Council. (2001). *Report of the Committee on Early Childhood Pedagogy Commission on Behavioral and Social Sciences and Education.* Washington, DC: Author.

Strickland, D.S., & Riley-Ayers, S. (2007). *Literacy leadership in early childhood.* New York: Teachers College Press and National Association for the Education of Young Children.

U.S. Department of Health and Human Services, Office of the Assistant Secretary for Planning and Evaluation. (2003). *Strengthening Head Start: What the evidence shows.* Washington, DC: Author.

Preface

Thinking back on my years as U.S. Assistant Secretary of Elementary and Secondary Education, 2001–2003, nothing gives me greater pleasure than to have contributed to what was then a small research program, the Early Childhood Educator Professional Development Program—a "little diamond in the rough" targeted to improving professional development in early education. The program was designed with a highly focused theory of action: namely to improve the quality of early education by enhancing the knowledge and skills of educators who worked in high-poverty communities. It was virtually the only program at the time that was focused on the needs of very young children, research-based, collaborative with other community-based organizations, and highly accountable for children's school readiness skills in the U.S. Department of Education.

The program had great potential, but it needed a stronger focus on evaluation. In contrast to Early Reading First, a research-based service program that I also helped develop, the Early Childhood Educator Professional Development Program was designed to be broad scaled with well-designed evaluation models that could be replicable, affordable, and scalable across other areas in the country. It was with this goal that I asked my good colleague, Michael Kamil, to join us in helping programs to buttress their designs, to better ensure that the monies spent would yield evidence that could essentially move the field toward better professional development programs.

As is evident in the chapters that follow, he fulfilled his promise—and more so. In the initial years of the program, professional development resided primarily in higher education institutions, with early childhood educators participating in college courses as the chief means of training. Nevertheless, an emerging body of evidence from these evaluations began to recognize the constraints and challenges of having only a one-size-fits-all approach. Programs responded by broadening the range of professional development activities. Recognizing the needs and challenges for the field of early childhood educators, programs began to use more practice-sensitive approaches. Among these alternatives were coaching, mentoring, and other forms of individualized intervention that were better tailored to the professional development of these educators in the wide array of early childhood programs.

As a result, readers will recognize throughout the chapters some central characteristics of these early childhood professional development programs. All are high-quality, sustained, and intensive. Programs focus on research-based strategies that provide developmentally appropriate instruction targeted to content-rich standards-based instruction. Progress monitoring and accountability using innovative tools for collecting information are threaded throughout each program. Rigorous evaluation approaches that recognize the special characteristics of the community are used. Programs highlight experimental and quasi-experimental designs.

As a result, today, unlike before, we can now make important causal statements about the effects of professional development on teacher quality and children's achievement. And what we know is this: When high-quality professional development is well targeted to the educators for whom it's designed, teacher quality improves and children's achievement accelerates. We have the evidence to make a difference.

Building on the work that each project contributed, we held an historic meeting at the University of Michigan, Ann Arbor, in 2008 to begin to develop a consensus of "what works." With the able assistance of Program Officer Rosemary Fennell, Michael and I invited representatives from some of the most exciting programs, primarily selected from the years 2006 and beyond, to contribute their findings and to highlight key take-away messages that might help policy makers in states, researchers, and practitioners develop programs. We needed to represent both community-based initiatives and higher education efforts, programs targeted to family child care and center-based care, programs that worked in high-poverty communities that spanned the country and that represented constitute voices seldom heard. As each program detailed its approaches, methodological strategies, and results, we found striking consistencies across data, leading to a consensus of factors that enhanced professional development and impact across a broad array of programs.

These are programs and projects that we highlight throughout this book. The book is organized with several key messages to keep in mind. In Section I, we highlight the needs, challenges, and opportunities for early childhood professional development. Given the issues that are raised, it becomes clear that we cannot merely apply the professional development models traditionally used in K–2 education to the early childhood profession. Subsequent Sections II and III emphasize alternative models, approaches that represent a better fit for the field. In each chapter, the authors highlight key take-away messages emphasizing practice-sensitive approaches that are widely scalable. Last, in Section IV we describe innovative tools for measuring progress and change, recognizing that accountability is the lynchpin that underlies quality improvements in education.

Together this research emphasizes that quality teaching is no accident. As William A. Foster once recognized, "It is always the result of high intention, sincere effort, intelligent direction and skillful execution." This is our charge to the profession in early childhood, and this is now our time of opportunity.

Acknowledgments

This book could not have come about without the heart, soul, and sheer intelligence of Rosemary Fennell, our project officer of the Early Childhood Educator Professional Development Program at the U.S. Department of Education. Rosemary has been dedicated to ensuring that children receive the highest quality practices from expert early childhood educators, recognizing that quality teaching has an enormous influence in children's lives. We owe her a tremendous debt of thanks for helping us connect with other professionals involved in this important work.

In addition, we sincerely appreciate the advice and guidance of Sarah Shepke at Paul H. Brookes Publishing Co. Sarah is an exceptional editor—thoughtful, wise, and forward thinking. This publication benefited tremendously from her talents and those of her team of editors.

Our book is a result of a 2-day workshop, bringing together the top scholars in the field of professional development in early childhood. We could not have been successful without the efforts of Colleen Neilson, who made the logistics of the conference look so easy and effortless, and the graduate students at the University of Michigan, including Rachel Schachter, Tanya Wright, Serene Koh, Julie Dwyer, and Christine Meyer, who observed, commented, and summarized the activities so deliberately and thoughtfully. Finally, we thank all the contributors to our volume. In their work to enhance the professional lives of early childhood teachers, they are making an enormous difference—every day—in helping young children develop and become good citizens and successful achievers.

To all the wonderful young children who will benefit from the education and loving care of highly qualified early childhood teachers

1

A Comprehensive Perspective on Early Childhood

Educator Professional Development

Michael L. Kamil

Despite the importance of early childhood education, there is not a unified perspective that combines research and policy on the professional development of early childhood educators. Rather, research in these and related issues has not systematically addressed issues of greatest importance to policy, and policy has often ignored important findings from research. This is clearly the case with professional development of early childhood educators. Very little rigorous research has been available to inform policy about the most effective ways in which to provide professional development for current or future early childhood educators. The chapters in this volume indicate the changing state of affairs: We are rapidly accumulating new evidence about how to provide professional development in a variety of contexts for diverse populations.

One of the traditional reasons for this situation is that it is very difficult for many researchers or policy makers to distance themselves from a deep concern for improving the lot of children and focus on the adults in the early childhood contexts. It is critical that there be studies in which the lens is focused on aspects of the early childhood education contexts other than simple child outcomes. Again, the chapters in this volume demonstrate that it is possible to focus on the preparation of early childhood educators while respecting the need to improve student achievement. While the knowledge represented in this volume would improve professional development if applied right now, we do need more work to extend our knowledge.

In what follows, a unified perspective on early childhood educators and their professional development, encompassing both research and policy, is developed. Implications for policy and research are elaborated as well as the benefits of a unified perspective. The focus of this chapter is specifically on issues of language and **literacy,** even while acknowledging the importance of early experiences in mathematics and social and emotional development, among many other variables. The important variables in professional development for early childhood education are elaborated, and the current work presented in the other chapters in this volume is related to those variables.

WHY IS EARLY CHILDHOOD EDUCATION IMPORTANT?

The need for early childhood education is a given. If children don't have early literacy (and other) experiences, they may never be able to take advantage of subsequent educational opportunities. Research from a number of areas has converged to confirm the need for such experiences prior to school. Policy has addressed these problems with a number of programs, albeit not from a unified perspective. Among these programs are **Title I; Head Start; Good Start, Grow Smart;** and **Early Reading First.**

Berliner (2009) showed the extreme influence of out-of-school influences on school achievement. Because lower socioeconomic status (SES) children may not be able to overcome the lack of experiences common to higher SES children without intensive **intervention,** early education becomes crucial. Although many of Berliner's recommendations center on noncognitive skills and abilities (e.g., medical care, addiction, pollution), his solutions include providing high-quality preschool for all children and providing summer programs to prevent summer loss in achievement.

WHAT IS BEING DONE ABOUT EARLY CHILDHOOD EDUCATION NOW?

The National Institute for Early Education Research (NIEER) collects and publishes statistics about the state of preschool every year, broken down by states: The programs of interest are those that are funded by the state and serve children ages 3 and 4 (and younger). In 2008, twelve states had no preschool programs statewide, but that does not necessarily mean that these states had no preschool students. It simply means that the states did not meet the NIEER criteria. Local districts may spend funds on these programs without having state reporting requirements.

The programs that NIEER examines are rated on three sets of standards: program quality, access, and resources. Of special interest to the issue of professional development are the quality standards. The quality standards are listed in Table 1.1. Of the 10 standards used to rate programs, only 4 of them have to do specifically with teacher quality.

These quality standards do not include an emphasis on teaching or instruction. Rather, these are criteria that can be rated without direct observation or special assessments. Consequently, there is a pressing need to unpack the notions of instruction and teacher quality both for policy and research.

All of the projects described in the chapters in this volume implemented far more complex teacher quality designs than those used to assess the state of affairs at the national level by NIEER.

Table 1.1. National Institute for Early Education Research program quality standards

Policy	State pre-K requirements
Early learning standards	National Education Goals Panel content areas covered by state learning standards for preschool-age children must be comprehensive
Teacher degree	Lead teacher must have a bachelor's degree, at minimum
Teacher specialized training	Lead teacher must have specialized training in a pre-K area
Assistant teacher degree	Assistant teacher must have a child development associate credential or equivalent, at minimum
Teacher in-service	Teacher must receive at least 15 hours/year of in-service professional development and training
Maximum class size (3-year-olds, 4-year-olds)	Maximum number of children per classroom must be 20 or lower
Staff–child ratio (3-year-olds, 4-year-olds)	Lowest acceptable ratio of staff to children in classroom (e.g., maximum number of students per teacher) must be 1:10 or better
Screening/referral and support services	Screenings and referrals for vision, hearing, and health must be required; at least one additional support service must be provided to families
Meals	At least one meal must be offered daily
Monitoring	Site visits must be used to demonstrate ongoing adherence to state program standards

From National Institute for Early Education Research. (2009). *The state of preschool 2009: State preschool yearbook* (p. 27). New Brunswick, NJ: National Institute for Early Education Research; adapted by permission.

LITERACY INSTRUCTION IN EARLY CHILDHOOD INSTRUCTION

Why focus on literacy? We have data that show that literacy is the best predictor of success in mathematics and science for students after eighth grade. ACT (2008) assessed performance on reading in Grade 8. Subsequently, they looked at the probability of passing future courses in mathematics and science. For students who were below benchmark in literacy, the probability of passing future courses in science was 1%. Students above benchmark had a 32% chance of passing future science courses. For mathematics, the comparable numbers are 15% for students below benchmark and a stunning 67% for those above benchmark. In and of itself, this is somewhat indirect evidence, but we can infer that giving students an early start in literacy is critical to later success.

We have several sources to guide the content of literacy instruction by early childhood educators. The following are four principles for early instruction in literacy identified by Strickland and Riley-Ayers (2006):

1. Oral language is the foundation for literacy development. It provides children with a sense of words and sentences and builds sensitivity to the sound system so that children can acquire **phonological awareness** and phonics.

2. Children's experiences with the world greatly influence their ability to comprehend what they read.

3. Learning to read and write starts long before first grade and has long-lasting effects.

4. Children's experiences with books and print greatly influence their ability to comprehend what they read.

These are general principles that point to the important content for early childhood instruction in literacy. Given the centrality of oral language in learning to read, it is imperative that children be given the opportunity to develop a rich oral language prior to entering school. While that does not imply that oral language development stops after students enter school, it does suggest that oral language is an important asset for learning in school. One clear difference between low and high SES children is the amount of vocabulary they are exposed to at home. Hart and Risley (1995) found that low SES children were exposed to from one third to one half the number of words that higher SES children encountered. Given the importance of vocabulary and oral language for learning to read, this deficit should clearly be addressed.

At the same time, oral language is most useful when students have a rich background they can bring to bear on language interactions with those around them. Thus, information about the world is important, even though school provides such information. The difference is that school experiences often build on a basic level of background knowledge. Again, students who possess such information will be able to leverage that information for school learning. One of the clear differences between more and less successful students in preschool and in early grades is the amount of information they have about the world (Hirsch, 2006; Neuman & Celano, 2006). It is critical that these differences be addressed if students are to be successful later in school.

Experiences with reading and writing clearly begin long before school and need to be encouraged and stimulated, particularly for children who do not have these experiences in their family context. Systematic interactions around books and print are also important for later learning.

Recent reviews of research on early literacy have clearly exposed two critical variables that are consistent with the four principles above (Dickinson & Neuman, 2006; Neuman, Copple, & Bredekamp, 2000). These research reviews have concluded that phonemic awareness and shared book reading are two practices that predict successful literacy learning. Phonemic awareness is the ability to manipulate sounds in language. It is not necessarily a skill to be taught or learned in conjunction with print, but some findings suggest that it is more effective when combined with print. Shared book reading is reading with one or more children without a great deal of interaction. The other form of shared book reading, interactive shared book reading, involves an adult reading a book to a child or a small group of children and using a variety of techniques to engage the children in the text. A third variety of shared book reading is **dialogic reading;** the adult and the child switch roles so that the child learns to become the storyteller with the assistance of the adult, who functions as an active listener and questioner. All three practices have been found to have at least potentially positive effects on oral language.

At the very least, these are clearly practices that should be incorporated in the early education of children. They should be part of the education or professional development of early childhood educators.

The National Early Literacy Panel (NELP, 2008) was charged with reviewing the research on early literacy to determine what abilities and skills were important for later literacy learning. They following six findings represent the most important of the NELP conclusions.

- *Alphabet knowledge (AK):* knowledge of the names and sounds associated with printed letters

- *Phonological awareness (PA):* the ability to detect, manipulate, or analyze the auditory aspects of spoken language (including the ability to distinguish or segment words, **syllables,** or phonemes), independent of meaning

- *Rapid automatic naming (RAN) of letters or digits:* the ability to rapidly name a sequence of random letters or digits

- *RAN of objects or colors:* the ability to rapidly name a sequence of repeating random sets of pictures of objects (e.g., *car, tree, house, man*) or colors

- *Writing or writing one's name:* the ability to write letters in isolation on request or to write one's own name

- *Phonological memory:* the ability to remember spoken information for a short period of time

The NELP also identified the following five additional factors as potentially beneficial:

- *Concepts about print:* knowledge of print conventions (e.g., left–right, front–back) and concepts (book cover, author, text)

- *Print knowledge:* a combination of elements of AK, concepts about print, and early decoding

- *Reading readiness:* usually a combination of AK, concepts of print, vocabulary, memory, and PA

- *Oral language:* the ability to produce or comprehend spoken language, including vocabulary and grammar

- *Visual processing:* the ability to match or discriminate visually presented symbols

The NELP is yet another source of information about early literacy that should be part of early childhood education for literacy. It should also be incorporated in teacher certification and professional development for early childhood educators even though not all of the predictor variables have direct instructional implications (e.g., RAN).

THE LOGIC OF RESEARCH ON
PROFESSIONAL DEVELOPMENT FOR LITERACY INSTUCTION

Most of the chapters in this volume have either an explicit or implicit perspective on the available research. Specific chapters that deal with these issues are Zaslow et al. (Chapter 2) and Doescher and Beudert (Chapter 8).

What we know from research on the effectiveness of professional development on the outcomes for students is from a relatively small but consistent body of literature. These studies are typically for teachers of older students in kindergarten through 12th grade (Cochran-Smith & Zeichner, 2005). While the content may not be entirely applicable to early childhood educators, the logic of the research would certainly be appropriate for all professional development and teacher education research.

In order to infer the effective causal link between professional development and student outcomes, three conditions need to occur. First, professional development must change teacher knowledge about the subject at hand. Second, there must be changes in teacher practice related to that new knowledge. Finally, student achievement must improve. These are the same criteria that were used to examine professional development research by the National Reading Panel (National Institute of Child Health and Human Development [NICHD], 2000).

This may appear to be an unnecessary set of criteria, but it is critical if causal connections are to be made between professional development and student outcomes. If teachers do not learn new knowledge, it is not clear how their practices will change in anything more than a random way. If teachers do acquire new knowledge as a result of professional development and do not use it to change classroom instruction, there is no reason to attribute any outcomes to professional development. Finally, even if the first two conditions are met, students must improve in order to demonstrate effective professional development.

Unfortunately, much professional development research does not adhere to this logic model and is thus not unambiguously interpretable (NICHD, 2000; Pang & Kamil, 2006). Future research needs to adhere to a clearer logic model so that causal inferences can be made about the effectiveness of professional development or teacher education.

Zaslow et al. (in press) have reviewed the research specifically on early childhood professional development. Although there is only a small body of research on these issues, they list the following as being consensus recommendations about necessary conditions for high-quality research in professional development, though not always thoroughly supported by rigorous research:

- "There are specific and articulated objectives for the professional development that are research-based, and a curriculum or defined set of activities to use with children."

- "Practice and theory are woven together in the professional development."

- "There is collective participation of teachers from the same classrooms or schools in professional development."

- "There are on-site models and **mentors** who can improve the **fidelity of implementation** of new techniques and skills."

- "The intensity/duration of the professional development is matched to the content being conveyed."

- "Educators are prepared to conduct child assessments and interpret their results as a tool for ongoing monitoring of the effects of professional development."

- "It is clearly linked to organizational philosophy and infrastructure and to local, state, and national standards for practice."

At the same time, Zaslow et al. (in press) identified some important needs in the research:

- The literature tends to focus on the *content* of professional development rather than the *processes* and *strategies* that can be used most effectively.

- The literature does not adequately address the issue of cultural and linguistic competence for early childhood educators.

- The methods and analytical strategies used in evaluations of professional development need more rigor.

- A final gap to note in the literature is the lack of focus on integrating content across topical areas.

The review clearly underscores the limited nature of what we know as fact from research and implicitly suggests an ambitious research agenda. Combined with a need to incorporate the logic model described previously, this program of research would expand the scope of our knowledge with regard to effective professional development for early childhood education. In what follows, issues relevant to research and policy are explored with the intent of providing a comprehensive view of what we need from research to translate into effective policy mandates to improve readiness for school among preschool children.

TEACHER QUALITY

Teacher quality is a topic that is, in some ways, central to all of the chapters in this volume, but several chapters relate directly to the issues as they are discussed in the following section: Peterson and Valk (Chapter 3); Doescher and Beudert (Chapter 8); Lambert, Sibley, and Lawrence (Chapter 4); Halle et al.

(Chapter 11); and Rubin, Sutterby, and Hoffman (Chapter 10). Most recent educational policies recognize the importance of teacher quality, but efforts to ensure the quality of teachers have not always been successful. One of the most common methods used by policy makers to ensure quality has been to rely on degrees or coursework for preservice and in-service teachers. The Committee on Early Childhood Pedagogy Report recommends that all children in an early childhood program be assigned a teacher who has at least a bachelor's degree (Bowman et al., 2000).

Despite the prevalent belief in teacher quality, there is substantial disagreement about the general value of degrees as a way to ensure better child outcomes. Goe (2007) conducted a research synthesis that found, at best, mixed results relating teacher quality to student outcomes. The strongest effects were found in mathematics. Goe concluded that there are many research issues that might obscure the true relationship between teacher quality and student outcomes. Among the most important is that the tests for measuring student achievement were not designed to measure teacher quality. Gordon, Kane, and Staiger (2006) concluded that teaching credentials have little predictive power for effective teaching. Roza and Miller (2009) also concluded that, on average, master's degrees in education bear no relation to student achievement. The findings do indicate that there is a relationship between degrees and student outcomes for mathematics and science, with the strongest effects being observed in secondary school.

Another factor that clearly impinges on teacher quality for early childhood is the relatively low literacy levels of many of the educators currently working with this population. Kaestle, Campbell, Finn, Johnson, and Mikulecky (2001) suggested the need for additional literacy support for early childhood educators. It is difficult to imagine how we can expect higher literacy outcomes when the individuals delivering the instruction may not have the necessary skills. This area needs careful consideration both by researchers and policy makers.

It is difficult to imagine that teacher quality is NOT related to student learning. The problems are in obtaining valid, reliable measures of teacher quality and then disentangling teacher quality from the many other variables affecting student outcomes. Clearly, this is an area in which much more research needs to be conducted before definite conclusions can be drawn. It also would appear that policy makers need to be wary of overstating the case for teacher quality and, in particular, be conservative in mandating specific ways of achieving teacher quality.

TECHNOLOGY AND PROFESSIONAL DEVELOPMENT

As a field that has traditionally emphasized personal contact, early childhood education has not always embraced new technologies. Nonetheless, various uses of technology are addressed by Wright (Chapter 13) and Sandefur et al. (Chapter 5).

Teaching is primarily a labor intensive occupation. The hope has always been that the appropriate use of developing technologies would be leveraged to reduce the intensity of the labor component. Pang and Kamil (2004) reviewed the published research literature on the uses of technology for professional development for reading teachers. They concluded that there was little or no evidence of the effectiveness of doing professional development with technology. Since then, Pianta and his colleagues (2008) and Powell, Diamond, and Burchinal (2009) have shown that, for early childhood educator professional development, the use of technology can be effective for improving not only teacher variables but also student outcomes. However, despite the promise of economy from technology, the web-based system, known as MyTeachingPartner (available at http://www.myteachingpartner.net/), still requires a great deal of labor. Those labor costs may offset other costs like travel to remote locations, producing a net savings.

There is a great deal of hope that emergent technologies will at least reduce the dependence on labor at all levels of the educational process, from classroom instruction to professional development. Perhaps the best course at present is not to reduce the labor intensity of teaching but to allow technology to make it more effective.

ASSESSMENT

One of the important needs in early childhood education in general is specific, appropriate assessments with desirable psychometric properties. While many of the chapters have information about assessments, central issues in assessment are specifically addressed by Warren et al. (Chapter 12) and Baker and Peterson (Chapter 7).

Research depends on precise measurements. One of the weakest links in the research chain is the varieties of assessments available for use in determining student outcomes. Many of the current assessments are not sufficiently precise to answer all of the questions being asked. Others assessments do not include normative scoring schemes for students in the populations under study. This mismatch could come about because of age differences or differences in language background or other relevant variables. Still other assessments require specialized training to administer and may therefore have limited use in research studies.

Fortunately this issue is receiving a great deal of attention. A report by the National Research Council laid out the properties of principled assessment for early childhood:

> If decisions about individual children or about programs are to be defended, the system of assessment must reflect the highest standards of evidence in three domains: the psychometric properties of the instruments used in the assessment system; the

evidence supporting the appropriateness of the assessment instruments for different ethnic, racial, language, functional status, and age group populations; and the domains that serve as the focus of the assessment. In addition, resources need to be directed to the training of assessors, the analysis and reporting of results, and the interpretation of those results. Such attention is especially warranted when making decisions about whether programs will continue to be funded by tax monies. (2008, pp. 341–376)

It is also critical that early childhood educators become more attuned to use both formal and informal assessments to refine or modify instruction. Assessments do not always have to be detailed instruments. Early childhood educators need to use observational data as well as more quantified and sophisticated data (when available) to improve instruction. This is often referred to as *formative assessment* and should be a part of all instruction. It is important in early childhood contexts because it has not always been part of the preparation of teachers for these populations.

At the very least all of these principles should be clearly represented in all program evaluations in early childhood education. They need to be represented in research studies as well.

COACHING

Coaching is so prevalent that it is often difficult to do research about its effectiveness. Several of the chapters have specifically explored parameters of coaching and mentoring: Sandefur et al. (Chapter 5); Sibley, Lawrence, and Lambert (Chapter 6); Doescher and Beudert (Chapter 8); and Hawkins et al. (Chapter 9).Coaching is a very popular, but underresearched, intervention for professional development. As more implementations emphasize coaching, research has been focusing on the issues of effectiveness of coaching as an intervention. There are several important issues that have led some to question the value of coaching and others to embrace it fully.

Among these critical issues is wide range of definitions for the various roles of coaches. This is compounded by the different expectations of coaches. Coaches can be directly involved in doing classroom observations, conducting teaching demonstrations, and providing feedback on instruction to teachers. Mentoring is also a variant on coaching. Mentors often assume the role of providing advice or assistance on matters not necessarily central to classroom instruction (see Chapter 6). For example, students who are interested in doing certification work may not be familiar with college procedures or the content of some disciplines necessary to graduate with a degree. Consequently, research and policy revolving around coaching must be very precise in delineating the specific roles and duties of coaches, mentors, literacy specialists, and so forth. Chapters in this volume explore some of these variations.

While standards exist for both elementary and middle and high school coaches, there are few similar efforts to delineate the prerequisite skills and abilities for early childhood coaches. A particular need here is the ability to work with adults and to understand adult learning as well as child learning. However, the ethic of caring about children often overrides the concerns with working with adults. The ability to teach preschool children is not the same as the ability to teach adults. Because professional development must focus on teaching adults how best to work with children, the need to be concerned with adult learning assumes a central, and critical, role.

DOSAGE AND DENSITY

How much professional development do early educators need? New information about this issue is provided in the chapter by Halle et al. (Chapter 11).

Dosage is a concept borrowed from medicine in which the concern is how much of a given drug is needed to be effective. In professional development the concerns have been more simplistic. Dosage is often measured in terms of hours, days, courses, or degrees without concern for the details of what is presented in those units. *Density* represents the concentration of professional development. It is apparent from accumulating research that this is not the most useful way of considering dosage, even though these units are clearly important.

Of considerable importance in dosage is the arrangement of professional development, or what can be described as density. Learning often is best when presented in a distributed format rather than as a complete block. Spreading out professional development may be more effective than blocking it in sessions that are close together in time. The considerations are important both in terms of absolute time as well as time relative to the entire program. That is, a program that lasts a year may not be affected by professional development that occurs at or near the end of the program.

Dosage, as Halle and her colleagues make note (see Chapter 11), is almost never measured or prescribed with regard to the needs of individual teachers. For example, certified teachers who receive professional development may need different dosages on different topics from noncertified early childhood educators. That is, the amount of attention to particular topics in any professional development may be more important than the total time allocated for the entire professional development.

Finally, the context in which professional development is delivered has a direct effect on the measurement of dosage. One illustration is the professional development delivered by coaches. If conducted correctly, interactions between teachers and coaches can often be much shorter but more targeted and specifically relevant to the immediate teaching context. By contrast, a formal course in teaching may be longer in terms of dosage but less specifically relevant to an educator's daily experience. This presents a problem for comparing dosage across formats of professional development. The formats of professional development range from formal college coursework to intensive workshops, informal coaching, or mentoring.

Not all of these can be compared in terms of "effective dosage" rather than trying to capture the concept of amount in a more simplistic concept. These are important concerns for both policy and research in terms of allocation of resources, effectiveness, and cost–benefit analyses.

EVALUATION, FIDELITY, AND ALIGNMENT

Conducting evaluations of the effectiveness of programs is a recurrent theme in many of these chapters. Many of the projects described implemented either experimental or quasiexperimental designs. Other chapters provide new knowledge about measuring fidelity. These chapters include: Baker and Peterson (Chapter 7); Warren et al. (Chapter 12); and Wright (Chapter 13).

Evaluation should be an integral part of all implementations. Policy should dictate that evaluations be conducted as a matter of course. Research to establish the effectiveness of programs requires principled evaluations. Evaluations are best conducted in as near to randomized control conditions as possible. Since early childhood settings often have low or specialized enrollments, truly randomized controls may not be able to be used. Instead, every attempt should be made to approximate that design, using quasiexperimental methods that involve randomly assigning intact classrooms or other units to treatment or control conditions.

As important as the general design is, it is at least equally important to be concerned about issues of fidelity and alignment. Fidelity is the degree to which the delivered instruction is the same as that which was intended by the program and program developers. Evaluations can only yield interpretable results if there is a high degree of fidelity in the implementation conditions. Unless there is a consistency about how the implementation is delivered, it is not possible to argue that the results can be attributed to the program or practice being used. This is not to suggest that there is an absolute level of fidelity that must be reached. We know that there is great variation between teachers in delivering the same program. What has to be ensured is that the implementation does not exceed "reasonable" variation in the treatment.

More complex is the notion of alignment. There are many levels on which alignment is an important consideration. Alignment between the instruction that is actually delivered and the assessments that are used to assess effectiveness is critical, as noted previously in the section on assessment. Teacher practices must align with the intent of the program or practices that are intended to be delivered. Professional development must align with the instruction to be delivered. When the professional development is about how to use the program, alignment is often a minor consideration. When the professional development goes beyond the program, it may prepare teachers to do good work that may not be part of the explicit goals of professional development. If a program is designed to improve literacy, professional development on science instruction may not have the desired effects.

One way of ensuring alignment is to be certain that the three conditions for causal connections between professional development and student outcomes are met. That is, teachers should learn new material, change behavior as a result of the new learning, and improve on relevant measures to the professional development.

When coaches are involved, the alignment issues are even more complex, involving the alignment of the professional development of the coaches with the instruction teachers are expected to deliver. In short, each layer of involvement creates another alignment issue.

CONCLUSION

The most important conclusion about the state of affairs in early childhood education is that we know a great deal about how to ameliorate the problems that attend readiness for school. Extant research provides a great deal of guidance. What is missing is a consistent delivery system, both in content and in pedagogy. To this end, a common set of standards in early childhood education would provide an important background for this. Preservice certification for these educators should also be standardized.

Assessments must match the population and have been standardized on such a population, as well as the skills being assessed. Moreover, there is a need to be certain that assessments align with what is being taught. For example, teaching phonemic awareness and assessing **comprehension** would not provide interpretable evidence about the relationship between instruction and student outcomes.

Teacher quality is critical and, while coursework is one avenue, professional development for educators who will not or cannot enroll in organized coursework is a more immediate solution. There are two kinds of professional development: how to implement a program and how to become a thoughtful, professional educator. These might be the same, but they are most often different. Whether college courses or coaching or on-site workshops or some combination of these or other formats is the most effective method of achieving teacher quality is a matter for research to determine in a much more systematic fashion than we have currently done. Policy needs to depend on such results from research for optimal resource allocation to early childhood educators.

The Early Childhood Educator Professional Development (ECEPD) program is authorized under Section 2151(e) of the Elementary and Secondary Education Act of 1965 (PL 89-10), as amended by the No Child Left Behind Act of 2001 (PL 107-110). ECEPD has focused specifically on the conditions and practices of professional development of early childhood educators in literacy. Such a program is critical if we are to address the needs of teachers who have very different characteristics from other educators. Much more intensive research is needed to continue to discover ways in which the preparation of early childhood educators can be enhanced. We need an intensive program of research on the preparation of high-quality early childhood educators. That program has to go beyond literacy, even while acknowledging its central role, to include social-emotional development, mathematics, and the other variables identified by Berliner (2009) that may prevent **at-risk** children from reaching their full potential in later education.

The focus of this program needs to be squarely on the adults in early childhood education contexts. We need to consider the effects of job stress, low wages, center-based versus school-based versus home-based education, student engagement, and parental involvement. There is an ambitious list of variables that have potential effects on early childhood education. In a time of scarce resources, it is crucial that we examine these variables carefully before we make policy decisions. Research and synthesis efforts represented in the chapters in this volume provide a solid beginning on that task. Those efforts need to be continued and expanded to address all of the issues in professional development for early childhood educators.

REFERENCES

ACT. (2008). *The forgotten middle: Ensuring that all students are on target for college and career readiness before high School.* Iowa City, IA: Author.

Berliner, D.C. (2009). *Poverty and potential: Out-of-school factors and school success.* Boulder, CO: Education and the Public Interest Center. Retrieved August 8, 2009, from http://epicpolicy.org/publication/poverty-and-potential

Bowman, B., Donovan, M., Burns, S. & the Committee on Early Childhood Pedagogy of the National Research Council. (Eds.). (2000). *Eager to learn: Educating our preschoolers.* Washington, DC: National Academies Press.

Cochran-Smith, M., & Zeichner, K. (Eds.). (2005). *Studying teacher education: The report of the AERA panel on research and teacher education.* Mahwah, NJ: Lawrence Erlbaum Associates.

Elementary and Secondary Education Act of 1965, PL 89-10, 20 U.S.C. §§ 241 *et seq.*

Goe, L. (2007). *The link between teacher quality and student outcomes: A research synthesis.* Washington, DC: National Comprehensive Center for Teacher Quality. Retrieved April 13, 2010, from http://tqcenter.learningpt.org/publications/LinkBetweenTQand StudentOutcomes.pdf

Gordon, R., Kane, T., & Staiger, D. (2006). *Identifying effective teachers using performance on the job* (Discussion Paper 2006-1). Washington, DC: The Brookings Institution.

Hart, B., & Risley, T.R. (1995). *Meaningful differences in the everyday experience of young American children.* Baltimore: Paul H. Brookes Publishing Co.

Hirsch, E.D. (2006). *The knowledge deficit: Closing the shocking education gap for American children.* Boston: Houghton Mifflin.

Kaestle, C.F., Campbell, A., Finn, J.D., Johnson, S.T., & Mikulecky, L.J. (2001). *Adult literacy and education in America: Four studies based on the National Adult Literacy Survey.* Washington, DC: National Center for Education Statistics.

National Early Literacy Panel. (2008). *Developing early literacy: Report of the National Early Literacy Panel.* Jessup, MD: National Institute For Literacy.

National Institute for Early Education Research. (2009). *The State of Preschool 2009: State Preschool Yearbook*. New Brunswick, NJ: National Institute for Early Education Research.

National Institute of Child Health and Human Development. (2000). *Report of the National Reading Panel. Teaching children to read: An evidence-based assessment of the scientific research literature on reading and its implications for reading instruction: Reports of the subgroups* (NIH Publication No. 00-4769). Washington, DC: U.S. Government Printing Office.

National Research Council. (2008). *Early childhood assessment: Why, what, and how?* Washington, DC: National Academies Press.

Neuman, S.B., & Celano, D. (2006). The knowledge gap: Implications of leveling the playing field for low- and middle-income children. *Reading Research Quarterly, 41,* 176–201.

Neuman, S.B., Copple, C., & Bredekamp, S. (2000). *Learning to read and write: Developmentally appropriate practice.* Washington, DC: National Association for the Education of Young Children.

No Child Left Behind Act of 2001, PL 107-110, 115 Stat. 1425, 20 U.S.C. §§ 6301 *et seq.*

Pang, E., & Kamil, M. (2004). Professional development and the uses of technology. In D. Strickland & M. Kamil (Eds.), *Professional development for teaching reading* (pp. 149–168). Norwood, MA: Christopher-Gordon.

Pang, E., & Kamil, M.L. (2006). Blending experimental and descriptive research: The case of educating reading teachers. In R. Subotnik & H. Walberg (Eds.), *Scientific basis of educational productivity* (pp. 45–84). Greenwich, CT: Information Age Publishing.

Pianta, R., Mashburn, A., Downer, Hamre, B., & Justice, L. (2008). Effects of web-mediated professional development resources on teacher-child interaction in prekindergarten classrooms. *Early Childhood Research Quarterly, 23,* 431–451.

Powell, D., Diamond, K., & Burchinal, M. (2009). *Effects of a professional development intervention on teaching processes and child language and literacy outcomes.* Paper presented at the Society for Research on Child Development, Denver, CO.

Roza, M., & Miller, R. (2009). Separation of degrees: State-by-state analysis of teacher compensation for master's degrees. In *Schools in crisis: Making ends meet* (Rapid Response brief). Seattle: University of Washington, Center on Reinventing Public Education.

Strickland, D.S., & Riley-Ayers, S. (2006). Early literacy: Policy and practice in the preschool years. *Preschool Policy Brief, National Institute for Early Education Research* (Issue 10).

Zaslow, M., Tout, K, Halle, T, Vick, J., & Lavelle, B. (in press). *Towards the identification of features of effective professional development for early childhood educators: A review of the literature.* Washington, DC: Child Trends and Policy and Program Studies Service, Office of Planning, Evaluation, and Policy Development, U.S. Department of Education.

I

Who Are Early Childhood Educators

Understanding the Needs, Challenges, and Opportunities

Research confirms the oft-repeated phrase from parents that "it all comes down to the teacher" when describing the quality of their child's school experience. Nothing can replace the power of a high-quality teacher during children's formative years. In fact, studies have shown repeatedly that teacher quality is the strongest predictor of children's **school readiness** skills over all other related variables.

Nevertheless, the field of early childhood has experienced both challenges and opportunities for improving teacher quality. Low wages and limited funding have traditionally plagued efforts to enhance teachers' knowledge, skills, and dispositions. However, there is a tremendous new sense of energy and commitment to the field of early childhood and its importance to children's success in reading and school achievement.

The introductory chapters in this section present ways in which we can overcome barriers to improving teacher quality. In Chapter 2, Zaslow and colleagues provide a much-needed framework for examining the emerging body of research on early childhood professional development. Together, these scholars identify four specific targets of professional development efforts, or areas in which professional development efforts are seeking to bring about improvements. The chapter provides a careful road map of what we know and what we need to find out.

In Chapter 3, Peterson and Valk highlight the challenges of professionalizing the early childhood workforce and emphasize promising strategies to meet these challenges. They also present a summary of best practices for meeting the challenges of early educators in professional development programs.

What becomes clear in these chapters is that we can overcome many of the traditional challenges to improving teacher quality. We have the knowledge. We now need to act on these solutions.

2

Emerging Research on Early Childhood Professional Development

Martha Zaslow, Kathryn Tout, Tamara Halle,
Jessica E. Vick Whittaker, and Bridget Lavelle

The research base on professional development for early childhood educators is an emerging one, with areas of accumulating evidence but also areas in which significant gaps remain. As the research moves toward both more rigorous and more specific identification of effective approaches toward early childhood professional development, it will be important to have a framework within which to place the evidence. As an organizing framework, this chapter identifies four targets of professional development efforts, or areas in which professional development efforts are seeking to bring about improvements. Based on a more detailed review (Zaslow, Tout, Halle, Vick, & Lavelle, in press), the chapter then provides a brief overview of selected research focusing on each of these target areas, noting how extensive and rigorous the research is in each area. The chapter concludes by identifying elements of effective professional development that are emerging *across* the research in these four target areas.

This chapter is based on the literature review completed as part of the Cross-site Evaluation of the Early Childhood Educator Professional Development Program conducted for the U.S. Department of Education under Contract Number ED-04-CO-0038/0002. The authors thank the members of the project's Technical Work Group—Kimberly Boller, Janice Im, Michael Kamil, Craig Ramey, Sharon Landesman Ramey, Kyle Snow, Marsha Sonnenberg, and Carol Vukelich—as well as anonymous reviewers, for their insightful and helpful feedback on drafts of the review. The authors thank their project officer, James Maxwell, as well as Rosemary Fennell for input and guidance on the completion of this literature review. They also thank Julia Wessel for her help in finalizing the chapter.

FOUR TARGETS OF EARLY CHILDHOOD PROFESSIONAL DEVELOPMENT ACTIVITIES

Efforts to strengthen the professional development of early childhood educators target four different areas:

1. The human and social capital of early educators

2. The effectiveness of institutions or organizations providing professional development

3. Children's outcomes in specific developmental domains, such as early literacy and early mathematics

4. The overall quality of children's experiences and outcomes

Figure 2.1 provides a visual summary of the four target areas as well as components within each that the research to date addresses.

The extent and rigor of the research focusing on these four target areas varies substantially. For Target Areas 3 and 4, there is a body of evaluation research examining and reporting on the effects of intervention studies (see Zaslow et al., in press, for detailed tables summarizing the research studies in Target Areas 3 and 4). In contrast, the research for Target Areas 1 and 2 has fewer evaluation studies. Instead, the research to date focusing on these target areas tends to be either descriptive in nature, documenting the need for efforts to strengthen early educators' knowledge and skills, or involves an examination of naturally occurring associations of characteristics of early educators and key outcomes, without manipulation and evaluation.

The following sections provide an overview of selected findings from the research for each of the four target areas.

Target Area 1: Strengthening the Human and Social Capital of Early Educators

Research on efforts to strengthen the human and social capital of early educators has focused on four specific issues:

- Correlates of increased educational attainment for early educators in terms of quality of the early childhood setting and young children's academic achievement and behavioral adjustment

- Correlates of the completion of training (i.e., professional development occurring outside of institutions of higher education)

- Levels of literacy among early educators and the potential to strengthen literacy

- Psychological well-being among early educators, and the potential importance of professional development approaches aimed at reducing stress and depression

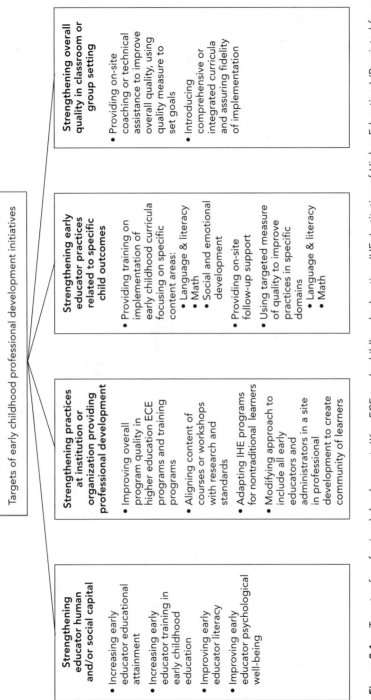

Targets of early childhood professional development initiatives

Strengthening educator human and/or social capital

- Increasing early educator educational attainment
- Increasing early educator training in early childhood education
- Improving early educator literacy
- Improving early educator psychological well-being

Strengthening practices at institution or organization providing professional development

- Improving overall program quality in higher education ECE programs and training programs
- Aligning content of courses or workshops with research and standards
- Adapting IHE programs for nontraditional learners
- Modifying approach to include all early educators and administrators in a site in professional development to create community of learners

Strengthening early educator practices related to specific child outcomes

- Providing training on implementation of early childhood curricula focusing on specific content areas:
  - Language & literacy
  - Math
  - Social and emotional development
- Providing on-site follow-up support
- Using targeted measure of quality to improve practices in specific domains
  - Language & literacy
  - Math

Strengthening overall quality in classroom or group setting

- Providing on-site coaching or technical assistance to improve overall quality, using quality measure to set goals
- Introducing comprehensive or integrated curricula and assuring fidelity of implementation

Figure 2.1. Targets of professional development. (Key, ECE, early childhood education; IHE, Institution of Higher Education.) (Reprinted from Zaslow et al., in press.)

Educational Attainment   It has long been concluded that the quality of early childhood settings (classroom and home-based care) is higher when those providing the care have completed more formal education (e.g., Burchinal, Cryer, Clifford, & Howes, 2002; Howes, Whitebook, & Phillips, 1992; National Institute of Child Health and Human Development [NICHD] Early Child Care Research Network, 2002; Phillips, Mekos, Scarr, McCartney, & Abott-Shim, 2000). Newer research, however, calls this conclusion into question. For example, analyses carried out with data from multiple major early childhood studies found little evidence that completion of a bachelor's degree was associated either with stronger observed quality or larger gain scores on measures of young children's academic achievement (Early et al., 2007). Researchers have suggested that the characteristics and motivations of those early educators who obtain higher education and remain in early education (rather than transition to elementary education) may have changed over time. They also raise the possibility that pressure to rapidly expand the numbers of early educators with higher education degrees in response to policy initiatives to increase access to early education may be resulting in pressures on institutions of higher education that lead to more variable quality in higher education programs (thus leading to the types of efforts described in Target Area 2). A gap exists in terms of describing not only educational attainment of early educators but also the quality of higher education programs they participate in (e.g., whether the program was accredited), the content of coursework (which varies substantially across degree granting programs), and whether the program requires a demonstration of skills through a supervised practicum or student teaching opportunities (Hyson, Tomlinson, & Morris, 2009).

Completion of Training   Looking at training (professional development that does not involve credit toward a higher education degree; Maxwell, Feild, & Clifford, 2006), an examination of findings from multiple studies reached two key conclusions: First, that overall, there were statistically significant effects of training aimed at improving the practices of early educators in interacting with young children. But second, that there was variation in findings across studies, with about a quarter of the evaluations considered showing no significant effects (Fukkink & Lont, 2007). The results caution that not all training approaches are effective. Just as there is a need to look in greater detail at what higher education for early childhood educators actually entails, for example, examining the quality, content, and amount of coursework, there is a parallel need to look at training approaches in a more differentiated manner.

Literacy Levels   Evidence suggests that low literacy may be an issue for a portion of early educators. Although the problem of low literacy likely varies by type of early care and education (e.g., prekindergarten, Head Start, child care), the National Adult Literacy Survey (Kaestle, Campbell, Finn, Johnson, & Mikulecky, 2001; National Center for Education Statistics, 2006) found that between 44% and 57% of child care workers perform at the lowest levels of proficiency on standardized literacy assessments.

Given the emphasis on promoting early language and literacy skills among preschool children (Halle, Calkins, Berry, & Johnson, 2003), the literacy skills of early childhood educators have been identified as a target for professional development efforts. However, the research to date on strengthening adult literacy has provided limited focus specifically on the needs of early educators. There may be specific skills in early childhood care and education settings, such as reading with fluency and expression, which are not emphasized generally in adult literacy courses. Similarly, Phillips and colleagues (2003) noted that assessments of adult literacy do not generally focus on aspects of adult literacy that may be particularly important in early childhood settings, such as oral language and book reading.

Psychological Well-Being   There is a small but growing body of evidence focusing on stress and depressive symptoms among early educators. For example, research by Hamre and Pianta (2004) documented clinically significant levels of depressive symptoms in about 10% of the sample of child care **providers** in the NICHD Study of Child Care and Youth Development. Caregivers reporting more depressive symptoms were observed as less sensitive in their interactions with young children and more withdrawn, and they showed fewer positive verbal interactions. Raver and colleagues (2008) cautioned that rates of depression may be higher among early educators working in low-income communities, in which child exposure to such stressors as domestic and community violence and economic hardship may be more severe. Gilliam (2005) reported that job stress among preschool teachers in Massachusetts is associated with expulsions of children from preschool.

Raver and colleagues (2008) have evaluated the effects of mental health consultation, providing guidance on behavior management for early educators in low-income communities. The intervention was associated with positive effects on classroom climate. These researchers suggested that early educators may be able to focus more on content such as language and literacy instruction when classroom climate is better.

Target Area 2: Strengthening the Effectiveness of Institutions or Organizations Providing Professional Development

Emerging research suggests the need for strengthening the quality of higher education programs in early development and education, strengthening the content of coursework provided through higher education or through training, and supporting **nontraditional learners** in pursuing higher education. The research in this target area is at a very early stage, primarily documenting the need for efforts rather than evaluating the effectiveness of such efforts.

Quality of Higher Education Programs   Hyson and colleagues (2009) noted that there are about 1,200 institutions of higher education with programs in early childhood. About 60% of these institutions provide associate's degrees, and 40% provide bachelor's degrees. Approximately 36,000 students graduate from these programs each year, making program quality a concern just from the point of view of the number of students affected by the programs.

However, research identifies further reasons for concern about program quality. Hyson and colleagues (2009) noted that of the approximately 450 institutions of higher education offering bachelor's and graduate programs in early childhood, fewer than half are recognized for quality by the National Association for the Education of Young Children (NAEYC) through the accreditation process of the National Council for the Accreditation of Teacher Education (NCATE). Although some institutions of higher education do not participate in the NCATE accreditation process, of those that do, approximately 25% have been unsuccessful in their first application over the past 3 years. A review of comments from applications that were not successful reveals some recurring tendencies that reflect concerns about quality. These include student assessments and assignments that are not in keeping with goals for teacher competencies identified in the NAEYC standards, assessments that focus on general teacher knowledge rather than knowledge of early childhood, lack of focus on application of knowledge in practice, field placements that lack supervision or are not in high-quality programs, and faculty without appropriate background in early childhood.

In order to learn about the perspectives of program administrators and faculty members, Hyson and colleagues (2009) carried out a survey of 250 program leaders. Responses identified both strengths and challenges in these programs. Strengths included emphases on students being able to implement high-quality early childhood curricula effectively and on improving program quality in key areas, such as improving assessments of student competencies, improving field placements, and strengthening coursework. However, program directors infrequently prioritized preparing their students to have supportive interactions with individual children or imparting the ability to access applied research. Most programs indicated a lack of budget or institutional support for building faculty. Many respondents to the survey either did not reply to a question about the research resources they used to guide program improvements or replied without pointing to the research resources they were using. Eighteen percent of programs described themselves as just in "survival mode."

Content of Coursework   Research by Roskos, Rosemary, and Varner (2006) suggested the need to strengthen the content of coursework offered through differing professional development formats: Child Development Associate **(CDA)** credentials, associate's degrees, and bachelor's degrees. This research involved an examination of materials used in coursework focusing on early literacy development (e.g., syllabi, course descriptions, field work assignments) at these three levels in a small sample of programs in Ohio. These researchers considered the alignment of the course materials with an external standard: the state's professional education curricula in reading pedagogy. They also examined whether the course materials indicated comprehensive treatment of early literacy through a balanced focus on knowledge, assessment, planning, and teaching, and through an emphasis on connecting knowledge and practice.

Although the content of coursework at the bachelor's degree level showed strong alignment with the external standard, there was weaker alignment in the associate's degree program and only minimal alignment in the coursework at the CDA level. Thus, the degree to which coursework was informed by external state standards varied substantially by the level of coursework. None of the programs showed a balanced emphasis on knowledge, assessment, planning, and teaching. They tended to overemphasize either theoretical topics or practice, and they failed to connect knowledge and practice.

Roskos and colleagues (2006) stressed that their study was a small-scale pilot study of the degree to which the content of coursework is aligned with external standards in the early literacy area, and of the degree to which it is balanced and comprehensive in emphasis. The study suffices to raise concern that there may be a need for a careful review and updating of the content of coursework, perhaps especially at entry levels of professional development.

Adult Learners An emerging research issue regarding the institutions providing professional development focuses on the way in which they engage adult learners. Many members of the early childhood workforce have characteristics that may serve as barriers to pursuing higher education in early childhood. Studies are beginning to focus on increasing both enrollment and retention in higher education programs by designing approaches that address the special needs of adult learners.

Whitebook and colleagues (2008) are carrying out a 5-year longitudinal descriptive study of a cohort approach to supporting adult learners in bachelor's degree programs in early childhood in six California colleges. The cohorts of students are nontraditional college students in that they tend to have GEDs or other certificates rather than high school diplomas, to have delayed entry into college beyond completion of the certificate or high school, to be attending college part time, to be working full time and financially independent while studying, to be supporting a dependent, and to be single parents. Students with these characteristics are more likely to leave college before completing a degree than other students because of competing demands from home or work, limited financial resources, or limited understanding of college requirements.

The approach being attempted and studied is a cohort approach, in which groups of students enroll and pursue courses together. They also receive financial assistance, are given flexibility in scheduling courses and field placements, and are offered tutoring and advising on how to fulfill degree requirements. Thus far, data collection has focused on student responses to the cohort structure and indicates that nearly all students find that this structure helps them to be successful in their coursework. In addition, a majority of participants feel that they benefit from the personal support of cohort members. Ongoing study will document whether the cohort approach supports retention and degree completion.

Target Area 3: Professional Development Focusing on Specific Child Outcomes

In contrast with the first two target areas to strengthen professional development for early educators, in the third target area—focusing on efforts to strengthen early educator instructional approaches in specific domains of children's development—there is a substantial research base with many studies involving comparative (including random assignment) evaluation designs. Studies focus especially on efforts to strengthen instruction in early language and literacy development and early mathematics and to support young children's social and emotional development. Although the research base here examines the effectiveness of specific professional development approaches, at the same time it is important to note that much of this research pertains to curricula, or the tools early educators use within the classroom. It is a clear limitation of this body of research that it provides limited description of the strategies used to help early educators actually use the tools, or how early educators are prepared through specific professional development activities.

Early Language and Literacy Development Early language and literacy encompasses multiple skills including, for example, the development of oral language skills, vocabulary development, phonological awareness, letter knowledge, print awareness, fluency, comprehension, and emergent writing skills (National Early Literacy Panel, 2008; National Reading Panel, 2000; Snow, Burns, & Griffin, 1998). The research in this area indicates that early childhood educators need to be trained and supported in the faithful execution of a variety of strategies to support children's language and literacy development in early childhood settings. Such strategies include—but are not limited to—using interactive book reading practices, arranging a separate and inviting book area, increasing environmental print, using props such as writing materials in play areas, and assessing individual children's language and literacy skills for the purpose of monitoring progress for individual children and for the effective implementation of the professional development program (National Reading Panel, 2000; Snow et al., 1998). Among 37 studies identified focusing on professional development to strengthen young children's early language and literacy, many emphasized more than one of these strategies within the same professional development intervention. (See Figure 2.2 for a listing of these studies that notes research designs used and outcome areas examined; further detail is available in Zaslow et al., in press.) On the one hand, the implication is that it is useful to employ multiple strategies simultaneously. On the other hand, it is difficult to disentangle which strategies are related to specific outcomes for educators and children when multiple strategies are used as a "package."

Study number	Citation	Design				Outcome areas examined			
		Exp	Quasi-exp	P/P with comp	P/P without comp	D	EK	EP	CO
1	Adger, Hoyle, and Dickinson (2004)					✓	✓		
2	Assel, Landry, Swank, and Gunnewig (2007)	✓						✓	✓
3	Baker and Smith (1999)			✓					✓
4	Byrne and Fielding-Barnsley (1995)			✓					✓
5	Dickinson and Brady 1 (2006)					✓		✓	
6	Dickinson and Brady 2 (2006)			✓				✓	✓
7	Dickinson and Brady 3 (2006)		✓					✓	
8	Dickinson and Brady 4 (2006)		✓					✓	
9	Dickinson and Brady 5 (2006)							✓	
10	Dickinson and Caswell (2007)		✓					✓	
11	Foorman and Moats (2004)				✓		✓	✓	✓
12	Fountain, Cosgrove, and Wood (2008)	✓						✓	✓
13	Gettinger and Stoiber (2007)			✓					✓
14	Jackson et al. (2006)		✓					✓	✓
15	Justice, Mashburn, Hamre, and Pianta (2008)					✓		✓	
16	Justice, Pence, and Wiggins (2008)	✓						✓	
17	Landry (2002)			✓				✓	✓

(continued)

Figure 2.2. Characteristics of language and literacy studies reviewed. (Key, CO, child outcomes; D, descriptive; EK, educator knowledge; EP, educator practice, Exp, experimental; P/P with comp, pre-post with comparison group; P/P without comp, pre-post without comparison group; Quasi-exp, quasi-experimental.) (Reprinted from Zaslow et al., in Press.)

Figure 2.2. *continued*

18	Landry, Assel, Gunnewig, and Swank (2008)	✓							✓	✓
19	Landry, Swank, Smith, Assel, and Gunnewig (2006)		✓					✓	✓	✓
20	Lonigan and Schatschneider (2008)	✓							✓	✓
21	Lonigan and Whitehurst (1998)	✓								✓
22	McCutchen et al. (2002)		✓					✓	✓	✓
23	McGill-Franzen, Allington, Yokoi, and Brooks (1999)	✓							✓	✓
24	National Center for Education Evaluation and Regional Assistance, Institute of Education Sciences (2007)		✓					✓	✓	✓
25	Neuman (1999)			✓					✓	✓
26	Neuman and Cunningham (2009)	✓						✓	✓	
27	O'Connor, Fulmer, Harty, and Bell (2005)			✓					✓	✓
28	Pence, Justice, and Wiggins (2008)	✓							✓	
29	Podhajski and Nathan (2005)			✓				✓		✓
30	Roskos, Rosemary, and Varner (2006)					✓	✓			
31	Wasik and Bond (2001)	✓							✓	✓
32	Wasik, Bond, and Hindman (2006)	✓							✓	✓
33	Whitehurst, Arnold, et al. (1994)	✓								✓

34	Whitehurst, Epstein, et al. (1994)	✓							✓
35	Whitehurst et al. (1999)	✓						✓	✓
36	Yaden et al. (2000)		✓						✓
37	Zevenbergen, Whitehurst, and Zevernbergen (2003)	✓							✓
Total studies reviewed: 37		15	8	8	1	4	8	26	26

Studies often used a variety of professional development delivery methods to convey the knowledge and practice components of early language and literacy development (e.g., employing coursework or workshops as well as on-site support). Only one study systematically compared providing coursework plus on-site professional development activities with coursework alone or "business as usual" (Neuman & Cunningham, 2009). This study indicated that there were no differences in educator knowledge across the different conditions, but there were benefits to educator practice of providing on-site work in addition to coursework. Further research is needed to assess whether on-site work alone could achieve comparable levels of benefit for teacher practice.

In addition to combining modes of professional development delivery, there are several additional promising practices that emerge from research focused on promoting children's early language and literacy skills. These include *establishing goals and objectives* for the professional development; *understanding the current classroom context* and being responsive to and respectful of the educator's current set of skills and contextual constraints; *providing resources* such as summaries of key take-home points of a training, curriculum manuals, activity guides, or reference lists; *engaging a cohort of educators,* including administrators, in professional development together within an institution; and *remaining faithful in implementation,* with better outcomes when the approach early educators were prepared for was more fully put into practice (Zaslow et al., in press).

Early Mathematical Skills Differences in mathematics achievement by children's socioeconomic status emerge by kindergarten entry. Furthermore, there is evidence that gains in children's achievement in mathematics during the year prior to kindergarten are related to the amount and

Study number	Citation	Design					Outcome areas examined		
		Exp	Quasi-exp	P/P with comp	P/P without comp	D	EK	EP	CO
1	Arnold, Fisher, Doctoroff, and Dobbs (2002)	✓					✓		✓
2	Casey, Erkut, Ceder, and Young (2008)	✓							✓
3	Clements and Sarama (2008)	✓						✓	✓
4	Sophian (2004)		✓						✓
5	Starkey, Klein, Clements, and Sarama (2008)	✓						✓	✓
6	Starkey, Klein, and Wakeley (2004)			✓					✓
7	Young-Loveridge (2004)			✓					✓
Total studies reviewed: 7		4	1	2	0	0	1	2	7

Figure 2.3. Characteristics of early mathematics studies reviewed. (*Key:* CO, child outcomes; D, descriptive; EK, educator knowledge; EP, educator practice, Exp, experimental; P/P with comp, pre-post with comparison group; P/P without comp, pre-post without comparison group; Quasi-exp, quasi-experimental.) (Reprinted from Zaslow et al., in press.)

quality of teachers' spontaneously occurring talk about mathematics (Klibanoff, Levine, Huttenlocher, Vasilyeva, & Hedges, 2006). These findings point to the possibility that professional development aimed at improving the amount and quality of early educators' talk about mathematical concepts, and other practices in the classroom or group, may improve young children's early mathematics achievement and narrow the early emerging gap by socioeconomic status.

A small set of evaluation studies is providing evidence in support of this hypothesis. (See Figure 2.3 for a listing of these studies that notes research designs used and outcome areas examined; further detail is available in Zaslow et al., in press.) These studies focus on the introduction of mathematics activities or an early childhood mathematics curriculum. As for the research on early literacy development, they tend to report far more detail on the activities or curricula than on how teachers are prepared to implement them (as noted previously, the content rather than processes of professional development).

A consistent theme in these studies is that young children have spontaneous interest in mathematics and informal knowledge of mathematical concepts. This interest and informal knowledge can provide a foundation for extending and deepening mathematical skills through a systematically developed set of activities. These activities do not need to be presented through didactic instruction, but with educator planning and structuring, they can involve engagement in exploration of materials, stories, games, and physical activities.

Among the seven studies evaluating interventions to support early educators in introducing mathematics content into early childhood classrooms, the curricula introduced varied in their comprehensiveness in terms of whether they aimed to strengthen a very specific mathematical concept, such as spatial reasoning skills (Casey, Erkut, Ceder, & Young, 2008); numeracy (Arnold, Fisher, Doctoroff, & Dobbs, 2002; Young-Loveridge, 2004); or the full range of mathematical concepts identified by the National Council of Teachers of Mathematics and NAEYC as important topical areas to cover in working with young children (e.g., Starkey, Klein, & Wakeley, 2004). Most of the professional development approaches in this set of interventions involved a combination of group training followed by on-site individualized visits to the early educators' work settings to support and monitor implementation, though there was substantial variation in the duration of the workshops or training and number of follow-up sessions.

All of the studies considered found evidence of effects of the interventions on child outcomes. However, the focus on whether there were effects on teacher knowledge and classroom practice was much less consistent (see Arnold et al., 2002, and Clements & Sarama, 2008, for findings indicating effects on teacher knowledge and classroom practice, respectively). This is in keeping with the concern raised previously that these studies focus much more on the curriculum and child outcomes than on early educators' knowledge and practice. These studies suggest that providing professional development in early mathematics can result in improvements in young children's mathematical skills, though more work is needed on how the effects are conveyed to children, especially the specific aspects of teacher knowledge, skill, and practice that are affected.

Social and Emotional Development

Early childhood educators place a high priority on learning how to manage behavior positively within the classroom. Disruptive behavior in early childhood classrooms or home-based groups detracts from learning experiences not only for the child exhibiting the negative behavior but also for the class as a whole (Raver et al., 2008).

Fourteen evaluation studies were identified involving early childhood professional development focused on improving children's social behavior: ten focused on strengthening the social skills of all of the children in the early childhood classrooms, though sometimes in combination with management of disruptive behavior, and four focused on approaches for working with children already showing problem behaviors, such as aggressive or socially withdrawn behaviors. (See Figure 2.4 for a listing of these studies that notes research designs used and outcome areas examined; further detail is available in Zaslow et al., in press.) As in the studies of early mathematical skills, the professional development approach in this set of studies often involved a combination of workshops with on-site consultation. However, there was again a substantial range in the intensity and structure of the training and on-site consultation. The level of expertise of the individuals providing the training and coaching also varied.

Most of the studies focusing on improving the social-emotional development of all of the children in a classroom or group found positive effects on teacher knowledge (e.g., Franyo & Hyson, 1999), teacher practice (e.g., Rhodes & Hennessy, 2000), or child outcomes (e.g., Domitrovich, Cortes, & Greenberg, 2007). In addition, all of the studies involving strengthening early educators' preparation to work with children already showing problem behaviors showed evidence of diminishing aggressive or withdrawn behavior (Hendrickson, Gardner, Kaiser, & Riley, 1993; Reynolds & Kelley, 1997; Schottle & Peltier, 1996; Webster-Stratton, Reid, & Hammond, 2004).

As in the studies of early mathematics, these studies do not all report on outcomes across both early educators (knowledge and skill) and the children (measures of social and emotional development and behavior); a gap that is important when seeking to understand how professional development affects the early educators and what the underlying processes contributing to child outcomes are. Programs with greater intensity as well as more specific curricula or classroom approaches tended to be those for which positive effects were reported. These studies provide encouraging evidence that professional development for early educators can improve classroom behavior overall and diminish problem behavior in children.

Target Area 4: Strengthening the Overall Quality of the Early Childhood Setting

A fourth target area involves strengthening professional development of early educators with the goal of improving the overall quality of the early childhood setting. Two approaches are found within this target area: the provision of professional development on comprehensive curricula, integrating multiple developmental domains rather than focusing on specific domains, and the use of broad measures of quality in early care and education to guide improvement efforts.

Comprehensive Curricula   Ten studies were identified that evaluated approaches to improving teachers' instructional practices in curricula that

Study number	Citation	Design					Outcome areas examined		
		Exp	Quasi-exp	P/P with comp	P/P without comp	D	EK	EP	CO
1	Brigman, Lane, Switzer, Lane, and Lawrence (1999)	✓							✓
2	Denham and Burton (1996)		✓						✓
3	Domitrovich, Cortes, and Greenberg (2007)	✓							✓
4	Franyo and Hyson (1999)	✓					✓		
5	Girolametto, Weitzman, and Greenberg (2004)	✓						✓	✓
6	Gowen (1987)				✓		✓	✓	
7	Hendrickson, Gardner, Kaiser, and Riley (1993)				✓			✓	✓
8	Lynch, Geller, and Schmidt (2004)	✓							✓
9	Raver et al. (2008)	✓						✓	
10	Reynolds and Kelley (1997)				✓		✓		✓
11	Rhodes and Hennessy (2000)			✓				✓	✓
12	Schottle and Peltier (1996)		✓						✓
13	Webster-Stratton, Reid, and Hammond (2001)	✓						✓	✓
14	Webster-Stratton, Reid, and Hammond (2004)	✓						✓	✓
Total studies reviewed: 14		8	2	1	3	0	3	7	11

Figure 2.4. Characteristics of social and emotional development studies reviewed. (*Key:* CO, child outcomes; D, descriptive; EK, educator knowledge; EP, educator practice, Exp, experimental; P/P with comp, pre-post with comparison group; P/P without comp, pre-post without comparison group; Quasi-exp, quasi-experimental.) (Reprinted from Zaslow et al., in press.)

integrated multiple developmental domains. (See Figure 2.5 for a listing of these studies that notes research designs used and outcome areas examined; further detail is available in Zaslow et al., in press.) Seven of these were part of the Preschool Curriculum Evaluation Research (PCER) initiative (U.S. Department of Education, 2008) and evaluated the implementation of interventions that, while differing in instructional philosophies, all aimed to promote children's development across domains in an integrated fashion. Two additional studies focused on a curriculum aimed at promoting children's executive function, or children's ability to control their behavior and emotions,

Study number	Citation	Design						Outcome areas examined		
		Exp	Quasi-exp	P/P with comp	P/P without comp	D	EK	EP	CO
1	Barnett et al. (2008)	✓							✓	✓
2	Bierman et al. (2008)	✓								✓
3	Chambers and Slavin (2008)	✓							✓	✓
4	Diamond, Barnett, Thomas, and Munro (2007)	✓								✓
5	Farran and Lipsey (2008)	✓							✓	✓
6	Lambert and Abbot-Shim (2008)	✓							✓	✓
7	Powell and File (2008)	✓							✓	✓
8	Priest and Zoellick (2008)	✓							✓	✓
9	Starkey, Klein, Clements, and Sarama (2008)	✓							✓	✓
10	Thornburg, Mayfield, Morrisson, and Scott (2008)	✓							✓	✓
Total studies reviewed: 10		10	0	0	0	0	0	8	10

Figure 2.5. Characteristics of comprehensive curricula studies reviewed. (Key: CO, child outcomes; D, descriptive; EK, educator knowledge; EP, educator practice, Exp, experimental; P/P with comp, pre-post with comparison group; P/P without comp, pre-post without comparison group; Quasi-exp, quasi-experimental.) (Reprinted from Zaslow et al., in press.)

inhibit impulses, and direct attention toward tasks (Barnett et al., 2008; Diamond, Barnett, Thomas, & Munro, 2007). And one further study evaluated a curriculum that integrated language and literacy development with social and emotional development, while also evaluating effects on executive function (Bierman et al., 2008). As for the domain-specific target area, the professional development approach most often (though not universally) followed in this set of studies involved initial training with follow-up consultation. In this set of interventions there was also follow-up ("booster") training.

The effects noted were not consistent across those studies examining change in overall classroom quality or educator practice. For example, the evaluation of an intervention focusing on strengthening young children's executive functioning found large effects on all measures used to assess classroom practices examined (Barnett et al., 2008), and one study of the implementation of a comprehensive curriculum for early childhood settings found effects on all aspects of classroom practices considered (Lambert & Abbott-Shim, 2008). However, three further studies reported mixed findings, with positive impacts on specific language and literacy instructional practices but not on overall classroom quality, and three of the PCER studies found no effects on educator practices. In addition, across all 10 studies, only isolated and mixed effects on child outcomes were reported. Only one of the comprehensive curricula—that focusing on children's executive function—reported positive effects both on classroom measures and child outcomes.

It is possible that apart from the professional development focusing on the single underlying child competence of executive functioning as foundational to learning across domains, the comprehensive curricula placed too many expectations at once on early educators, or did not match the extent and comprehensiveness of professional development with the complexity of the curricula. However, there is a lack of systematic evaluation of variation in professional development approaches and dosages for implementing the curricula, making it impossible to isolate either the nature of the curricula or the specific professional development as underlying the results. A further possibility is that the relative lack of effects overall on educator practices and child outcomes is related to the initial level of knowledge or skills of the early educators. It is possible that professional development for comprehensive curricula requires a higher initial level of educator knowledge and skill.

General Approaches in Professional Development

In a further set of studies, the focus was explicitly on the processes of professional development rather than on curricula to be implemented. This is an important departure from the studies reviewed in other target areas. Eleven studies were identified with this goal, most asking whether professional development of different kinds improves overall observed classroom quality and the quality of

Study number	Citation	Design				Outcome areas examined			
		Exp	Quasi-exp	P/P with comp	P/P without comp	D	EK	EP	CO
1	Arnett (1989)		✓					✓	
2	Campbell and Milbourne (2005)			✓				✓	
3	Cassidy, Buell, Pugh-Hoese, and Russell (1995)			✓			✓	✓	
4	Fantuzzo et al. (1997)	✓						✓	
5	Fantuzzo (1996)	✓						✓	
6	Fiene (2002)	✓					✓	✓	
7	Kontos, Howes, and Galinsky (1996)			✓			✓	✓	
8	Palsha and Wesley (1998)				✓			✓	
9	Pianta, Mashburn, Downer, Hamre, and Justice (2008)	✓						✓	
10	Wesley (1994)				✓			✓	
11	Whitaker et al., (2007)		✓						
Total studies reviewed: 11		4	2	3	2	0	3	10	0

Figure 2.6. Characteristics of general approaches studies reviewed. (Key: CO, child outcomes; D, descriptive; EK, educator knowledge; EP, educator practice, Exp, experimental; P/P with comp, pre-post with comparison group; P/P without comp, pre-post without comparison group; Quasi-exp, quasi-experimental.) (Reprinted from Zaslow et al., in press.)

teacher–child interactions. (See Figure 2.6 for a listing of these studies that notes research designs used and outcome areas examined; further detail is available in Zaslow et al., in press.) Whereas many of the other studies included in this review encompassed measures of change in children's development, only one of the studies in this set considered child outcomes (and the results were not yet available), underscoring the focus on educator practice, an important emphasis, yet limiting the scope and conclusions that can be drawn. The approaches used to improve overall program quality in this set of studies included community college coursework, training in coordination with on-site consultation, on-site consultation without a workshop or training component, web-mediated professional development, and joint participation in training by educators and parents. This set of studies includes both home-based and center-based early care and education settings.

Findings are mixed, with some studies pointing to changes in overall classroom quality and teacher–child interaction. The review of the evidence suggests the importance of individualization, sufficient intensity, and the need for opportunities for observation and practice as factors important to change in overall quality in early childhood settings. Findings also point to the potential importance of including all of the teachers in a classroom or program, in addition to center or program administrators, rather than working with educators in isolation.

The research reviewed here points to the emergence of professional development approaches that focus simultaneously on strengthening early educator knowledge (through training or college coursework) and practice (through on-site or web-based individualized modeling and feedback). An important next step will be the delineation of specific strategies used in each of these, and attempts to isolate more fully the individual strategies and combinations of strategies that underlie improvements in educator knowledge and practice and in child outcomes.

EMERGING PATTERNS
ACROSS THE FOUR TARGET AREAS

We have noted that the research on professional development is at a relatively early stage, hindered by a focus on the content early educators are asked to implement rather than also focusing on how early educators are prepared to provide this content. Significant questions remain about which features of professional development for early childhood educators, singly and in combination, are most effective for improving both educator and child outcomes. However, the literature does point to an initial set of conclusions that can serve as starting points in the identification of effective practices in early childhood professional development (see Zaslow et al., in press, for further details on these general conclusions).

The evidence suggests that professional development for early childhood educators is more effective when

- **There are specific and articulated objectives for professional development.**

There is evidence that effects on early educator practice are larger when training goals are specified rather than open-ended (Fukkink & Lont, 2007). An observational measure of quality can be used to provide specific and articulated goals for quality improvement (QUINCE Research Team, 2009). In the areas of early language and literacy development as well as early mathematical skills, consensus documents that summarize research about what is appropriate and important for young children to know provides a strong basis for specifying the content of curricula and approaches for preparing early educators to implement them (Clements & Sarama, 2008; Ginsburg et al., 2006; National Early

Literacy Panel, 2008; National Reading Panel, 2000; Snow et al., 1998; Starkey et al., 2004).

- **Practice is an explicit focus of the professional development, and attention is given to linking the focus on early educator knowledge and practice.**

In the research reviewed, there is a growing emphasis on strengthening early educator practice directly rather than focusing only on increasing early educator knowledge. This emphasis is in keeping with the principles of adult learning summarized by the National Research Council (2001). In the studies reviewed, such approaches usually involved a combination of coursework or training with individualized modeling and feedback on interactions with children in the early childhood setting (though in some instances the professional development involved only the individualized on-site component and in others, the individualized modeling and feedback was provided online rather than in the classroom or home-based care setting; Assel, Landry, Swank, & Gunnewig, 2007; Campbell & Milbourne, 2005; Clements & Sarama, 2008; Dickinson & Brady, 2006; Fantuzzo, 1996; Fantuzzo et al., 1997; Gettinger & Stoiber, 2007; Landry, 2002; Neuman & Cunningham, 2009; Palsha & Wesley, 1998; Pianta, Mashburn, Downer, Hamre, & Justice, 2008; Raver et al., 2008). There is promising evidence of the effectiveness of these approaches. Yet not all practice-focused professional development approaches have shown positive effects. It will be very important in future work to identify the specific processes underlying positive effects and to distinguish the specific features of practice-focused approaches that are and are not effective (Sheridan, Edwards, Marvin, & Knoche, 2009; Zaslow, 2009). In addition, there is a need for more work focusing on the issue of whether the presentation of information through coursework or training alone results in improvements in early educator practice and child outcomes (Burchinal, Hyson, & Zaslow, 2008; Early et al., 2007), or whether professional development aimed at strengthening knowledge needs to be closely tied to practice, for example, by intentionally interspersing training and opportunities for application (see, e.g., Dickinson & Brady, 2006).

- **There is collective participation of teachers from the same classrooms or schools in professional development.**

Joint participation in professional development can help to create a "community of practice" (Sheridan et al., 2009) and help to assure that changes endure. Including program directors or administrators can protect early educators from receiving conflicting guidance about what practices to implement. In addition, there is greater continuity in children's experiences if the professional development for educators of different age groups is consistent in focus (Assel et al., 2007; Baker & Smith, 1999; Bierman, Desimone, Porter, & Garet, 2000; Bierman et al., 2008; Burchinal et al., 2008; Donovan, Bransford, & Pelligrino, 1999).

- **The dosage of the professional development is matched to the content being conveyed.**

As noted elsewhere in this book, the *extent* of professional development provided can vary widely. Furthermore, dosage is not a simple total of extent of hours of professional development, but also involves patterning (e.g., frequency of training sessions and whether and how they are interspersed with opportunities for application). Rather than pointing to a particular dosage of professional development, the research suggests that intensity, duration, and other markers of dosage need to be aligned with the goals of the professional development. For example, as we have noted, language and literacy development involves multiple components. Professional development aimed at improving all aspects of early language and literacy development needs to be more intensive than professional development aimed at a single aspect (Donovan et al., 1999; Raikes et al., 2006; Whitehurst, Arnold, et al., 1994).

- **Educators are prepared to conduct child assessments and interpret their results as a tool for ongoing monitoring of the effects of professional development.**

Assessments provide a source of information for early educators about where progress is being made and where children need further input and support. Assessments also help early educators understand that their knowledge and skills are contributing to children's development (Foorman & Moats, 2004; Garet et al., 2008; Gettinger & Stoiber, 2007; O'Connor, Fulmer, Harty, & Bell, 2005).

- **It is appropriate for the organizational context and is aligned with standards for practice.**

We are learning that early childhood professional development will vary in its effects according to the organizational context, such as the extent to which there is ongoing monitoring and supervision (Fuligni, Howes, Lara-Cinimoso, & Karoly, 2009; Vu, Jeon, & Howes, 2008). Beyond the immediate program environment, professional development approaches also need to take into account and be aligned with state standards regarding pedagogy and early learning guidelines (Roskos et al., 2006).

REFERENCES

Adger, C.T., Hoyle, S.M., & Dickinson, D.K. (2004). Locating learning in in-service education for preschool teachers. *American Educational Research Journal, 41*(4), 867–900.

Arnett, J. (1989). Caregivers in day-care centers: Does training matter? *Journal of Applied Developmental Psychology, 10*(4), 541–552.

Arnold, D.H., Fisher, P.H., Doctoroff, G.L., & Dobbs, J. (2002). Accelerating math development in Head Start classrooms. *Journal of Educational Psychology, 94*, 762–770.

Assel, M.A., Landry, S.H., Swank, P.R., & Gunnewig, S. (2007). An evaluation of curriculum, setting, and mentoring on the performance of children enrolled in pre-kindergarten. *Reading and Writing, 20,* 463–494.

Baker, S., & Smith, S. (1999). Starting off on the right foot: The influence of four principles of professional development in improving literacy instruction in two kindergarten programs. *Learning Disabilities Research and Practice, 14*(4), 239–253.

Barnett, W.S., Jung, K., Yarosz, D.J., Thomas, J., Hornbeck, A., Stechuk, R., et al. (2008). Education effects of the Tools of the Mind curriculum: A randomized trial. *Early Childhood Research Quarterly, 23,* 299–313.

Bierman, B.F., Desimone, L., Porter, A.C., & Garet, M.S. (2000). Designing professional development that works. *Educational Leadership, 57*(8), 28–32.

Bierman, K.L., Domitrovich, C.E., Nix, R.L., Gest, S.D., Welsh, J.A., Greenberg, M.T., et al. (2008). Promoting academic and social-emotional school readiness: The Head Start REDI program. *Child Development, 79,* 1802–1817.

Brigman, G., Lane, D., Switzer, D., Lane, D., & Lawrence, R. (1999). Teaching children school success skills. *Journal of Educational Research, 92*(6), 323–330.

Burchinal, M.R., Cryer, D., Clifford, R.M., & Howes, C. (2002). Caregiver training and classroom quality in childcare centers. *Applied Developmental Science, 6*(1), 2–11.

Burchinal, M., Hyson, M., & Zaslow, M. (2008). Competencies and credentials for early childhood educators: What do we know and what do we need to know? *National Head Start Association Dialog Briefs, 11*(1), 1–7.

Byrne, B., & Fielding-Barnsley, R. (1995). Evaluation of a program to teach phonemic awareness to young children: A 2- and 3-year follow-up and a new preschool trial. *Journal of Educational Psychology, 87*(3), 488–503.

Campbell, P.H., & Milbourne, S.A. (2005). Improving the quality of infant-toddler care through professional development. *Topics in Early Childhood Special Education, 25*(1), 3–14.

Casey, B., Erkut, S., Ceder, I., & Young, J.M. (2008). Use of a storytelling context to improve girls' and boys' geometry skills in kindergarten. *Journal of Applied Developmental Psychology, 29,* 29–48.

Cassidy, D.J., Buell, M., Pugh-Hoese, S., & Russell, S. (1995). The effect of education on child care teachers' beliefs and classroom quality: Year One Evaluation of the TEACH early childhood associate degree scholarship program. *Early Childhood Research Quarterly, 10*(2), 171–183.

Chambers, B., & Slavin, R. (2008). Curiosity Corner: Success for All Foundation (SFA sites: Florida, Kansas, and New Jersey). In Preschool Curriculum Evaluation Research Consortium, *Effects of preschool curriculum programs on school readiness (NCER, 2008–2009)* (pp. 75–84). Washington, DC: U.S. Department of Education, Institute of Education Sciences, National Center for Education Research.

Clements, D.H., & Sarama, J. (2008). Experimental evaluation of the effects of a research-based preschool mathematics curriculum. *American Educational Research Journal, 45,* 443–494.

Denham, S.A., & Burton, R. (1996). A social-emotional intervention for at-risk 4-year-olds. *Journal of School Psychology, 34,* 225–245.

Diamond, A., Barnett, W.S., Thomas, J., & Munro, S. (2007). Preschool program improves cognitive control. *Science, 318,* 1387–1388.

Dickinson, D.K., & Brady, J.P. (2006). Toward effective support for language and literacy through professional development. In M. Zaslow & I. Martinez-Beck (Eds.), *Critical issues in early childhood professional development* (pp. 141–170). Baltimore: Paul H. Brookes Publishing Co.

Dickinson, D.K., & Caswell, L. (2007). Building support for language and early literacy in preschool classrooms through in-service professional development: Effects of the Literacy Environment Enrichment Program (LEEP). *Early Childhood Research Quarterly, 22,* 243–260.

Domitrovich, C.E., Cortes, R.C., & Greenberg, M.T. (2007). Improving young children's social and emotional competence: A randomized trial of the preschool "PATHS" curriculum. *Journal of Primary Prevention, 28,* 67–91.

Donovan, M.D., Bransford, J.D., & Pelligrino, J.W. (Eds.). (1999). *How people learn: Bridging research and practice.* Washington, DC: National Academies Press.

Early, D., Maxwell, K., Burchinal, M., Bender, R., Ebanks, C., & Henry, G. (2007). Teachers' education, classroom quality, and young children's academic skills: Results from seven studies of preschool program. *Child Development, 78*(2), 558–580.

Fantuzzo, J. (1996). The Head Start teaching center: An evaluation of an experiential, collaborative training model for Head Start teachers and parent volunteers. *Early Childhood Research Quarterly, 11*(1), 79–99.

Fantuzzo, J., Childs, S., Hampton, V., Ginsburg-Block, M., Coolahan, K.C., & Debnam, D. (1997). Enhancing the quality of early childhood education: A follow-up evaluation of an experiential, collaborative training model for Head Start. *Early Childhood Research Quarterly, 12,* 425–437.

Farran, D., & Lipsey, M. (2008). Bright Beginnings and Creative Curriculum: Vanderbilt University (Tennessee site). In Preschool Curriculum Evaluation Research Consortium, *Effects of preschool curriculum programs on school readiness (NCER, 2008–2009)* (pp. 41–54). Washington, DC: U.S. Department of Education, Institute of Education Sciences, National Center for Education Research.

Fiene, R. (2002). Improving child care quality through an infant caregiver mentoring project. *Child & Youth Care Forum, 31*(2), 79–87.

Foorman, B.R., & Moats, L.C. (2004). Conditions for sustaining research-based practices in early reading instruction. *Remedial & Special Education, 25*(1), 51–60.

Fountain, C., Cosgrove, M., & Wood, J. (2008). Early Literacy and Learning Model (ELLM): University of North Florida (Florida-UNF site). In Preschool Curriculum Evaluation Research Consortium, *Effects of preschool curriculum programs on school readiness (NCER, 2008–2009)* (pp. 99–108). Washington, DC: U.S. Department of Education, Institute of Education Sciences, National Center for Education Research.

Franyo, G.A., & Hyson, M.C. (1999). Temperament training for early childhood caregivers: A study of the effectiveness of training. *Child & Youth Care Forum, 28*(5), 329–349.

Fukkink, R., & Lont, A. (2007). Does training matter? A meta-analysis and review of caregiver training studies. *Early Childhood Research Quarterly, 22*(3), 294–311.

Fuligni, A.S., Howes, C., Lara-Cinimoso, S., & Karoly, L. (2009). Diverse pathways in early childhood development: An exploration of early educators in public preschools, private preschools and family child care homes. *Early Education and Development, 20*(3), 507–526.

Garet, M.S., Cronen, S., Eaton, M., Kurki, A., Ludwig, M., & Jones, W. (2008). *Effects of preschool program curriculum programs and school readiness: Report from the Preschool Curriculum Evaluation Research Initiative.* Washington, DC: Institute for Education Sciences, National Center for Education Evaluation and Regional Assistance.

Gettinger, M., & Stoiber, K. (2007). Applying a response-to-intervention model for early literacy development in low-income children. *Topics in Early Childhood Special Education, 27,* 198–213.

Gilliam, W.S. (2005). *Prekindergartners left behind: Expulsion rates in state prekindergarten systems.* Retrieved June 18, 2009, from http://www.med.yale.edu/chldstdy/faculty/pdf/Gilliam05.pdf

Ginsburg, H.P., Kaplan, R.G., Cannon, J., Cordero, M.I, Eisenband, J.G., Galanter, M., et al. (2006). Helping early childhood educators to teach mathematics. In M. Zaslow & I. Martinez-Beck (Eds.), *Critical issues in early childhood professional development* (pp. 171–202). Baltimore: Paul H. Brookes Publishing Co.

Girolametto, L., Weitzman, E., & Greenberg, J. (2004). The effects of verbal support strategies on small-group peer interactions. *Language, Speech, & Hearing Services in Schools, 35*(3), 254–268.

Gowen, J.W. (1987). Facilitating play skills: Efficacy of a staff development program. *Early Childhood Research Quarterly, 2,* 55–66.

Halle, T., Calkins, J., Berry, D., & Johnson, R. (2003). *Promoting language and literacy in early childhood care and education settings.* Washington, DC: Child Care and Early Education Research Connections. Retrieved January 31, 2010, from http://www.researchconnections.org/childcare/resources/2796/pdf

Hamre, B.K., & Pianta, R.C. (2004). Self-reported depression in nonfamilial caregivers: Prevalence and associations with caregiver behaviors in child-care settings. *Early Childhood Research Quarterly, 19,* 297–318.

Hendrickson, J.M., Gardner, N., Kaiser, A., & Riley, A. (1993). Evaluation of a social interaction coaching program in an integrated day-care setting. *Journal of Applied Behavior Analysis, 26,* 213–225.

Howes, C., Whitebook, M., & Phillips, D. (1992). Teacher characteristics and effective teaching in child care: Findings from the National Child Care Staffing Study. *Child & Youth Care Forum, 21*(6), 399–414.

Hyson, M., Tomlinson, H.B., & Morris, C. (2009). Quality improvement in early childhood teacher education: Faculty perspectives and recommendations for the future. *Early Childhood Research and Practice, 11*(1). Retrieved January 31, 2010, from http://ecrp.uiuc.edu/v11n1/hyson.html

Jackson, B., Larzelere, R., St. Clair, L., Corr, M., Fichter, C., & Egertson, H. (2006). The impact of Heads Up! Reading on early childhood educators' literacy practices and preschool children's literacy skills. *Early Childhood Research Quarterly, 21,* 213–226.

Justice, L., Mashburn, A., Hamre, B., & Pianta, R. (2008). Quality of language and literacy instruction in preschool classrooms serving at-risk pupils. *Early Childhood Research Quarterly, 23,* 51–68.

Justice, L., Pence, K., & Wiggins, A. (2008). Language-Focused Curriculum: University of Virginia (Virginia site). In Preschool Curriculum Evaluation Research Consortium, *Effects of preschool curriculum programs on school readiness (NCER, 2008–2009)* (pp. 109–116). Washington, DC: U.S. Department of Education, Institute of Education Sciences, National Center for Education Research.

Kaestle, C.F., Campbell, A., Finn, J.D., Johnson, S.T., & Mikulecky, L.J. (2001). *Adult literacy and education in America: Four studies based on the National Adult Literacy Survey.* Washington, DC: National Center for Education Statistics.

Klibanoff, R.S., Levine, S.C., Huttenlocher, J., Vasilyeva, M., & Hedges, L.V. (2006). Preschool children's mathematical knowledge: The effect of teacher "math talk." *Development Psychology, 42,* 59–69.

Kontos, S., Howes, C., & Galinsky, E. (1996). Does training make a difference to quality in family child care? *Early Childhood Research Quarterly, 11*(4), 427–445.

Lambert, R.G., & Abbott-Shim, M. (2008). Creative Curriculum: University of North Carolina at Charlotte (North Carolina and Georgia sites). In Preschool Curriculum Evaluation Research Consortium, *Effects of preschool curriculum programs on school readiness (NCER, 2008–2009)* (pp. 55–64). Washington, DC: U.S. Department of Education, Institute of Education Sciences, National Center for Education Research.

Landry, S.H. (2002). *Supporting cognitive development in early childhood.* Paper presented at the Summit on Early Childhood Cognitive Development: Ready to Read, Ready to Learn, Little Rock, AR.

Landry, S., Assel, M., Gunnewig, S., & Swank, P. (2008). Doors to Discovery and Let's Begin with the Letter People: University of Texas Health Science Center at Houston (Texas site). In Preschool Curriculum Evaluation Research Consortium, *Effects of preschool curriculum programs on school readiness (NCER, 2008–2009)* (pp. 85–98). Washington, DC: U.S. Department of Education, Institute of Education Sciences, National Center for Education Research.

Landry, S.H., Swank, P.R., Smith, K.E., Assel, M.A., & Gunnewig, S.B. (2006). Enhancing early literacy skills for preschool children: Bringing a professional development model to scale. *Journal of Learning Disabilities, 39*(4), 306–324.

Lonigan, C.J., & Schatschneider, C. (2008) Literacy Express and DLM Early Childhood Express supplemented with Open Court Reading Pre-K: Florida State University (Florida-FSU site). In Preschool Curriculum Evaluation Research Consortium, *Effects of preschool curriculum programs on school readiness (NCER, 2008–2009).* Washington, DC: U.S. Department of Education, Institute of Education Sciences, National Center for Education Research.

Lonigan, C.J., & Whitehurst, G.J. (1998). Relative efficacy of parent and teacher involvement in a shared-reading intervention for preschool children from low-income backgrounds. *Early Childhood Research Quarterly, 13*(2), 263–290.

Lynch, K.B., Geller, S.R., & Schmidt, M.G. (2004). Multi-year evaluation of the effectiveness of a resilience-based prevention program for young children. *Journal of Primary Prevention, 24,* 335–353.

Maxwell, K.L., Feild, C.C., & Clifford, R.M. (2006). Defining and measuring professional development in early childhood research. In M. Zaslow & I. Martinez-Beck (Eds.), *Critical issues in early childhood professional development* (pp. 21–48). Baltimore: Paul H. Brookes Publishing Co.

McCutchen, D., Abbott, R.D., Green, L.B., Beretvas, S.N., Cox, S., Potter, N.S., et al. (2002). Beginning literacy: Links among teacher knowledge, practice, and student learning. *Journal of Learning Disabilities, 35*(1), 69–86.

McGill-Franzen, A., Allington, R.L., Yokoi, L., & Brooks, G. (1999). Putting books in the classroom seems necessary but not sufficient. *Journal of Educational Research, 93*(2), 67–75.

National Center for Education Evaluation and Regional Assistance, Institute of Education Sciences (2007). *National Evaluation of Early Reading First: Final report to Congress* (NCEE 2007-4007). Washington, DC: U.S. Department of Education.

National Center for Education Statistics. (2006). *National Assessment of Adult Literacy (NAAL): A first look at the literacy of America's adults in the 21st century.* Washington, DC: Author.

National Early Literacy Panel. (2008). *Developing early literacy: Report of the National Early Literacy Panel.* Washington, DC: National Institute for Literacy.

National Institute of Child Health and Human Development Early Child Care Research Network. (2002). Child-care structure—process—outcome: Direct and indirect effects of child care quality on young children's development. *Psychological Science, 13*(3), 199–206.

National Reading Panel. (2000). *Teaching children to read: An evidence-based assessment of the scientific research literature on reading and its implications for reading instruction.* Washington, DC: National Institute of Child Health and Human Development.

National Research Council. (2001). *Eager to learn: Educating our preschoolers.* In Committee on Early Childhood Pedagogy, B.T. Bowman, M.S. Donovan, & M.S. Burns (Eds.), *Commission on Behavioral and Social Sciences and Education.* Washington, DC: National Academies Press.

Neuman, S.B. (1999). Books make a difference: A study of access to literacy. *Reading Research Quarterly, 34*(3), 286–310.

Neuman, S.B., & Cunningham, L. (2009). The impact of professional development and coaching on early language and literacy instructional practices. *American Educational Research Journal, 46,* 532–266.

O'Connor, R.E., Fulmer, D., Harty, K.R., & Bell, K.M. (2005). Layers of reading intervention in kindergarten through third grade: Changes in teaching and student outcomes. *Journal of Learning Disabilities, 38*(5), 440–455.

Palsha, S.A., & Wesley, P.W. (1998). Improving quality in early childhood environments through on-site consultation. *Topics in Early Childhood Special Education, 18*(4), 243–253.

Pence, K.L., Justice, L.M., & Wiggins, A.K. (2008). Preschool teachers' fidelity in implementing a comprehensive language-rich curriculum. *Language, Speech, & Hearing Services in Schools, 39,* 329–341.

Phillips, D., Crowell, N., Whitebook, M., & Bellm, D. (2003). *English literacy levels of the early care and education workforce: A profile and associations with quality of care.* Berkeley, CA: Center for the Study of Child Care Employment.

Phillips, D., Mekos, D., Scarr, S., McCartney, K., & Abbott-Shim, M. (2000). Within and beyond the classroom door: Assessing quality in child care centers. *Early Childhood Research Quarterly, 15*(4), 475–496.

Pianta, R.C., Mashburn, A.J., Downer, J.T., Hamre., B.K., & Justice, L. (2008). Effects of web-mediated professional development resources on teacher-child interactions in pre-kindergarten classrooms. *Early Childhood Research Quarterly, 23,* 431–451.

Podhajski, B., & Nathan, J. (2005). Promoting early literacy through professional development for childcare providers. *Early Education and Development, 16*(1), 23–41.

Powell, D., & File, N. (2008). Project Approach: Purdue University and University of Wisconsin-Milwaukee (Wisconsin site). In Preschool Curriculum Evaluation Research Consortium, *Effects of preschool curriculum programs on school readiness (NCER, 2008–2009)* (pp. 143–152). Washington, DC: U.S. Department of Education, Institute of Education Sciences, National Center for Education Research.

Priest, J.S., & Zoellick, L. (2008). Creative Curriculum with Ladders to Literacy: University of New Hampshire (New Hampshire site). In Preschool Curriculum Evaluation Research Consortium, *Effects of preschool curriculum programs on school readiness (NCER, 2008–2009)* (pp. 65–74). Washington, DC: U.S. Department of Education, Institute of Education Sciences, National Center for Education Research.

QUINCE Research Team. (2009). *Delivering and evaluating on-site consultation in a 5-state collaborative study.* Paper presented at the Meetings of the National Association of Resource and Referral Agencies, Washington, DC.

Raikes, H.H., Torquati, J.C., Hegland, S., Raikes, H.A., Scott, J., Messner, L., et al. (2006). Studying the culture of quality early education and care: A cumulative approach to measuring characteristics of the workforce and relations to quality in four Midwestern states. In M. Zaslow & I. Martinez-Beck (Eds.), *Critical issues in early childhood professional development* (pp. 111–136). Baltimore: Paul H. Brookes Publishing Co.

Raver, C.C., Jones, S.M., Li-Grinning, C.P., Metzger, M., Champion, K.M., & Sardin, L. (2008). Improving preschool classroom processes: Preliminary findings from a randomized trial implemented in Head Start settings. *Early Childhood Research Quarterly, 23,* 10–26.

Reynolds, L.K., & Kelley, M.L. (1997). The efficacy of a response cost-based treatment package for managing aggressive behavior in preschoolers. *Behavior Modification, 21*(2), 216–230.

Rhodes, S., & Hennessy, E. (2000). The effects of specialized training on caregivers and children in early-years settings: An evaluation of the foundation course in playgroup practice. *Early Childhood Research Quarterly, 15*(4), 559–576.

Roskos, K., Rosemary, C.A., & Varner, M.H. (2006). Alignment in educator preparation for early and beginning literacy instruction: A state-level case example. In M. Zaslow & I. Martinez-Beck (Eds.), *Critical issues in early childhood professional development* (pp. 255–282). Baltimore: Paul H. Brookes Publishing Co.

Schottle, D.A., & Peltier, G.L. (1996). Should schools employ behavior management consultants? *Journal of Instructional Psychology, 23*(2), 128–130.

Sheridan, S.,M., Edwards, C.P., Marvin, C.A., & Knoche, L.L. (2009). Professional development in early childhood programs: Process issues and research needs. *Early Education and Development, 20*(3), 377–401.

Snow, C.E., Burns, M.S., & Griffin, P. (Eds.). (1998). *Preventing reading difficulties in young children.* Washington, DC: National Academies Press.

Sophian, C. (2004). Mathematics for the future: Developing a Head Start curriculum to support mathematics learning. *Early Childhood Research Quarterly, 19,* 59–81.

Starkey, P., Klein, A., Clements, D., & Sarama, J. (2008). Pre-K Mathematics supplemented with DLM Early Childhood Express Math software: University of California, Berkeley/University at Buffalo, State University of New York (California/New York sites). In Preschool Curriculum Evaluation Research Consortium, *Effects of preschool curriculum programs on school readiness (NCER, 2008–2009)* (pp. 131–142). Washington, DC: U.S. Department of Education, Institute of Education Sciences, National Center for Education Research.

Starkey, P., Klein, A., & Wakeley, A. (2004). Enhancing young children's mathematical knowledge through a pre-kindergarten mathematics intervention. *Early Childhood Research Quarterly, 19,* 99–120.

Thornburg, K.R., Mayfield, W., Morrison, J., & Scott, J. (2008). Project Construct: University of Missouri-Columbia (Missouri site). In Preschool Curriculum Evaluation Research Consortium, *Effects of preschool curriculum programs on school readiness (NCER, 2008–2009)* (pp. 153–162). Washington, DC: U.S. Department of Education, Institute of Education Sciences, National Center for Education Research.

U.S. Department of Education. (2008). *Effects of preschool program curriculum programs and school readiness: Report from the preschool curriculum evaluation research initiative.* Washington, DC: Institute for Education Sciences, National Center for Education Evaluation and Regional Assistance.

Vu, J.A., Jeon, H., & Howes, C. (2008). Formal education, credential, or both: Early childhood program classroom practices. *Early Education and Development, 19*(3), 479–504.

Wasik, B.A., & Bond, M.A. (2001). Beyond the pages of a book: Interactive book reading and language development in preschool classrooms. *Journal of Educational Psychology, 93*(2), 243–250.

Wasik, B.A., Bond, M.A., & Hindman, A. (2006). The effects of a language and literacy intervention on Head Start children and teachers. *Journal of Educational Psychology, 98(1),* 63–74.

Webster-Stratton, C., Reid, M.J., & Hammond, M. (2001). Preventing conduct problems, promoting social competence: A parent and teacher training partnership in Head Start. *Journal of Clinical Child Psychology, 30,* 283–302.

Webster-Stratton, C., Reid, M.J., & Hammond, M. (2004). Treating children with early-onset conduct problems: Intervention outcomes for parent, child, and teacher training. *Journal of Clinical Child and Adolescent Psychology, 33*(1), 105–124.

Wesley, P.W. (1994). Innovative practices: Providing on-site consultation to promote quality in integrated child care programs. *Journal of Early Intervention, 18*(4), 391–402.

Whitaker, S., Kenzie, M., Kraft-Sayre, M.E., Mashburn, A., & Pianta, R.C. (2007). Use and evaluation of web-based professional development services across participant levels of support. *Early Childhood Education Journal, 34,* 379–386.

Whitebook, M., Sakai, L., Kipnis, F., Almaraz, M., Suarez, E., & Bellm, D., (2008). *Learning together: A study of 6 BA completion cohort programs in early care and education. Year 1 report.* Berkeley: University of California, Berkeley, Center for the Study of Child Care Employment.

Whitehurst, G.J., Arnold, D.S., Epstein, J.N., Angell, A.L., Smith, M., & Fischel, J.E. (1994). A picture book reading intervention in day care and home for children from low-income families. *Developmental Psychology, 30,* 679–689.

Whitehurst, G.J., Epstein, J.N., Angell, A.L., Payne, A.C., Crone, D.A., & Fischel, J.E. (1994). Outcomes of an emergent literacy intervention in Head Start. *Journal of Educational Psychology, 86,* 542–555.

Whitehurst, G.J., Zevenberegen, A.A., Crone, D.A., Shultz, M.D., Velting, O.N., & Fischel, J.E. (1999). Outcomes of an emergent literacy intervention from Head Start through second grade. *Journal of Educational Psychology, 91*(2), 261–272.

Yaden, D.B., Tam, A., Madrigal, P., Brassell, D., Massa, J., Altamirano, L.S., et al. (2000). Early literacy for inner-city children: The effects of reading and writing interventions in English and Spanish during the preschool years. *The Reading Teacher, 54*(2), 186–189.

Young-Loveridge, J.M. (2004). Effects of early numeracy of a program using number books and games. *Early Childhood Research Quarterly, 19,* 82–98.

Zaslow, M. (2009). Strengthening the conceptualization of early childhood development initiatives and evaluations. *Early Education and Development, 20*(3), 527–536.

Zaslow, M., Tout, K., Halle, T., Vick, J., & Lavelle, B. (in press). *Towards the identification of features of effective early childhood professional development: A review of the literature.* Prepared for the U.S. Department of Education, Office of Planning, Evaluation and Policy Development, Policy and Program Studies Service.

Zevenbergen, A., Whitehurst, G., & Zevenbergen, J. (2003). Effects of a shared-reading intervention on the inclusion of evaluative devices in narratives of children from low-income families. *Applied Developmental Psychology, 24,* 1–15.

3

Beyond Babysitting

Challenges and Opportunities in Early Childhood Education

Shira M. Peterson and Constance Valk

The recent political focus on standards and accountability in early childhood education has led to widespread efforts to provide effective professional development experiences for early childhood educators. Professional development programs are challenged to increase educators' knowledge and skills, improve the quality of teaching practices, and in turn, improve outcomes for children. However, there has been little prior research on whether these programs effectively meet the needs of the adult population they serve. Early childhood educators typically have low levels of academic preparation, income, and job stability, and thus they are more likely to face challenges for professional development compared with their elementary school counterparts (Raikes et al., 2006). Additional differences exist *within* the early educator population, such that infant-toddler caregivers have lower education and income levels than preschool educators and are less likely to view themselves as professionals. The high proportion of inadequate infant care in the United States is so troubling that the Carnegie Corporation characterized it as a "quiet crisis," making the need for effective professional development for these caregivers even more acute (Carnegie Corporation, 1994; Helburn et al., 1995; National Institute of Child Health and Human Development [NICHD] Early Child Care Research Network, 2000; Whitebook, Howes, & Phillips, 1990). High-quality care for very young children entails having caregivers who understand the fundamental importance of attachment relationships in children's development, who know how to apply research to practice, and who can communicate this knowledge to parents and colleagues (Honig, 2002). In light of the fact that about 80% of the paid early educator work force care for infants and toddlers, it is imperative that programs are designed to address the particular challenges faced by this adult population in the context of professional development, especially for those caregivers who may not consider themselves professionals and lack the confidence or motivation to change their beliefs or practices (Burton et al., 2002).

This chapter discusses the challenges of professional development within the early childhood work force. It includes summaries of 1) previous research on characteristics of the early childhood work force; 2) the challenges faced by infant-toddler educators participating in a mentoring program funded by an Early Childhood Educator Professional Development (ECEPD) grant in Rochester, New York; 3) the strategies implemented by the mentoring program for meeting the challenges of early educators in professional development programs; and 4) the outcomes of this mentoring program.

CHARACTERISTICS OF THE EARLY CHILDHOOD WORK FORCE

A number of features of the early educator work force are likely to create challenges for participation and success in any professional development program.

Financial Resources and Life Stressors

Early education is one of the lowest paid professions in the United States. The mean hourly wage of a child care worker is $9.79 (U.S. Department of Labor, 2009); based on the average number of hours they work, this amounts to annual earnings of approximately $19,600. About 44% of caregivers do not receive any health insurance benefits from their job (Raikes et al., 2006). Providers for whom child care is their sole family income may experience multiple hardships associated with living in poverty, such as work–family stress, isolation, depression, health problems, and effects of community violence (Conger & Donnellan, 2007; Curry, Latkin, & Davey-Rothwell, 2008). Low pay coupled with difficult life circumstances likely contribute to the extremely high rates of turnover in early child care and education—among the highest of any profession. Lack of financial resources also can create hardships in terms of paying for professional development programs or purchasing necessary books or materials. Some states offer funding programs for professional development, such as New York State's Educational Incentive Program, yet many caregivers do not know how to navigate these systems.

Psychological Well-Being

It is likely that the rates of depression and emotional burnout are higher among educators working with children in low-income communities (Raver et al., 2008). Data from the NICHD Study of Child Care and Youth Development reveal that about 10% of early educators report symptoms of clinical depression, and these caregivers were found to engage in less sensitive and less positive interactions with children (Hamre & Pianta, 2004).

Academic Skills

Based on a large-scale study conducted in 2001, the Midwest Child Care Research Consortium estimated that about 17% of center-based caregivers held at least a bachelor's degree, 13% held a teaching certificate, and 17% held a child development associate (CDA) credential. Infant-toddler caregivers and family child care providers had the lowest levels of formal education (Raikes et al., 2006). Prekindergarten (pre-K) teachers have higher levels of formal education: According to a 2001 multistate study by the National Center for Early Development and Learning, about 18% of pre-K teachers hold a bachelor's degree, and 41% have higher than a bachelor's degree (Early et al., 2006). Educators with lower education levels tend to be less involved in professional development programs (Fuligni, Howes, Lara-Cinisomo, & Karoly, 2009) and may encounter difficulty in professional development programs that require high-level academic work.

Professional Orientation

Although the majority of early educators say they regard their job as a career or profession (Raikes et al., 2006), only between one third and one half of child care workers belong to a professional organization or subscribe to a professional journal (Jorde-Bloom, 1989; Whitebook & Sakai, 2003). Educators working at large, for profit, or full-day programs tend to have lower levels of professional orientation than those working in smaller centers, nonprofit programs, and half-day programs (Jorde-Bloom, 1989). A low level of professional orientation is also a predictor of job turnover (Jorde-Bloom, 1996; Stremmel, 1991; Whitebook & Sakai, 2003). In addition, infant-toddler caregivers are less likely than preschool caregivers to regard themselves as professionals (Raikes et al., 2006).

Several studies have documented high levels of job dissatisfaction among child care workers, a factor that is associated with a low level of professional orientation (Jorde-Bloom, 1996; Pope & Stremmel, 1992; Stremmel, 1991; Whitebook et al., 1990). Low levels of job satisfaction have been linked with increased rates of emotional exhaustion (Stremmel, Benson, & Powell, 1993), burn out (Manlove, 1993), and turnover (Catapano, 2001). In addition, job dissatisfaction has been associated with low levels of intrinsic interest in professional development (Daly Wagner & French, in press).

CHALLENGES ASSOCIATED WITH PROFESSIONAL DEVELOPMENT

Today many early childhood educators are being required to obtain a bachelor's degree in order to maintain their teaching positions; yet, child care workers face significant hurdles in balancing their full- or part-time job with higher education. Many educators who are already in the work force and concurrently pursuing a degree in higher education may be characterized as *nontraditional students,* defined as

> Having four or more of the following characteristics: delayed postsecondary enroll-
> ment beyond the year of high school completion; part-time attendance for at least
> part of the academic year; full-time employment while attending school; financial
> independence as defined by eligibility criteria for financial aid; responsibility for
> dependents; single-parenthood; and a lack of a high school diploma (vs. a GED,
> other certificate, or no formal completion). (Whitebook, Sakai, Gerber, & Howes,
> 2001, p. 5)

Researchers have acknowledged that the terms *traditional student* and *non-traditional student* are outdated, as nontraditional students make up the majority of students in many higher education settings (Dukakis, Bellm, Seer, & Lee, 2007; Whitebook et al., 2001). Nonetheless, students who meet these criteria face serious challenges succeeding in formal educational programs. A survey of students in California early education teacher preparation programs found that the major challenges for these students included competing work and family responsibilities, a lack of academic preparation, low levels of proficiency with spoken and written English, and insufficient financial aid (Whitebook et al., 2001). Nontraditional students also tend to have lower grade point averages, take longer to finish college, and are less likely to complete degree programs (Chen, 2005; Choy, 2002).

Still another challenge is the literacy levels of those who enter the early childhood profession. For example, in a secondary analysis of the National Adult Literacy Assessment, Kaestle and colleagues (2001) found that 44% of child care workers performed in the two lowest levels of proficiency in the prose and document literacy areas, and 55% performed in the two lowest levels in the quantitative proficiency area. Furthermore, a study examining the literacy skills of early childhood professionals working in Head Start classrooms, public pre-K classrooms, child care centers, and family child care homes in California reported that 31% of the lead and assistant teachers in these early care and education settings placed in the "limited proficiency" category as measured by the Test of Applied Literacy Skills (Phillips, Crowell, Whitebook, & Bellm, 2003).

Other challenges for early educators in higher education can stem from a lack of social or cultural capital to prepare them for navigating the institutional practices of college (Bourdieu, 1993). Early educators from working class backgrounds may experience a "cultural mismatch" between their life experiences and the culture of formal education, making it difficult for them to identify with the social practices associated with higher education or to feel integrated into the college community (Berger, 2000; Tinto, 1993). Those who are first-generation college students may lack understanding of processes such as enrollment and financial aid and have less family support, in part because family members are not able to serve as role models (Tym, McMillion, Barone, & Webster, 2004). First-generation college students who are from low-income backgrounds are likely to face even greater challenges that stem from the combination of a lack of cultural capital and low levels of family support (Thayer, 2000).

On-site training and individualized approaches such as mentoring or coaching programs are designed to ease some of these burdens by bringing professional development services directly to the child care setting. Though these opportunities are designed specifically for early educators, participants may still face challenges in comprehending content, completing required assignments, or translating knowledge into practice. Early educators who lack confidence in their professional role may resist changing their beliefs or practices despite intensive, individualized mentoring (Awaya et al., 2003). However, there is little known about what strategies are effective for motivating individuals who are not ready to change.

Little research has addressed the question of how professional development programs can effectively meet the needs of early educators who face the challenges described in this section. The following section describes strategies that were designed to meet the unique needs of infant-toddler caregivers through a mentoring program funded by an Early Childhood Educator Professional Development (ECEPD) grant in Rochester, New York.

STRATEGIES FOR ENGAGING INFANT-TODDLER CAREGIVERS IN A PROFESSIONAL DEVELOPMENT MENTORING PROGRAM

The Rochester early childhood community, with the help of an ECEPD grant in 2004, initiated several communitywide programs to increase the quality of early care and education in high-poverty areas. The grant established new college courses, a communication network for parents and caregivers, a resource center on early childhood professional development opportunities in the community, and a model infant-toddler child care demonstration site. Mentoring of early childhood caregivers and teachers serving children from birth to preschool was an important component of the project.

The Early Education Mentoring System was developed at Children's Institute as a research-based approach to mentoring that incorporated the following strategies for effective professional development and adult learning:

1. *A strong relationship between mentor and mentees.* The selection of mentors and the pairing of mentors and mentees are critical steps (Bellm, Whitebook, & Hnatiuk, 1997; Fraser, 1998).

2. *Good assessment and clear, reciprocal communication.* Preobservation conferencing, postobservation feedback, and discussion are essential (Lyons, 2002; Wood & McQuarrie, 1999).

3. *Observation* followed by focused discussions, specific plans for improvement, and a time to reflect (Murphy, 1999).

4. Mentors meet as a *community of learners* to reduce isolation, provide a forum for exchanging ideas, and promote continuous improvement (Rogoff, Matusov, & White, 1996; Senge, 1990).

Although mentoring programs based in universal pre-K were already in place, this was the first mentoring program offered for infant-toddler caregivers in the region. The program administrators found that the infant-toddler caregiver population was characterized by unique challenges that fundamentally affected the implementation of the mentoring program. Findings presented next are based on qualitative analysis of data collected during the ECEPD grant. Data sources include enrollment surveys, mentor logs, written minutes of mentor group and supervisory meetings, mentor focus groups, and mentor interviews.

Enrollment data demonstrated that, compared with the participants in the preschool mentoring program, infant-toddler caregivers had much lower levels of formal education. Most had only a high school diploma, if that. Analysis of data from mentors' logs revealed that many infant-toddler caregivers had limited literacy skills, and a few could not read at all. Several caregivers had limited English proficiency.

Written minutes from mentor meetings revealed several emergent findings about the characteristics of mentees in the program. Mentors observed that most infant-toddler caregivers generally did not consider themselves professionals. Parents often thought of them as babysitters, and many had not had the opportunity to take on the challenge of college course work. Most infant-toddler caregivers did not seek out or make use of research and resources. Practices for them were informed by tradition, observing colleagues, intuition that sprung from their experiences as a parent, or even chance—which sometimes aligned with best practice, but more often did not. One of the mentors described how her mentee chose books to read to the toddlers in her care: "She just picked up any book, without regard to whether or not it was age appropriate. She had no idea that books might be chosen to match the developmental age of children, and wasn't interested in figuring out alternative way to choose books."

STRATEGIES FOR ADDRESSING CHALLENGES TO PROFESSIONALIZATION

This section describes key strategies that were used by mentors to address challenges faced by infant-toddler caregivers in terms of their participation and success in the mentoring program.

Adapting Academic Language

Mentors used their monthly meetings to problem-solve ways to present information to caregivers in a comprehensible format. They designed and shared handouts that were easy to read and discussed ways to assist the mentees without needing reading skills (e.g., techniques of modeling). Sometimes technical language was avoided. For example, instead of talking about "goal-setting," mentors would say, "Think about what you'd like to try next."

One of the assessments used in the project was the Infant/Toddler Environment Rating Scale–Revised (**ITERS-R**; Harms, Cryer, & Clifford, 2003). Trained master observers would observe in the infant-toddler classrooms each year and relay the data to Children's Institute for scoring. The mentors wanted to use the ITERS-R with their mentees to help them self-assess but knew that it would be overwhelming in its booklet form. One of the supervising mentors worked with a subgroup of infant-toddler mentors to break the book down into easy-to-use parts to use with mentees. Each of the subscales was broken down by indicators, with examples of how to achieve quality in the particular area.

Caregivers often complained that they were unable to implement best practices because of a lack of equipment or lack of knowledge on the part of the child care center director. Mentors would address this issue by helping mentees to articulate their needs to directors in a professional way, often by suggesting specific language they might use or even helping them to write a written request.

Using Culturally Responsive Strategies

Some mentors were exceptionally successful when they explained new concepts to mentees using *culturally responsive* strategies, defined as "using the cultural knowledge, prior experiences, frames of reference, and performance styles of ethnically diverse students to make learning encounters more relevant to and effective for them" (Gay, 2000). This was achieved when mentors were able to connect with and build on the life experiences of their mentees. In order to initiate a discussion about language modeling, one of our African American mentors challenged her African American mentees to "stop the ghetto talk" in their classrooms. As someone who shared similar life experiences and ethnic background, she could speak as a peer. When mentors did not share a similar background with a mentee, they could still implement culturally responsive strategies by deliberately building on the mentee's life experiences and then reflecting on the success of these strategies in engaging the mentee. For example, one mentor was surprised to learn that a caregiver's family tradition included spoon-feeding children until age 3 years or older. The mentor used this conversation as an opportunity to discuss variation in cultural traditions and the importance of communication with parents about their values and beliefs regarding child rearing.

Mentors were able to share culturally responsive strategies during their monthly collegial group meetings. One mentor shared the observation that her Spanish-speaking mentees preferred that the mentor offer her direct suggestions rather than use indirect questioning, which was interpreted as "beating around the bush" or having a "hidden agenda." One mentee put it this way: "Just say what you think we should do, and we'll try to do it."

Concentrating on the Long-Term Relationship

Many infant-toddler caregivers were not accustomed to setting goals for making changes in their practice, so change was slow to come. This was frustrating for new mentors who wanted to just jump in and make meaningful changes. Because the mentors were eager to share the information they had learned in their own training and put the content into practice, it was particularly discouraging for them to have to write "no action taken"(on the part of the mentee) on the observation pages where goals and process were logged.

It became the role of the supervisor to view caregivers' seeming inertia within the context of the long-term mentoring relationship. One of the supervising mentors wrote the following to a mentor in a monthly feedback report: "I would not say that no progress has been made with [your mentee], it just seems that progress is slow and sometimes regresses. I suggest that you add no new goals, and just work patiently on the ones in place."

Trainers used *The Mentor's Guide* by Lois J. Zachary (2000) as a reference during trainings and supervisory conferences to remind mentors that there are, as in the development of a child, predictable phases of the mentoring relationship. Mentors and their mentees, according to Zachary, navigate through these phases:

1. *Preparing:* clarify expectations and roles, assess viability of relationship

2. *Negotiating:* agree on goals, content, and process

3. *Enabling:* implement learning, promote professional growth, offer feedback

4. *Coming to closure:* evaluate and celebrate achievements, discuss whether and how the relationship will continue

Each of these phases is unique to the particular relationship. They cannot be taken for granted or skipped over. It is not until the enabling stage that progress toward goals can happen. Mentoring, if done right, is an investment of time.

Focusing on the Positive

Having mentors list the shortcomings of mentees would have been an easy thing to do. Mentors, steeped in content and experience, often observed a multitude of practices that were contrary to what educators know is good for children. Poor practices often outweighed the good in some mentees' classrooms. Supervising mentors constantly reinforced the need to validate what was good, and ignore, at first, what needed to change. Validation is important for all learners, but for care-givers who are not accustomed to thinking about making changes in their prac-tices, validation was even more important. In order to build a relationship and prepare the mentee for improving practice, trust had to be established. What the mentors wanted the mentee to hear was: "My mentor knows that I have the inter-est of these children at heart. My mentor is here to support me, not supervise me. My mentor thinks I'm a good person."

A format was established for conferencing with mentees, with a focus on val-idation before delving into goals for improvement. It is not easy for some mentors to focus on validation. Supervisory meetings with mentors quickly became a way to vent and relate the negative in the observations, and then to focus on the ways to emphasize the positive with the mentee in the next mentor–mentee conference. Even in the enabling stage, mentors were cautioned to work on one or two goals at a time, rather than on the long list of goals they would have liked to have tackled.

One of the infant-toddler mentors told the following story of the inroads she had achieved because of her focus on the positive: "The director asked the mentee to describe for the other teachers what it was like to have a mentor. She told them a mentor gave her a place to discuss issues, trusted her to know the answers, and gave her the space and encouragement to find her own solutions. This answer seemed just the right description of what we're trying to do. This mentee has greatly improved her confidence level about the importance and value of her work and is starting to think about ways she might help other teachers."

Adapting to the Mentee's Stage of Change

A theme that almost always emerged from mentor collegial group meetings was that of resistance to change. This particularly seemed to be an issue with students who lacked a strong professional identity and who were not used to using infor-mation from outside sources to inform practice. Mentors frequently shared their frustration with the seemingly contradictory behaviors they were seeing. One mentor described it this way: "My mentee agreed that she needed to move the furniture in a different arrangement, but it's been a month now and nothing has happened. How can I get her to actually make the changes we both agreed need-ed to happen?"

After listening to the mentors' frustration, the program leaders began to research the topic of readiness to change. One of the most influential theories in this area is the Transtheoretical Model (TTM; Prochaska & DiClemente, 1983), which is widely used in counseling programs to tailor services to participants' stage of change (precontemplation, contemplation, preparation, action, mainte-nance; Table 3.1). These stages were based on profiles of individuals involved in counseling programs for smoking cessation (DiClemente et al., 1991).

Table 3.1. Stages of change

Stage	Characteristic of caregivers	Supportive processes
Stage 1: Precontemplation (Not ready to make a change)	Avoid thinking or talking about their caregiving practices Are not interested in learning more about caring for young children Are unaware or unconcerned about the effect of their behavior on children May have attempted change in the past with unsuccessful results May be defensive or in denial about the need to change	Help the caregiver see the emotional consequences of his or her practices (e.g., "It must be hard for you when the kids' behavior is out of control"). Help the caregiver envision him- or herself with a more positive experience. If the caregiver does not make progress toward Stage 2, it may be best to remove him or her from the program.
Stage 2: Contemplation (Not ready to change on their own)	Would like to improve their practices and are aware that this requires a change Feel overwhelmed by the costs of change Are ambivalent, or torn between the costs and benefits of change, so are unable to take action	Help the caregiver recognize the underlying beliefs that may be keeping him or her from changing (e.g., I have no time, I'm not smart enough). Help the caregiver accept personal responsibility for making a change Help the caregiver truly believe he or she can make the change.
Stage 3: Preparation (Ready to change)	Intend to make a change in their practices Are ready to receive information through courses, role models, or reading Are beginning to develop a commitment to change Are devising a plan of action	Match the caregiver's interest and ability to help him or her create a feasible plan for change. Provide information as needed in the way of modeling, guided observation of other caregivers, or other resources. Support the caregiver in developing positive habits that will help him or her in making changes (e.g., time management, stress management, assertiveness skills). Affirm actions that move the caregiver toward lasting change.
Stage 4: Action (Actively engaged in change)	Are actively engaged in making positive changes in their practices	Help the caregiver make sure his or her goals are realistic.

	Set goals for themselves and follow through with them Observe the effects of their practices on themselves and the children	Engage in active problem-solving and reflection (e.g., "How did it go? What would you do differently next time?") Suggest ways to avoid -relapsing into old habits (e.g., social support, self-rewards, reminders).
Stage 5: Maintenance (Maintaining change with vigilance)	Work hard to maintain positive practices Continually reflect on and improve their practices Make a conscious effort to avoid setbacks or relapses of old habits	Celebrate the caregiver's accomplishments. Encourage the caregiver to act as a mentor to others and as a leader in the professional community.

From Peterson, S.M. (2008). *Applying the Transtheoretical Model of behavior change to child care providers enrolled in professional development programs.* Rochester, NY: Children's Institute, Inc.; adapted by permission.

Researchers have also identified 10 "processes of change" that are related to individuals' progress in counseling programs. TTM-based counseling programs are designed to increase the processes of change most likely to benefit individuals at each stage of change (Prochaska & Velicer, 1997).

Building on this prior research in the field of counseling, the program leaders developed a system to apply TTM so that mentors could tailor their services to fit their mentees' stage of change. Dr. Peterson (the first author of this chapter) along with consultant Alida Merrill designed a training guide for mentors, *Applying the Transtheoretical Model of Behavior Change to Early Childhood Educators Receiving Mentoring Services* (Peterson, 2008). The training led the mentors through the typical stages of change and provided examples of recommended mentoring strategies (see Table 3.1).

The program leaders also designed a measure for the mentor to rate each mentee's stage of change along with several associated processes of change (see Appendix 3.1). Analysis of the data collected from this measure showed that mentees who were "not ready to change" (those in the precontemplation and contemplation stages) comprised more than one third of all mentees.

Learning about the stages of change perspective helped to reduce the mentors' anxiety and frustration level. As one mentor remarked, "Now I understand why she won't change. It's just like the developmental stages of children—you can't force a child to run before he can walk."

OUTCOMES OF THE INFANT-TODDLER MENTORING PROGRAM

Results of the evaluation suggest that the ECEPD mentoring program had an impact on infant-toddler caregivers' professional behaviors and practices.

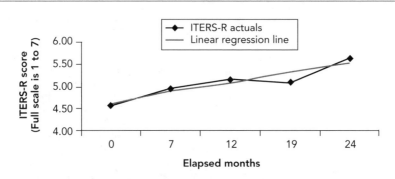

Figure 3.1. Infant/Toddler Environment Rating Scale–Revised (ITERS-R) Group 4 (all mentored classrooms) trend line analysis. Mean scores by elapsed time. Regression line change coefficient (increase) .038 per month; significant at $p < .05$, r-squared = .867

Although we cannot demonstrate that the results were purely because of mentoring, the emphasis that mentors placed on the importance of continuing education certainly influenced mentees to pursue increased professional development. Mentors reported that their mentees engaged in professional development activities, including enrolling in GED programs, CDA credential programs, infant-toddler credential programs, and higher education classes; becoming a member of the National Association for the Education of Young Children (NAEYC); attaining a higher position in their center; submitting an article for publication; and receiving a minigrant.

Another indicator of outcomes was the improvement in the quality of the infant-toddler caregivers' classroom environments. Infant-toddler caregivers who received mentoring significantly increased their classroom ITERS-R score from an average of 4.5 to an average of 5.6 over the course of 2 years (almost half of one standard deviation; see Figure 3.1).

Although not definitive, these results provide evidence that the intensive, sustained, one-on-one mentoring intervention coupled with knowledge gained from coursework had an impact on improving the quality of care offered by infant-toddler caregivers.

CONCLUSION

The experiences of the ECEPD mentoring program confirm prior research findings that early educators face significant challenges in participating and succeeding in professional development programs. Mentoring programs can address these challenges by providing sustained and responsive support for learning that is tailored to the individual's skills, needs, and readiness to change.

Basic to the success of maximizing learning for early educators is the expectation that they can learn and grow. By carrying out this belief into our practices in early educator professional development programs, we will move forward with the goal that all children have access to the high-quality early care and education environments that they deserve.

REFERENCES

Awaya, A., McEwan, H., Heyler, D., Linsky, S., Lum, D., & Wakukawa, P. (2003). Mentoring as a journey. *Teaching and Teacher Education, 19,* 45–56.

Bellm, D., Whitebook, M., & Hnatiuk, P. (1997). *The early childhood mentoring curriculum: A handbook for mentors.* Washington, DC: Center for the Child Care Work Force.

Berger, J.B. (2000). Optimizing capital, social reproduction, and undergraduate persistence: A sociological perspective. In J.M. Braxton (Ed.), *Reworking the student departure puzzle* (pp. 95–126). Nashville, TN: Vanderbilt University Press.

Bourdieu, P. (1993). *The field of cultural production.* New York: Columbia University Press.

Burton, A., Whitebook, M., Young, M., Bellm, D., Wayne, C., Brandon, R.N., et al. (2002). *Estimating the size and components of the U.S. child care work force and caregiving population.* Seattle: University of Washington, Human Services Policy Center.

Carnegie Corporation. (1994). *Starting points: Meeting the needs of our youngest children.* New York: Author.

Catapano, S. (2001). Why do they stay? Teachers make a career in the classroom. *Child Care Information Exchange, 142,* 66–69.

Chen, S. (2005). *First generation students in postsecondary education: A look at their college transcripts* (NCES 2005-171). Washington, DC: U.S. Department of Education, National Center for Education Statistics.

Choy, S. (2002). *Nontraditional undergraduates: Findings from "The Condition of Education 2002"* (NCES 2002-102). Washington, DC: U.S. Department of Education, National Center for Education Statistics.

Conger, R.D., & Donnellan, M.B. (2007). An interactionist perspective on the socioeconomic context of human development. *Annual Review of Psychology, 58,* 175–199.

Curry, A., Latkin, C., & Davey-Rothwell, M. (2008). Pathways to depression: The impact of neighborhood violent crime on inner-city residents in Baltimore, Maryland, USA. *Social Science Medicine, 67*(1), 23–30.

Daly Wagner, B., & French, L. (in press). Motivation, work satisfaction, and teacher change among early childhood teachers. *Journal of Research in Childhood Education, 24*(2).

DiClemente, C.C., Prochaska, J.O., Fairhurst, S., Velicer, W.F., Rossi, J.S., & Velasquez, M. (1991). The process of smoking cessation: An analysis of precontemplation, contemplation and contemplation/action. *Journal of Consulting and Clinical Psychology, 59,* 295–304.

Dukakis, K., Bellm, D., Seer, N., & Lee, Y. (2007). *Chutes or ladders? Creating support services to help early childhood students succeed in higher education.* Berkeley: University of California at Berkeley, Center for the Study of Child Care Employment.

Early, D.M., Ritchie, S., Burchinal, M., Howes, C., Clifford, R.M., Barbarin, O., et al. (2006). Are teachers' education, major, and credentials related to classroom quality and children's academic gains in pre-kindergarten? *Early Childhood Research Quarterly, 21*(2), 174–195.

Fraser, J. (1998). *Teacher to teacher: A guidebook for effective mentoring.* Portsmouth, NH: Heinemann.

Fuligni, A. S., Howes, C., Lara-Cinisomo, S., & Karoly, L. (2009). Diverse pathways in early childhood professional development: An exploration of early educators in public preschools, private preschools, and family child care homes. *Early Education and Development, 20*(3), 507–526.

Gay, G. (2000). *Culturally responsive teaching: Theory, research, and practice.* New York: Teachers College Press.

Hamre, B.K., & Pianta, R.C. (2004). Nonfamilial caregiver self-reported depression: Prevalence and associations with caregiver behavior in child care settings. *Early Childhood Research Quarterly, 19,* 297–318.

Harms, T., Cryer, D., & Clifford, R. M. (2003). *The Infant/Toddler Environment Rating Scale–Revised.* New York: Teachers College Press.

Helburn, S., Culkin, M.L., Morris, I., Mocan, N., Howes, C., Phillipsen, L., et al. (1995). *Cost, quality, and child outcomes in child care centers: Executive summary.* Denver: University of Colorado.

Honig, A.S. (2002). *Secure relationships: Nurturing infant/toddler attachment in early care settings.* Washington, DC: National Association for the Education of Young Children.

Jorde-Bloom, P. (1989). Professional orientation: Individual and organizational perspectives. *Child and Youth Care Quarterly, 18*(4), 227–242.

Jorde-Bloom, P. (1996). The quality of work life in NAEYC accredited and nonaccredited early childhood programs. *Early Education and Development, 7*(4), 301–317.

Kaestle, C.F., Campbell, A., Finn, J.D., Johnson, S.T., & Mikulecky, L.J. (2001). *Adult literacy and education in America: Four studies based on the National Adult Literacy Survey.* Washington, DC: National Center for Education Statistics.

Lyons, C.A. (2002). Becoming an effective literacy coach: What does it take? In E.M. Rodgers & G. Pinnell (Eds.), *Learning from teaching in literacy education: New perspectives on professional development* (pp. 93–118). Portsmouth, NH: Heinemann.

Manlove, E.E. (1993). Multiple correlates of burnout in child care workers. *Early Childhood Research Quarterly, 8,* 499–518.

Murphy, C.U. (1999). Use time for faculty study. *Journal of Staff Development, 20*(2), 20–25.

National Institute of Child Health and Human Development (NICHD) Early Child Care Research Network. (2000). Characteristics and quality of child care for toddlers and preschoolers. *Applied Developmental Science, 4*(3), 116–135.

Peterson, S.M. (2008). *Applying the Transtheoretical Model of behavior change to child care providers enrolled in professional development programs.* Rochester, NY: Children's Institute.

Phillips, D., Crowell, N., Whitebook, M., & Bellm, D. (2003). *English literacy levels of the early care and education work force: A profile and associations with quality of care.* Berkeley, CA: Center for the Study of Child Care Employment.

Pope, S., & Stremmel, A. (1992). Organizational climate and job satisfaction among child care teachers. *Child and Youth Care Forum, 21,* 39–52.

Prochaska, J.O., & DiClemente, C.C. (1983). Stages and processes of self-change of smoking: Toward an integrative model of change. *Journal of Consulting and Clinical Psychology, 51,* 390–395.

Prochaska, J.O., & Velicer, W.F. (1997). The Transtheoretical Model of health behavior change. *American Journal of Health Promotion, 12,* 38–48.

Raikes, H.H., Torquati, J.C., Hegland, H., Raikes, A., Scott, J., Messner, L., et al. (2006). Studying the culture of quality early education and care. In M. Zaslow & I. Martinez-Beck

(Eds.), *Critical issues in early childhood professional development* (pp. 111–136). Baltimore: Paul H. Brookes Publishing Co.

Raver, C.C., Jones, S.M., Li-Grining, C.P., Metzger, M., Champion, K.M., & Sardin, L. (2008). Improving preschool classroom processes: Preliminary findings from a randomized trial implemented in Head Start settings. *Early Childhood Research Quarterly, 23*, 10–26.

Rogoff, B., Matusov, E., & White, C. (1996). Models of teaching and learning: Participation in a community of learners. In D. Olson & N. Torrance (Eds.), *Handbook of education and human development: New models of learning, teaching, and schooling* (pp. 388–414). London: Basil Blackwell.

Senge, P. (1990). *The fifth discipline: The art and practice of the learning organization.* New York: Doubleday.

Stremmel, A. (1991). Predictors of intention to leave child care work. *Early Childhood Research Quarterly, 6*, 285–298.

Stremmel, A., Benson, M., & Powell, D. (1993). Communication, satisfaction, and emotional exhaustion among child care center staff: Directors, teachers, and assistant teachers. *Early Childhood Research Quarterly, 8*, 221–233.

Thayer, P.B. (2000). Retention of students from first generation and low income backgrounds. *Opportunity Outlook, 2–8.* Washington, DC: Council for Opportunity in Education.

Tinto, V. (1993). *Leaving college: Rethinking the causes and cures of student attrition* (2nd ed.). Chicago: University of Chicago Press.

Tym, C., McMillion, R., Barone, S., & Webster, J. (2004). *First-generation college students: A literature review.* Round Rock, TX: Texas Guaranteed Student Loan Corporation.

U.S. Department of Labor. (2009). *Occupational employment statistics, May 2008.* Washington DC: Bureau of Labor Statistics.

Whitebook, M., Howes, C., & Phillips, D. (1990). *Who cares? Child care teachers and the quality of care in America: Final report, National Child Care Staffing Study.* Oakland, CA: Child Care Employee Project.

Whitebook, M., & Sakai, L. (2003). Turnover begets turnover: an examination of job and occupational instability among child care center staff. *Early Childhood Research Quarterly, 18*, 273–293.

Whitebook, M., Sakai, L., Gerber, E., & Howes, C. (2001). *Then and now: Changes in child care staffing, 1994–2000. Technical report.* Washington, DC: Center for the Child Care Work force.

Wood, F.H., & McQuarrie, J.F. (1999). On-the-job learning. *Journal of Staff Development, 20*(3), 10–13.

Zachary, L.J. (2000). *The mentor's guide: Facilitating effective learning relationships.* San Francisco: Jossey Bass.

Mentor/Coach Survey: Stage of Change Scale 1.0

Mentor/coach name: ______________ Caregiver name: ______________ Date: ________

Instructions: For each row, circle the phrase that best completes the sentence: "When it comes to her/his child care practices, this person…."

Stage of change	Does not intend to make any changes	Is thinking about making a change but not ready to act	Has a plan to make a change	Is acting on a plan for change	Is working to maintain changes
Awareness	Does not think s/he needs to make any changes	Thinks s/he could make some changes in the future	Is ready to make a change	Has a particular area s/he is working on changing	Constantly thinks about how to improve
Seeking information	Is not interested in learning new information	Sometimes thinks about information s/he has heard	Is open to learning new information	Is looking for new information (e.g., taking a class, reading)	Always learns a lot about the areas s/he wants to change
Effect on children	Does not see how making a change would affect children	Thinks making a change might affect children	Believe that when s/he makes a change, it will help children	Sees how a change s/he made has helped helped the children	Constantly tries to improve so s/he can best help children
Overcoming obstacles	Sees no reason to make any changes	Feels overwhelmed by the thought of changing	Believes s/he can change, even though it isn't easy	Works to make changes, even when it isn't easy	Works hard to make sure s/he doesn't go back to her/his old ways
Social support	Does not have peers that encourage change	Would like to try something that s/he has seen someone do	Has a role model that encourages him/her to change	Has several peers that encourage change	Is active in a community that supports change
Professional identity	Does not think of himself/herself as a professional	Thinks s/he would feel more professional if s/he made a change	Is beginning to think of himself/herself as a professional	Feels like a professional because of a change s/he has made	Feels like a true professional because s/he constantly tries to improve his/her practices

Appendix 3.1. Mentor/Coach Survey: Stage of Change Scale 1.0. Copyright © 2008 by Children's Institute, Inc., Rochester, NY. All rights reserved. Do not reproduce without permission of Children's Institute, Inc., 585-295-1000, http://www.childrensinstitute.net

II

What Practices
Are Promising

Federal funding has begun to help support a burgeoning research base on quality teaching practices. This research has led to the identification of an emerging body of best practices for training and professional development among early childhood educators. We now know, for example, that merely adapting approaches to professional development used with K–12 teachers is not optimal. Rather, through a better understanding of the challenges and opportunities in the field, we have now identified an array of practice-sensitive approaches better tailored to meet the needs of early childhood teachers.

The chapters in this section offer important and timely research-based solutions for enhancing teacher quality in a wide variety of early childhood settings. In Chapter 4, Lambert and colleagues provide a broad overview of current activities in early childhood professional development and propose a model for developing expertise and sources of teacher support as the field progresses toward full professional status. The next two chapters demonstrate how these activities may work in the field and discuss their subsequent effects on teacher development. In Chapter 5, Sandefur and colleagues describe the research base and a model of coaching that has shown enormous promise for nontraditional learners. Similarly, in Chapter 6 Sandefur and colleagues focus on how mentoring, in addition to coaching, can provide much-needed supports that uniquely address the needs of the early childhood work force. These scholars make a significant contribution to the literature by pinpointing the distinguishing elements of mentoring and helping policy makers better understand the critical role and contribution of the mentor's knowledge, skills, and dispositions to adult learning and professional development.

Finally, and importantly, in Chapter 7, Baker and Peterson examine new methodological strategies to enable researchers to monitor progress in field-based interventions and to make necessary adjustments to enhance the potential for improving teacher quality in community-based settings.

4

Choosing Content

Richard G. Lambert, Annette Sibley, and Robert Lawrence

What makes a job a profession? What makes a worker a professional? A *profession* is a group of people who share a common occupation, have completed a set of requirements to enter that occupation, and agree to abide by specified standards of practice (Harvey, 2009). A *professional* is an autonomous practitioner who possesses specialized knowledge and skills; applies those skills using independent professional judgment; and takes responsibility for his or her own professional conduct, reflective practice, and professional growth (Burbules & Densmore, 1991). However, when considering the state of the early childhood work force at the time of this writing, the question quickly changes: To what extent do these definitions apply to those working in our system of education and care in the United States? And, furthermore, how can professional development help early childhood teachers view their work as more than just a job, and rather as a professional career?

To answer this question, it is important to examine the fundamental features that professions have in common. First, professions control who enters their field. This can be accomplished by establishing minimum qualifications for those recognized as members of the profession. These qualifications can include educational levels, training requirements, and achievement on written and/or performance evaluations. Professions also collaborate with governmental regulatory authorities to formally codify these qualifications as licensure or certification standards. Second, professions establish guidelines for the appropriate roles and responsibilities of their members. Many professions include in these definitions the common goals and commitments their members share as they strive to serve the public good (Burbules & Densmore, 1991; Harvey, 2009). Third, professions translate these guidelines into systems of self-regulation. These systems often include formal codes that establish standards of practice, ranging from criteria for the minimum required to constitute adequate service delivery, to ethical standards for acceptable professional conduct, to standards for high-quality practice, all of which extend beyond an individual practitioner's own moral or ethical commitments to establish a group consensus (Professions Australia, 2004). Furthermore, professions self-regulate by establishing processes for governance of the profession itself, performance evaluation of their members, and the review of and possible sanctions following allegations of misconduct. Some professions collaborate with governmental authorities to translate standards of practice into regulatory statutes and legal mandates.

Professions that have achieved consensus regarding who can practice and what practitioners do focus on more advanced and collective activities, often facilitated through professional organizations. Specifically, professions recognize excellence. Formalized levels of distinction, awards for professional accomplishment, and acknowledgement of career milestones are strategies that professions use to identify practitioners of high quality for both the membership and those served by the profession. These recognitions can even be incorporated into public policy. The Generalist/Early Childhood certificate from the National Board for Professional Teaching Standards (2009) is an example of this type of professional recognition for teachers, which can lead to higher compensation in some state educational systems. National Association for the Education of Young Children (NAEYC) certification (NAEYC, 2007) and the North Carolina STAR Rating System (North Carolina Division of Child Development, 2009) are examples of the recognition of early childhood program quality, which can lead to higher funding and reimbursement levels.

Professions advocate for public policies that benefit both the membership and those served by the profession. Many professional organizations fund both individuals and committees charged with raising public awareness about and support for specific governmental policies on a variety of issues such as funding, research, requirements for licensure or certification, and legal sanctions for unethical behavior. The Research and Evaluation Department of the National Head Start Association (NHSA; 2009) and the Governmental Relations Committee of the Division for Early Childhood (2009) of the Council for Exceptional Children are two organizations that participate in this type of professional activity.

Finally, professions have organized systems of support for their members that include ongoing, high-quality research-based and standards-driven professional development (Boone, 2001). All of the major professional organizations that serve the early childhood work force offer training at conferences and other events, as do state and local education agencies.

The remainder of this chapter focuses on sources of content for early childhood professional development and proposes models for both the foci and sources of teacher support as the field progresses toward full professional status.

FROM A TRADITION OF COMPLIANCE TOWARD RESEARCH-BASED CONTENT

Although a complete treatment of the ongoing debate regarding the existence of a subculture among America's impoverished—with unique values, experiences, and adaptations to the demands of living with low resources in a wealthy society (Goode & Eames, 1996; Lewis, 1966; Payne, 2003)—is beyond the scope of this chapter, substantial questions remain when considering the realities of the early childhood work force within a profession in transition. Many early childhood teachers have low literacy levels, a history of low wages, their own experiences in poverty, and personal histories with traditions of compliance rather than professionalism. The early childhood work force faces many challenges and barriers as it adapts to what is slowly becoming a middle class profession with changing educational and licensure requirements and the implementation of more complex curricular models. Similarly, teachers who work in low-income neighborhoods and do not come from a background of poverty themselves face the demands associated with adapting their teaching strategies to the needs of the children and families they serve.

In October 2000, the National Research Council and the Institute of Medicine released a report titled *From Neurons to Neighborhoods: The Science of Early Childhood Development.* The report was designed to promote an understanding of the basic science of early childhood development, including its underlying neurobiology, for the purpose of informing both public and private sector investments in young children and their families. The report called for a long-term investment by all segments of society—including the business community, private philanthropy, both faith-based and secular voluntary organizations, professional associations, and government at all levels—to work together to strengthen families, educate parents, and provide professional assistance for young children and their families who need help.

Concurrently, in support of state and federal commitments to move toward better trained and qualified teachers, NAEYC developed standards for the preparation of early childhood professionals. These standards present a "shared vision of excellence for all early childhood professionals across education and training settings" (NAEYC, 2006). It is widely believed that quality pedagogical practices include a complex set of skills, content knowledge, and disposition (National Council for the Accreditation of Teacher Education, 2007; Tarrant, Greenberg, Kagan, & Kauerz, 2009). The national standards established by NAEYC link to desired outcomes at colleges and universities and in community-based and other professional development settings, and they focus on five distinct competencies for teachers working in early childhood programs.

These competencies address the knowledge, skills, and abilities that early childhood teachers should demonstrate, including the following (NAEYC, 2006):

1. *Knowledge of the range of influences on child development*—including cultural contexts, economic conditions, health status, and learning styles—and an ability to apply knowledge to improve social interactions, assessment, and instruction

2. *Respect for relationships with all families,* irrespective of their structure, language, ethnicity, and child's ability or disability

3. *Use of effective assessment strategies* to guide decisions about curriculum and instruction

4. *Use of content knowledge in academic subject areas* to give all children the experiences that promote their comprehensive development and learning

5. *Demonstration of self-motivated, ongoing learning, collaboration, and reflective and critical thinking* in their role as early childhood professionals

CURRENT CONDITIONS

Under the best conditions, professional development in the early childhood field contains a wide range of content that is delivered through a variety of methods. For example, a review of the program for the 2009 NAEYC National Institute for Early Childhood Professional Development identified a range of session topics, including the developmental value of play, parent involvement and home school partnerships, use of outdoor space, content specific teacher child interactions (e.g., art, music, literacy, math, oral language), curriculum and implementation fidelity, assessment, and coaching and mentoring strategies (NAEYC, 2009). Leaving aside the limited access that many practitioners have to events such as this conference, a detailed review of the actual content of these sessions and the process of delivery would be required to determine exactly how much of a given session was engaging to the audience, met the real needs of practitioners, and contained research-based content.

In practice, early childhood professional development plays a variety of roles for teachers and program administrators. Figure 4.1 outlines a proposed model that can serve as a classification system for the hierarchy of content that early childhood professional development activities contain. The first, and lowest, level refers to *Social Support*. Historically, professional development activities across the education profession have been inadequately evaluated, and evaluation has rarely extended beyond the simple and immediate reaction of the participants (Kirkpatrick, 1998; Kirkpatrick & Kirkpatrick, 2005). Therefore, strategies that teachers feel good about at the time and offer a sense of social support from colleagues have often been perpetuated, despite a lack of evidence-based content. The second level in the model refers to *Induction*. Administrators often use professional development events to disseminate policy and procedural information, particularly with new teachers. The third level, *Compliance*, refers to the substantial amount of time that early childhood practitioners spend in professional development activities related to dissemination of information about safety and health standards, environmental quality, and systemic policy mandates. Even if one were able to assume that all of the content of such events was necessary, more experienced practitioners may not benefit from repeated exposure to the same content. The fourth level in the model refers to *Curriculum* and includes all the time practitioners spend in professional development activities related to the

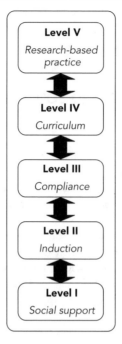

Figure 4.1. A model for classifying the content of professional development activity.

lesson planning, materials, assessment, activities, and implementation fidelity of the curriculum model used by their center or school, whether or not the model is research based. The fifth, and highest, level in the model is *Research-Based Practice* and refers to the relatively small portion of the total professional development exposure for practitioners that focuses on changing specific practices and teacher–child interactions in accordance with research findings.

Teachers need each of these types of content at different points in their career, and this model illustrates the competing demands for professional development time that administrators need to negotiate and broker in order to meet the needs of both funding sources and teachers, all with limited resources. Each level in the model shares some overlapping content with the level that precedes and/or follows it, and the higher levels necessitate a foundation in place from the lower levels. However, it is important to note that much of the content of early childhood professional development activity is focused on things other than evidence-based practice and higher order teacher functions, such as reflection about practice, intentional teaching, and professional growth. Furthermore, it is unrealistic to expect that professional development activities that do focus on translating evidence-based practice into specific teaching strategies will result in improved teacher–child interactions and child outcomes, particularly outside of a coordinated system of training content and follow-up coaching (Neuman & Cunningham, 2009).

TOWARD RESEARCH-BASED SOURCES OF CONTENT

How do professions determine the sources of content for the professional development of their members? To answer this question, we must need to build upon the previous discussion of professions and professionalism. Professions establish standards of practice and quality that are rooted in the research literature of their discipline. In early childhood education, school readiness or early learning standards have had a significant impact on policy and practice (Kagan & Scott-Little, 2004) and continue to evolve and respond to the research knowledge base of the field (Neuman & Roskos, 2005). Most states now have such standards, although they vary in terms of the extent to which standards for children's growth, development, and learning are tied to state learning standards for the school-age years. They also vary as to how connected they are to child assessments, standards for program quality, and systems of teacher support (Scott-Little, Lesko, Martella, & Milburn, 2007).

We propose a model for the sources of early childhood professional development content that includes a macro level, or professionwide process, and an interrelated micro level, or teacher-specific process. Figure 4.2 illustrates how this process flows from research-based standards in the upper left corner to teacher self-directed learning in the lower right corner, with the top row representing the macro level and the bottom row representing the micro level. In the ideal case, the early childhood professional organizations in a given state would work with the state authorities to develop, refine, and update the early learning standards for

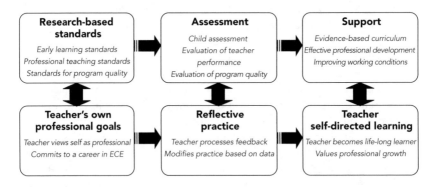

Figure 4.2.   A model for the sources of early childhood professional development content. The top row represents the macro level, and the bottom row represents the micro level. (*Key:* ECE, early childhood education.)

children, standards for teaching practice, and standards for program quality, all of which would be interconnected and rooted in the research base. These standards would in turn lead to systems of child assessment, teacher performance evaluation, and program quality evaluation. Ideally these systems would be based on multiple indicators and data sources and on measurements obtained at the level under evaluation (child, teacher, or program) as opposed to being based solely on aggregations of lower level indicators. Furthermore, the indicators would be developed and validated considering the particular purpose and use for which they are intended within an overall system of evaluation and teacher support, and they would be accompanied by guidelines for proper interpretation (Lambert, 2003).

Data from these assessment systems would in turn drive a comprehensive system of teacher support that includes evidence-based curriculum and materials, and effective professional development, both in terms of content and delivery methods. In addition, assessment would inform a broad system of teacher support that includes professional salary levels and career pathways that reduce attrition and occupational stress. The teacher work force, as it becomes more professionalized, would respond with greater levels of commitment to the profession. Individual teachers would view themselves increasingly as professionals and would set goals for their own practice that are rooted in the research-based standards. The cumulative effect of these individual goals across the profession would be a greater demand for research-based professional development, particularly as teachers learn to process the feedback they receive from the assessment systems and become more reflective about their practice. Teachers would, with the proper supports, learn to become self-directed learners, taking responsibility for their own professional development.

In summary, the model suggests that the content of early childhood professional development needs to be based on standards for early learning, teaching practice, and program quality. These standards need to be tied directly to research evidence. Early childhood professional organizations can play an important role in promoting awareness of local, state, and national standards and in conducting training sessions about the standards for practitioners. Assessment systems that are directly tied to the standards help make the standards come to life for teachers and administrators, particularly as they learn to interpret objective evidence of their progress toward meeting the standards. Assessment systems also need to be credible, useful, timely in their feedback, and aligned with national standards for assessment systems. For example, child assessment systems can be aligned with the guidelines from the National Research Council report on early childhood assessments (Snow & Van Hamel, 2008). Teacher performance appraisal systems can be aligned with *The Personnel Evaluation Standards: How to Assess Systems for Evaluating Educators* (Gullickson & Howard, 2008), and systems for evaluating program quality can be aligned with the *Program Evaluation Standards: How to Assess Evaluations of Educational Programs* (Sanders, 1994).

STANDARDS DRIVING CONTENT

Systems of teacher support can be tied to early childhood standards as well. Both content and delivery methods can be evidence-based, and both content and the particular support processes can be data driven and individualized at the teacher or program level as indicated by the standards-based assessment systems. For example, the National Staff Development Council (2009) issued a report titled *Professional Learning in the Learning Profession.* The report contains national standards, tied to research evidence, that outline the conditions under which teacher professional development is most effective. Although the research base that supports these standards is not specific to early childhood educators, and the early childhood research base does not yet provide clear consensus about the most effective delivery methods for professional development (Zaslow & Martinez-Beck, 2006), the report offers guidelines that can transfer in spirit to the development of systems for supporting the early childhood work force.

Specifically, the report suggests that professional development for teachers needs to be data driven and directly linked to assessment and analysis of teaching practices and student learning. The content should be aligned with, coincide with, and integrated into teacher instructional planning and curriculum implementation. When the content is seen as immediately relevant to teachers, focused on curricular content, and specific to actual teaching practices and teacher–child interactions, it is more likely to be applied in the classroom. The report also suggests that professional development cannot succeed as an unconnected chain of one-shot events. It is much more useful for teachers and more likely to be implemented in the classroom if it is intensive, sustained, and continuous over time; supported by coaching, modeling, observation, and feedback; and connected to teacher's collaborative work in professional learning communities. These standards support early childhood research findings indicating that professional development training improves teacher practice only if participants are actively involved, the model provides teachers with both early childhood theory and practical application, the sessions are ongoing with each session building on earlier sessions, the trainer observes and provides feedback on classroom implementation, and the participants are provided opportunities to reflect on what they have learned and share their accomplishments and challenges (Epstein, 1993).

A detailed review of the research literature that could support standards, and in turn assessment and professional development content for the early childhood work force across all domains of development, is beyond the scope of this chapter. However, we will examine examples of three potential sources of content that are both rooted in the research knowledge base and stem from the model: 1) research-based standards, 2) research-based formal assessment, and 3) informal assessment of individual teacher needs within comprehensive systems of teacher support. We will focus on language and literacy, although a similar process could be used by administrators to plan staff development activities and identify the needs of their teachers in other domains of development.

Research evidence has suggested that intentional teaching to support the language and literacy domain of child development requires that teachers possess a sophisticated level of content-specific knowledge (Dickinson & Brady, 2006), an ability to build on children's prior knowledge, and an awareness of the context-specific experiences that children bring to the classroom (Neuman, Roskos, Wright, & Lenhart, 2007). Given the association between overall program quality and the background of teachers (Bowman, Donovan, & Burns, 2001) and the connection between program quality and the quality of teaching in the area of language and literacy (Snow, Griffin, & Burns, 2005), program administrators interested in improving practice in this area are faced with the difficult work of synthesizing a large amount of information into a meaningful professional development plan for their teachers. For a comprehensive discussion of the research base that supports suggested professional development content for early childhood teachers in the area of language and literacy, refer to Dickinson and Brady (2006).

To illustrate how just a few research-based standards or guidelines can offer early childhood practitioners a rich set of suggestions for the content of professional development related to language and literacy, we will review an NAEYC position paper, the most recent report from the National Early Literacy Panel, and the portion of the North Carolina Early Learning Standards that addresses early literacy.

Administrators just beginning to explore research-based standards for themselves and their teachers can refer to the guidelines from the NAEYC (1998) position paper titled *Learning to Read and Write: Developmentally Appropriate Practices for Young Children,* which provides an overview of the NAEYC and International Reading Association joint report on the same topic. The report emphasizes the importance of early reading and writing as a part of the early education process for young children and the role early childhood teachers play in making reading and writing enjoyable for children as they experience it in a school setting for the first time. The report stresses the need for intentional instructional planning and ongoing assessment to drive individualized intervention in addition to the unique needs of English language learners and their families. However, many teachers do not understand either the process of using assessment to determine the unique needs of individual children or how to individualize instruction. Professional development can help introduce them to the core components of teaching young children.

The National Institute for Literacy (2009) report titled *Developing Early Literacy: Report of the National Early Literacy Panel* offers an overview of many of the early skills and abilities that are linked to later academic outcomes for children. Exposing early childhood teachers to this information can help them internalize the rationale for and critical importance of high-quality intentional teaching in the area of language and literacy. The report illustrates how high-quality preschool environments can have an impact on the school readiness and future academic success of the children they serve, which further motivates early childhood teachers to take a professional and ever-expanding approach toward their work with young children. The report makes it clear that rich and complex language stimulation in the early childhood classroom can have a lasting impact on young children and suggests specific strategies that teachers can focus on to create such an environment: 1) code-focused interventions, 2) shared reading-focused interventions, 3) rich use of oral language in interactions with children, and 4) partnerships with the home environment to connect language stimulation at home with stimulation in the classroom. Administrators can use these broad guidelines as they begin the processes of educating themselves on the topic, diagnosing the needs of their teachers as a group when planning training, and identifying the needs of specific teachers when planning individualized support.

In the 1990s, state education agencies or child care regulation bodies began developing standards that can also be used to help guide local professional development plans (Scott-Little, 2006). The *North Carolina Early Learning Standards* are one such example (North Carolina Office of School Readiness, 2005). These standards attempt to offer a comprehensive examination of multiple domains of development, including a language and literacy section that provides a rich and accessible outline of the developmental processes at work in young children, birth to age 5, as they begin to develop in this area. The standards stress that high-quality preschool classroom environments filled with print, books, literacy activities, and rich conversations with supportive adults are linked to later child academic success. The standards also remind teachers of the importance of rich stimulation in the language of the home environment for those children learning English.

The standards outline four broad areas of critical development within the language and literacy domain: receptive language, **expressive language,** foundations for reading, and foundations for writing. For each broad area, the standards provide clear and accessible *definitions* of the concepts involved, clear explanations of widely held *expectations* for developmental milestones and tasks, specific guidelines regarding *teaching strategies* and teacher–child interactions that can facilitate the development of young children, and *strategies for families* interested in stimulating their child's development and reinforcing the stimulation in the classroom. For example, in the area of receptive language, the standards outline 7 specific expectations for development (e.g. "Children begin to understand increasingly complex sentences, including past, present, and future tenses"), 10 strategies for educators (e.g. "Introduce new words and concepts by labeling what children are doing and experiencing while providing opportunities for conversations"), and 8 strategies for families (e.g. "Have fun with words. Singing songs and playing rhyming and word games [nursery rhymes, poems, finger plays] help children develop an understanding of different sounds").

By starting with broad position papers from their respective professional organizations, moving to research reports that outline and translate the current evidence of the research knowledge base, and ending with the particular set of standards that define high-quality practice in a given locale, program administrators can begin to connect the professional development they plan for their teachers to the research base as they become professional leaders themselves.

ASSESSMENT DRIVING CONTENT

This section discusses strategies that early childhood programs can use to establish comprehensive, data-driven systems of professional development. The first step is the development of systems for assessment that systematically document child developmental progress; teacher performance, including teaching practices and fidelity of curriculum implementation; teacher characteristics; classroom quality; and program quality. This involves the selection of measures that are rooted in the research base and possess the necessary measurement properties to provide reliable, valid, and culturally sensitive feedback for their particular context. Administrators must next decide who collects each source of data and how it will be used. Some measures of child developmental progress can be collected best by teachers, whereas others may be best collected by independent assessors. Measures of teacher performance and program quality may be best collected by outside observers who supervise the teachers, however, teachers and coaches may benefit from self-assessments on the same measures. Finally, administrators need to be trained to use all of this data to identify programwide deficits that can lead to professional development goals for their teachers as a group. This can involve organizing professional learning communities made up of teachers with similar needs. Administrators can also begin to understand how to analyze the data from individual classrooms to drive the systems of individualized support (coaching, mentoring, and accessing self-study resources).

As an example, we will examine the information provided by several measures of the quality of teaching practices our research team has used to evaluate specific approaches to coaching early childhood teachers. These measures are rooted in the research base, designed to measure the impact of professional development on the intermediate outcomes of classroom quality, and can be used by program administrators to define high-quality teaching practices in the area of language and literacy. Specifically, the Teacher Behavior Rating Scale (Landry, Gunnewig, Assel, Crawford, & Swank, 2004) gives detailed feedback on the quantity and quality of very specific teaching behaviors. The Early Language and Literacy Classroom Observation Tool (**ELLCO**) Pre-K (Smith, Brady, & Anastasopoulos, 2008) provides a comprehensive look at the language richness of the classroom environment and provides evidence of teaching quality in targeted areas of practice. In addition, the Use of Center Time measure (Lambert & Brewer, 2006) examines the extent to which teachers remain engaged with children during child-directed activities in the daily schedule and provide feedback regarding the extent to which they intercede to extend and enrich children's activities.

Collectively, these measures provide a comprehensive overview of the topics that can be targeted for professional development. Along with implementation fidelity data related to the specific curricular model used by our research partner programs, much of this data has been used at the aggregate level to plan the content of training events and at the individual teacher level to plan coaching interventions. This process begins by organizing the data into areas of professional practice. Then as the data are analyzed by content area, if patterns of less-than-ideal practice emerge across a majority of teachers, this suggests the need for training and follow-up supports. As individual teachers are identified that have specific weaknesses that are not shared by the majority of teachers, those teachers can be referred to resources, mentors, or coaches for targeted assistance.

Stimulating the use of children's oral language is one of the broad areas covered by these measures. Specific feedback can be provided to teachers in areas such as conducting class meetings to discuss and review the learning opportunities for the day, having stimulating conversations with young children, asking open-ended questions, and generally encouraging children's use of language by creating a language-rich and cognitively complex classroom environment. Feedback is also provided in the area of book reading regarding teaching practices, such as orienting children to printed material in the context of book reading; introducing new vocabulary in the context of book reading; and leading discussions with children before, during, and after book reading. These measures can also offer feedback about teaching practices related to the alphabet and writing, such as fostering letter recognition in young children and helping children associate letter names with sounds. Phonological awareness is covered by items related to teaching listening, sentence segmentation, syllable blending and segmenting, rhyming, phoneme blending and segmentation, and alliteration, as well as how well a teacher integrates phonological awareness into daily activities.

These measures can also offer feedback regarding a variety of general high-quality teaching practices. For example, observers can report about writing centers and the extent to which they are integrated it into daily activities. Observational data can be collected regarding how well a teacher remains engaged with children during child-directed times in the schedule; supports, extends, and encourages interactions among children; and plans small-group activities. Such a wealth of feedback about teacher practices can help identify both collective areas of need that can point to training and individual needs to support coaching for programs and teachers functioning at varying levels.

The North Carolina Beginning Teacher Support Program is an example of data-driven mentoring within a comprehensive system of support for early childhood teachers. The program includes tuition assistance for teachers pursuing a North Carolina Birth-to-Kindergarten license. It includes a process whereby teachers can satisfy their student teaching requirements while continuing to work in their current job. Each teacher working in a nonpublic school setting (e.g., child care center, Head Start), following their initial licensure, is provided with a mentor and evaluator for a 3-year process of performance evaluation and data-driven mentoring. The performance evaluations are performed using the Prekindergarten/Kindergarten Teacher Performance Appraisal Instrument (Lambert, Rowland, Wheeler, Ullrich, & Bird, 2008). This measure was specifically created to evaluate teachers in early childhood classrooms according to the North Carolina Early Learning Standards. In addition, each teacher receives four evaluations each year (three formative and one summative), each with a pre- and postevaluation conference. The mentor and teacher receive the feedback from each observation, and collectively they establish an Individual Growth Plan and Staff Development Log. Finally, each the teachers are provided with salary supplements and benefits once they complete their degrees so that they can remain in their work setting and receive school system salary levels. Although this system represents a substantial commitment of state resources, it is a model for how data-driven mentoring and professional development can function within a comprehensive system of teacher support.

CONTENT EMERGING WITHIN THE COACHING PROCESS

If a straightforward translation of the results of external evaluations of a teacher's job performance, interactions with children and their families, and the quality of the classroom environment into professional development goals and requirements was all that was needed to improve teaching practices, coaches could focus solely on delivering content. However, a great deal of professional judgment is often required to develop the optimal professional development plan for individual teachers. Several models can be helpful in training coaches to individualize the professional development experience for teachers by tying content directly to a synthesis of assessment information and a diagnosis of the unique characteristics and needs of the individual teacher. One example of an individualized and data-driven model of coaching is the consultation model (Palsha & Wesley, 1998). In this model, both the consultant and consultee collaborate, review the results of assessments, and create solutions to mutually identified problem areas (Brown, Pryzwansky, & Schulte, 1987; Buysse & Wesley, 2004).

Another model of individualized data-driven coaching is outlined in *The Coach's Guide to The Creative Curriculum for Preschool: A Step-by-Step Resource for Individualizing Professional Development* (Heroman, Jablon, Stetson, Aghavan, & Dodge, 2009). This approach includes a process for using data from the *Creative Curriculum for Preschool Implementation Checklist* (Dodge, Colker, & Heroman, 2003) to diagnose areas of need, set professional development goals with the teacher, and plan coaching interventions. The model also contains specific strategies for diagnosing the teacher's level of career development (Katz, 1972), including the teacher's stress level, work experience, and readiness for innovation. This information is used to match specific coaching strategies to both areas of needed content and to the depth and style that is most appropriate for the particular teacher.

For example, consider the following commonly occurring situations:

Becky is a veteran child care worker and the data from external observations indicate that she has multiple weaknesses and needs substantial assistance across several areas of practice. Although she is not resistant to discussions of the data, and seems open to outside input, she really has not had many high-quality role models in her career and really does not understand how much she could do to improve the quality of her classroom.

Brian is a young, newly licensed teacher with limited experience in the classroom. He is fresh from teacher training and is working in a Head Start center where there are no other degreed teachers. He does not see the need for mentoring, is somewhat resistant to discussions of the results of observations, and does not understand how much mentoring can help him, both with adjustment to the professional practice of teaching and related to quality improvement.

Carla is a mid-career teacher. She has been working at the same child care center for 11 years. Carla is overwhelmed with behavior management issues in the classroom and many stresses in her personal life. She is a single mother with three children of her own ranging in age from 3 to 8 years. She is not overtly resistant to coaching but is experiencing a great deal of stress in her personal and professional life and sees the coaching process as another external mandate that is likely to simply impose more demands on her already busy daily schedule.

Teachers such as these could share many of the same relative weaknesses. However, an experienced coach would be sensitive to each teacher's individual circumstances and help him or her co-create an individualized professional development plan that is realistic and sensitive to his or her unique needs. An experienced coach can synthesize scores from performance evaluations, classroom observations, and child assessments with the information they have gathered informally through their own interactions with the teacher to steer the discussion to the most important initial goals and initial focal topics for coaching. Furthermore, a well-designed and comprehensive system of teacher support could include features that address the needs of teachers throughout the career development process.

For example, the coach may need to focus on simple, achievable goals with Becky, and may gradually increase the complexity of the changes that she tries to encourage as she sees Becky increasing her skills and knowledge, and thereby her readiness for further innovation and improvement. The system of support could offer Becky the opportunity to visit model classrooms and meet potential role models. With Brian, the coach may choose to demonstrate instructional strategies in the classroom to both build credibility and model good practice. The system of support could offer Brian specific induction programs designed to help new teachers adjust to the profession. With Carla, the coach may start by offering behavior management strategies and emotional support. The system of support could offer Carla the opportunity to join a learning community of other educators at similar stages in their careers, which could help provide tangible social and emotional support.

A professional coach can focus early in the relationship on building rapport and trust with the teacher and can simply begin by observing and asking questions. The coach can then move on to completing one of the observational tools and asking the teacher to complete a self-assessment using the same tool. The process of developing an individualized professional development plan can begin with a discussion of these two assessments, looking for common ground. An experienced coach can also help make the content of training and the results from external observations relevant to the teacher by practical examples and applications in the classroom. The coach can help the teacher understand the rationale behind scores on observational measures and the importance of the content of the items in terms that the teacher understands. Perhaps the most important element of this process is the rich discussion and exchange between the teacher and coach as they identify and agree on needs and develop both a professional development plan and set of goals for which the teacher can take ownership. A comprehensive system of teacher support can not only offer coaching or mentoring programs but also can target all stages of a teacher's career with specific supports from induction programs to formal pathways to professional recognition and opportunities to become a coach or mentor for those identified as exemplary.

CONCLUSION

This chapter has focused on one aspect of professional development—sources of content. We presented a model suggesting that professional development content for teachers needs to fit seamlessly into a comprehensive system of support that helps attract, nurture, and retain high-quality educators of young children. Furthermore, such content needs to be rooted in and driven by current research and made practical, actionable, and concrete for practitioners by research-based standards and assessment systems.

Program administrators interested in developing a comprehensive system of support for their teachers are faced with a number of decisions. They need to become familiar with the research-based standards that are applicable in their locale, develop a system of assessment that will measure progress toward the standards, and develop a system of professional development that will meet the needs of their work force. This process includes several smaller steps as well. Administrators need to become aware of the degree of readiness for formal training and education among their work force. They need to decide how they will complement formal training and education with ongoing support such as professional learning communities, mentoring, or coaching. They need to develop specific strategies for matching teachers with coaches, mentors, and/or professional learning communities to maximize the benefits for teachers, considering the unique strengths and needs of the individuals involved. They need to decide how they will ask teachers to document and be recognized for their professional development accomplishments, for example through the use of personal portfolios of training content received and implemented. They may also be faced with questions about how to integrate professional development content with the content teachers are exposed to in college coursework. Administrators, particularly those in small programs, may have limited resources for professional development and may need to create and maintain lists of resources that are available in their communities that can them meet the needs of their teachers. For many smaller programs, the most useful and long lasting professional development experiences may come through collaborations with broader systems of support at the community, regional, and state levels.

As the field of early childhood education matures into a profession and makes progress in the current transition from a culture of compliance to a culture of professionalism, we need to remember that the process of developing high-quality teachers shares much more in common with making fine wine according to organic farming methods than it does with mixing Kool-Aid. There will be no easy answers or quick fixes. Focusing too much on short-term results at the expense of long-term benefits to children and families may allow us to occasionally stumble upon methods for making Beaujolais, but will never lead us to the best strategies for making carefully aged Merlot. As we take the long-range perspective as a profession, we will need to develop strategies for identifying teachers who are worthy of substantial investment, while recognizing both the stages of career development that teachers pass through and the unique needs that each stage presents.

Making a commitment to the long-range development of individual teachers is like picking the right grapes and then investing in a process of continually nurturing the vineyards so they produce plentiful harvests of high-quality grapes year after year. Winemaking is of course a fine art that has been developed over centuries and takes a lifetime to master. Identifying and lessening the impact of the many barriers individual programs and teachers will face in this process of professionalization will not be easy. The organic winemaker removes the pesticides and fertilizers and plants food plots to attract back the natural wildlife and restore the natural and balanced ecosystem, composting all the unused materials along the way. Similarly, local, state, and national early childhood policy makers will need to help our system of care develop into a unified and balanced system that is integrated into the broader professional early education community.

REFERENCES

Boone, T. (2001). Constructing a profession. *Professionalization of Exercise Physiology, 4*(5). Retrieved May 2001 from http://faculty.css.edu/tboone2/asep/Constructing Aprofession.html

Bowman, B.T., Donovan, M.S., & Burns, M.S. (Eds.). (2001). *Eager to learn: Educating our preschoolers.* Washington, DC: National Academies Press.

Brown, D., Pryzwansky, W., & Schulte, A. (1987). *Psychological consultation: Introduction to theory and practice.* Boston: Allyn & Bacon.

Burbules, N., & Densmore, K. (1991). The limits of making teaching a profession. *Educational Policy, 5*(1), 44–63.

Buysse, V., & Wesley, P.W. (2004). A framework for understanding the consultation process: Stage by stage. *Young Exceptional Children, 7*(2), 2–9.

Dickinson, D.K., & Brady, J.P. (2006). Toward effective support for language and literacy through professional development. In M. Zaslow & I. Martinez-Beck (Eds.), *Critical issues in early childhood professional development.* Baltimore: Paul H. Brookes Publishing Co.

Division for Early Childhood. (2009). *Policy/Advocacy.* Retrieved July 28, 2009, from http://www.dec-sped.org/PolicyAdvocacy

Dodge, D.T., Colker, L.J., & Heroman, C. (2003). *The Creative Curriculum for Preschool Implementation Checklist.* Washington, DC: Teaching Strategies.

Epstein, A.S. (1993). *Training for quality: Improving early childhood programs through systemic inservice training* (Monographs of the High/Scope Educational Foundation, 9). Ypsilanti, MI: HighScope Press.

Goode, J.G., & Eames, E. (1996). An anthropological critique of the culture of poverty. In G. Gmelch & P. Zenner (Eds.), *Urban life: Readings in urban anthropology.* Prospect Heights, IL: Waveland Press.

Gullickson, A.R., & Howard, B. (2008). *The personnel evaluation standards: How to assess systems for evaluating educators* (2nd ed.). Thousand Oaks, CA: Corwin.

Harvey, L. (2009). *Analytic quality glossary.* Retrieved July 28, 2009, from http://www.qualityresearchinternational.com/glossary

Heroman, C., Jablon, J., Stetson, C., Aghavan, C., & Dodge, D.T. (2009). *The coach's guide to The Creative Curriculum for Preschool: A step-by-step resource for individualizing professional development.* Bethesda, MD: Teaching Strategies.

Kagan, S.L., & Scott-Little, C. (2004). Early learning standards: Changing the parlance and practice of early childhood education? *Phi Delta Kappan, 85*(5), 388–396.

Katz, L. (1972). Developmental stages of preschool teachers. *Elementary School Journal, 73*(1), 50–54.

Kirkpatrick, D.L. (1998). *Evaluating training programs* (2nd ed.). San Francisco: Berrett-Koehler Publishers.

Kirkpatrick, D.L., & Kirkpatrick, J.D.(2005). *Evaluating training programs: The four levels.* La Vergne, TN: Ingram Publisher Services.

Lambert, R. (2003). Considering purpose and intended use when making evaluations of assessments: A response to Dickinson. *Educational Researcher, 32*(4), 1–4.

Lambert, R., & Brewer, D. (2006). *Use of center time.* Charlotte, NC: The Center for Educational Measurement and Evaluation.

Lambert, R., Rowland, B., Wheeler, C., Ullrich, A., & Bird, J. (2008). *Evaluator's guide: Pre-Kindergarten and Kindergarten Teacher Performance Appraisal Instrument.* Raleigh: North Carolina Department of Public Instruction.

Landry, S.H., Gunnewig, S., Assel, M., Crawford, A., & Swank, P. (2004). *Teacher Behavior Rating Scale.* Unpublished manuscript.

Lewis, O. (1966). The culture of poverty. *Scientific American, 215*(4), 19–25.

National Association for the Education of Young Children. (1998). *Learning to read and write: Developmentally appropriate practices for young children.* Available online at http://www.naeyc.org/files/naeyc/file/positions/PSREAD98.PDF

National Association for the Education of Young Children. (2006). *On standards for programs to prepare early childhood professionals.* Retrieved July 28, 2009, from http://208.118.177.216/about/positions/pdf/programStandards.pdf

National Association for the Education of Young Children. (2007). *NAEYC early childhood program standards and accreditation criteria: The mark of quality in early childhood education.* Washington, DC: Author.

National Association for the Education of Young Children. (2009). *National Institute for Early Childhood Professional Development.* Retrieved July 28, 2009, from http://www.naeyc.org/institute

National Board for Professional Teaching Standards. (2009). *The standards: Generalist/early childhood.* Retrieved July 28, 2009, from http://www.nbpts.org/the_standards/ standards_by_cert?ID=17&x=42&y=9

National Council for the Accreditation of Teacher Education. (2007). *Professional standards for the accreditation of teacher preparation institutions.* Retrieved July 28, 2009, from http://www.ncate.org/documents/standards/NCATE%20Standards%202008.pdf

National Head Start Association. (2009). *Research and evaluation.* Retrieved July 28, 2009, from http://www.nhsa.org/research/research_and_evaluation

National Institute for Literacy. (2009). *Developing early literacy: Report of the National Early Literacy Panel.* Retrieved July 28, 2009, from http://www.nifl.gov/publications/ pdf/NELPReport09.pdf

National Research Council and Institute of Medicine. (2000) *From neurons to neighborhoods: The science of early childhood development.* Washington, DC: National Academies Press.

National Staff Development Council. (2009). *Professional learning in the learning profession.* Retrieved July 28, 2009, from http://www.nsdc.org/stateproflearning.cfm

Neuman, S.B., & Cunningham, L. (2009). The impact of professional development and coaching on early language and literacy instructional practices. *American Educational Research Journal, 46*(2), 322–353.

Neuman, S.B., & Roskos, K. (2005). The state of state prekindergarten standards. *Early Childhood Research Quarterly, 20,* 125–145.

Neuman, S.B., Roskos, K., Wright, T., & Lenhart, L. (2007). *Nurturing knowledge: Linking literacy to math, science, social studies, and much more.* New York: Scholastic.

North Carolina Office of School Readiness. (2005). *Foundations – NC's early learning standards.* Retrieved July 28, 2009, from http://www.osr.nc.gov/ProfDevandResources/ foundationsEarly_learning.asp

North Carolina Division of Child Development. (2009). *Star Rated License: Overview.* Retrieved July 28, 2009, from http://ncchildcare.dhhs.state.nc.us/parents/pr_sn2_ ov_sr.asp

Palsha, S.A., & Wesley, P.W. (1998). Improving quality in early childhood environments through on-site consultation. *Topics in Early Childhood Special Education, 18*(4), 243–253.

Payne, R.K. (2003). *A framework for understanding poverty* (3rd ed.). Highland, TX: Aha! Process.

Professions Australia. (2004). *About Professions Australia: Definition of a profession.* Retrieved July 28, 2009, from http://www.professions.com.au/defineprofession.html

Sanders, J.R. (1994). *The program evaluation standards: How to assess evaluations of educational programs* (2nd ed.). Thousand Oaks, CA: Sage Publications.

Scott-Little, C. (2006). *Standing at the crossroads: Next steps to maximize the potential benefits of early learning standards.* Retrieved January 29, 2010, from http://www.naeyc.org/files/yc/file/200609/ScottLittleBTJ.pdf

Scott-Little, C., Lesko, J., Martella, J., & Milburn, P. (2007). Early learning standards: Results from a national survey to document trends in state-level policies and practices. *Early Childhood Research and Practice, 9*(1). Retrieved July 28, 2009, from http://ecrp.uiuc.edu/v9n1/little.html

Smith, M.W., Brady, J.P., & Anastasopoulos, L. (2008). *Early Language and Literacy Classroom Observation Tool (ELLCO) Pre-K.* Baltimore: Paul H. Brookes Publishing Co.

Snow, C., Griffin, P., & Burns, M. (2005). *Knowledge to support the teaching of reading: Preparing teachers for a changing world.* San Francisco: Jossey-Bass.

Snow, C., & Van Hamel, S.B. (Eds.). (2008). *Early childhood assessment: Why, what, and how.* Washington, DC: National Academies Press.

Tarrant, K., Greenberg, E., Kagan, S.L., & Kauerz, K. (2009). The early childhood work force. In S. Feeney, A. Galpar, & C. Seefeldt (Eds.), *Continuing issues in early childhood education* (3rd ed.). Upper Saddle River, NJ: Reason Education.

Zaslow, M., & Martinez-Beck, I. (Eds.). (2006). *Critical issues in early childhood professional development.* Baltimore: Paul H. Brookes Publishing Co.

5

Coaching

It's Not Just for Little League

Sarah Jo Sandefur, Amye R. Warren,
Anne B. Gamble, Jenny M. Holcombe, and Heather K. Hicks

Labor coach, Little League coach, and (more recently) *life coach* are familiar titles in the national lexicon, but another kind of coach is gaining recognition as a potentially essential element in professional development training for improved teacher practice in the early childhood setting: the professional development coach. Professional development coaching can occur in many different ways, but it is usually most valuable to have the individualized support of an experienced coach to encourage desired strategies in the teacher's own environment.

For example, there is a difference between Child A who watches a video on effective batting techniques and Child B who stands on home plate, bat in hand, awaiting a pitch, while an experienced player explains how to swing at the perfect moment. Intuition and experience would suggest that Child B has the greater potential for connecting with the ball. Many early childhood teachers, like Child A, have watched the video (or attended the workshop or taken the course) to learn effective teaching practices with young children. However, like Child B, it is assumed that teachers who have had the individualized support of an experienced coach modeling and encouraging the desired strategies in the teacher's own setting are more likely to connect with children in an educative way.

Research is at a premium that supports a causal connection between professional development in general, inclusive of the coaching element specifically, and the ultimate positive impact on the child learner. This chapter examines coaching in professional development as essential to improving the quality of early childhood education, both in building capacity in teachers and improving children's achievement (Wei, Darling-Hammond, Andree, Richardson, & Orphanos, 2009).

This chapter also explores the aspect of coaching within a professional development model that ultimately may increase children's knowledge and skills

The authors would like to thank Calithea Steward, Project REEL's coach coordinator, for her critical insights into successful coaching in professional development models.

through improving teachers' practice. First, we examine the potential benefits of and barriers to effective coaching as identified in the extant literature. Next, we examine the successes and challenges of a directive coaching model used in two professional development projects that addressed a widely diverse cadre of teachers. Then, we summarize what we have learned from the literature and our own projects as the foundation from which to design future professional development models, and we describe what we still need to know. Finally, we relate our findings to questions about professional development within the teacher work force.

WHAT IS COACHING FOR TEACHERS IN PROFESSIONAL DEVELOPMENT PROGRAMS?

Professional development that focuses on child achievement and teacher accountability has garnered intensive attention in the past decade, particularly since the enactment of the No Child Left Behind Act of 2001 (PL 107-110). However, the rush to include coaching in professional development programs to build teacher capacity is a fairly recent phenomenon to attempt to fill the gap between knowledge and effective application that has not been accomplished by previous education, training, or practical experience. But coaching is a topic for which there is little rigorous research, particularly in the area of early literacy (Deussen, Coskie, Robinson, & Autio, 2007; Neuman & Cunningham, 2009).

The term *coaching* in general is used "when a more knowledgeable professional works closely with another professional to increase productivity or to meet some predetermined outcome" (Deussen et al., 2007, p. 5). The term *coaching* is used in this chapter specifically to refer to an apprenticeship model of an experienced mentor who helps other teachers become more effective, reflective, and evaluative in their daily work with children through individualized, ongoing, and intensive professional development (Darling-Hammond & McLaughlin, 1995; Dole, 2004; International Reading Association, 2004; West, 2009).

Specifically, coaches for professional development purposes can be categorized into two approaches: 1) more *directive,* helping identify a teacher's weakness or implement a specific program; or 2) more *reflective,* helping a teacher deepen understandings about his or her role in supporting learning (Deussen et al., 2007). Because of the low educational levels and high teacher turnover in the early childhood work force in general, and specifically in our projects described later in this chapter, the coaching model described herein is a directive one: to improve teacher practice by interjecting specific social-emotional, language, literacy, and mathematical strategies into the setting. Neuman and Cunningham (2009) use a "diagnostic/prescriptive" model, designed to be on-site, balanced and sustained, facilitative of reflection, and highly interactive, which allows for descriptive (not evaluative) feedback and offers opportunities to prioritize the teacher's needs. In addition, although the International Reading Association's 2004 definition of coaching is specifically directed to the "reading coach," it offers the following framework by which to describe a coach's qualifications and responsibilities: 1) successful teaching at the levels of the teachers they will coach; 2) in-depth knowledge of development, curriculum, instruction, and assessment; 3) experience working with teachers to improve their knowledge and skills; 4) excellent presentational skills and knowledge of adult learner characteristics; and 5) complex abilities to observe, model, and provide feedback in a way that engenders positive relationships with teachers.

WHAT DO WE ALREADY KNOW ABOUT COACHING?

Although there is compelling evidence that professional development is the linchpin for improved teacher attitude, knowledge, and skills, additional information is needed to draw firm conclusions about the specific characteristics of professional development that lead to improved child outcomes (Fukkink & Lont, 2007; Yoon, Duncan, Lee, Scarloss, & Shapley, 2007).

Although extensive anecdotal evidence suggests that professional development serves as a change agent for teachers, professional development continues to be situated in a culture of "make-and-take" workshops with disjointed, fragmented content. It has historically followed a course of workshops in which the material was presented in a superficial way, the presenters and/or the content were evaluated by the attendees, and the teachers were to return to their settings to supplement or change their practice with little planning, no support, and no follow-up (Dickinson & Brady, 2006). Topics for these professional development sessions were often selected by trainers unfamiliar with teachers' background or experience, and workshops were offered that may or may not have addressed their classroom needs (Deussen et al., 2007). Often, the only evaluation that was undertaken was the teachers' response as to their satisfaction with the workshop training or a survey to determine their beliefs and philosophies about the child care industry (Welch-Ross, Wolf, Moorehouse, & Rathgeb, 2006). Calls for high-quality professional development are still being made, as professional development programs that are "characterized by coherence, active learning, sufficient duration, collective participation, a focus on content knowledge, and a reform rather than traditional approach" are still in short supply (Yoon et al., 2007, p. 1).

Fukkink and Lont's (2007) meta-analysis of caregiver training studies identified the importance of both the teacher's general educational level and specialized formal/informal professional development experiences in the quality of early childhood settings, as both are linked to child care quality measures. The authors also examined research of children's developmental outcomes and identified studies that suggested that children benefitted from more educated and trained teachers, evidenced by their increased language skills, social skills, and school readiness. However, they cautioned against the conclusion that early childhood education and training are always positively correlated to child benefits, as diverse studies have found that education and training for teachers 1) had a positive impact on infants and toddlers but not on preschoolers (Phillips, Mekos, Scarr, McCartney, & Abbott-Shim, 2000), 2) was not related to quality in the infant-toddler classrooms (Phillipsen, Burchinal, Howes, & Cryer, 1997), or 3) was not found to have an impact on the educational outcomes of any of the age groups of young children in the early childhood setting (Burchinal et al., 2000). The authors emphasized the challenges of studying professional development. Most of the research is correlational rather than causal. Researchers admit to the complications of 1) teasing out teacher competence based on professional development as a separate variable from work experience, and 2) separating the coexisting influences of formal education in combination with professional development experiences (Fukkink & Lont, 2007). Also, if prior research has failed to specify the content and research framework that strengthens the training, then no conclusions can be drawn about what knowledge and skills teachers need to improve their practice and how the specific knowledge and skills that lead to improved child outcomes could best be delivered.

Ultimately a teacher's professional development should have a positive, measurable impact on child outcomes, and there has been a call for research to identify a causal connection between professional development and improved student achievement (Deussen et al., 2007; Fukkink & Lont, 2007). A meta-analysis of 1,300 studies on the impact of professional development on student achievement resulted in identifying only nine studies that met the rigorous What Works Clearinghouse evidence standards (Yoon et al., 2007). The What Works Clearinghouse is a web site offered by the U.S. Department of Education's Institute of Education Sciences as a source for evidence-based practices in multiple topics, such as early childhood education. Although none of the nine studies focused on professional development in the prekindergarten setting, the evidence is compelling that teachers who received an average of 49 hours of professional development were able to improve children's outcomes by 21 percentile points with as little as 14 hours of professional development, evidencing a significant effect on student achievement (Yoon et al., 2007).

Although this finding regarding time on task is important, further studies that establish the definitive connection between well-defined elements of professional development and student achievement are necessary. These studies, however, pose tremendous challenges. High-quality empirical evidence on the sequence from enhanced teacher knowledge and skills, to improved classroom teaching, to higher student achievement is required to support the relationship between professional development to student outcomes. These studies must 1) be based on designs with high internal and external validity, 2) have statistical power, 3) be executed with high fidelity, 4) use sensitive measures, and 5) employ appropriate analytic models. The few studies available for the Yoon et al. (2007) analysis indicate the difficulty of designing such research.

Coaching seems to be the logical bridge from the workshop to classroom application for teachers to learn the knowledge, skills, and attitudes of their profession (Bowman, Donovan, & Burns, 2001; Poglinco & Bach, 2004). In their review of the literature on coaching, Deussen et al. (2007) found mixed results about the value of coaching on teacher performance. They found support for coaching in the research of Showers and Joyce (1996), Neufeld and Roper (2003), and others, in that teachers who had received coaching were more likely to use new strategies effectively than those who had not received coaching. However, they also found challenges to the efficacy of coaching in the several studies that suggested that teachers who received coaching were not any more effective in the classroom than those who had no coaching (Gutierrez, Crosland, & Berlin, 2001; Veenman, Denessen, Gerrits, & Kenter, 2001). What has been suggested to resolve this kind of conflicting evidence is rigorous research methodologies that examine the intersection of the teacher's education, the professional development content, and the delivery methods of that content that would improve effectiveness of teachers from myriad backgrounds (Welch-Ross et al., 2006).

Neuman and Cunningham's (2009) research utilizes a quasi-experimental design to examine the delivery of early childhood language and literacy content to home- and center-based teachers through three different conditions: professional development only (through a formal community college course); professional development with ongoing classroom coaching; and a control group, who received neither professional development nor coaching. The results of this study are important for several reasons. First, it found that a professional development course alone (45 contact hours over one semester) had negligible effects on teacher practices in early language and literacy. Second, the group that received both the coursework (45 hours) and ongoing coaching (65 contact hours over 1 year) experienced statistically significant improvement over the other treatment conditions. Third, a critical finding was that the professional development course and ongoing coaching for the home-based practitioners put them on par with the center-based teachers, who were initially rated higher on language and literacy practices.

Although it did not extend to the measurement of the children's early literacy and language development in the three treatment groups, Neuman and Cunningham's (2009) research is of dramatic importance to the field of early childhood professional development in its findings that coaching seemed to be the variable most critical in a professional development design. In addition, the authors suggested a cautionary note to others engaged in early childhood professional development: Although the coursework provided as the formal training for teachers was of high quality (designed to meet the standards of professional organizations, cross-referenced with environmental measures, aligned with assessment, and staffed by highly qualified instructors), the course alone did not improve teachers' practice in their settings. Other studies (Early et al., 2007; Justice, Mashburn, Hamre, & Pianta, 2008; Phillipsen et al., 1997) corroborate the finding that education alone (coursework, degree, certification,) does not ensure quality in early childhood settings. Tout, Zaslow, and Berry (2006) clarified in their meta-analysis that higher levels of education, especially in early childhood development, are related to higher quality programs for young children but that the literature does not yet confirm specific levels of education or types of professional development required for improved child outcomes.

Other studies support the inclusion of coaching in professional development designs. Dickinson and Caswell (2007) determined that on-site support of early childhood teachers as part of a literacy-focused professional development initiative named Literacy Environment Enrichment Program (LEEP) was the design element that was central to teacher improvement. The authors' case study of the teacher–supervisor teams revealed that the supervisors adopted the role of coach. Trusting relationships developed between teachers and supervisors that were more supportive of sustained teacher change than the supervisors' previous role as "enforcer" of rules and regulations. Although LEEP did not connect teacher growth to improved child outcomes, LEEP realized moderate to large positive effects on all teacher measures for language and literacy support with the exception of writing, for which the results were small in effect. Podhajski and Nathan (2005) designed BUILDING BLOCKS for Literacy, an intensive weekend (2-day) education program for early childhood teachers that was followed by 6 months of on-site mentoring to support teachers' applications of key concepts and activities in their daily routines. Children whose teachers participated in BUILDING BLOCKS for Literacy showed significant improvement in their early literacy skills, and perhaps more importantly, the number of children who were considered at-risk for future reading problems was decreased as compared with the control group.

Another study (Jackson et al., 2006) that examined the impact of literacy-focused professional development through both formal instruction and coaching included measures of both the teachers' growth and the child outcomes. All teachers in the treatment groups participated in the *HeadsUp! Reading* televised professional development course, but a smaller subgroup participated in a mentoring program with highly qualified trainers/consultants who provided in-classroom support for teachers for 8–24 hours of individualized support over a 2-month period. The findings evidenced statistically significant improvement for the preschool children of the treatment groups over those in the control group. However, the addition of teacher mentoring did not result in greater gains for the children, although teachers improved in some classroom literacy practices. The limited sample size and timing (late in training and of only 2 months' duration) were likely confounding factors in this null relationship between coaching and teacher improvement.

HOW IS COACHING IMPROVING TEACHER PERFORMANCE? EXPERIENCES WITH TWO PROFESSIONAL DEVELOPMENT DESIGNS

The question about the effectiveness of coaching in early childhood professional development is one that is still largely unanswered. As discussed previously, certain studies (Dickinson & Caswell, 2007; Neuman & Cunningham, 2009;

Podhajski & Nathan, 2005) have advanced the field with their findings that coaching was the variable responsible for higher quality teaching and/or learning, but we are relatively early in the research timeline about coaching in terms of dosage (frequency and duration), intensity, content details, delivery modes, and more. Researchers still need to examine a convergence of multiple studies that meet quasi-experimental, and preferably experimental, methodology linking professional development inclusive of coaching to child outcomes. However, with early childhood education professional development research gaining focus on a national scale, we are hopeful for a dramatic increase in research that will answer some ongoing questions in the field. Our experiences with two professional development projects, both inclusive of coaching as a significant feature of the design, contribute to understandings about the role and characteristics of an effective coach in the early childhood setting.

We relied heavily on coaching to anchor the workshop information and material to actual classroom (or setting) practice in our two professional development projects: the community-based Early SUCCESS (Strategies for Urban Child Care, Education, Support, and Services, 2002–2004) and the statewide Project REEL (Resources for Early Educator Learning, 2005–2008). Both SUCCESS and REEL were based on the multiple elements of effective teacher professional development that require rigor, ambitious objectives and goals, consistency, and sustained attention (Darling-Hammond & McLaughlin, 1995; Garet, Porter, Desimone, Birman, & Yoon, 2001; Guskey, 2003). We also drew from the characteristics of effective professional development as detailed in the No Child Left Behind Act of 2001 (PL 107-110), as well as the National Staff Development Council's (2001) *Standards for Staff Development*. The professional development plans for teachers in both SUCCESS and REEL were designed to

1. Be intensive, of high quality, and from research-validated practices for the purpose of increasing the number of children who were prepared for social and academic success

2. Be a series of formal (workshops) and informal (coaching) experiences that were focused, based on a long-term plan, and ongoing to the extent that teachers had sufficient time to learn and practice new instructional skills

3. Be aligned with state standards, assessments, and curriculum, while encouraging teacher and director collaboration

4. Be fully evaluated by using multiple instruments to demonstrate the impact on teacher quality and children's knowledge/skills

5. Support teachers in implementing screenings and other appropriate measures to determine children's progress, ensuring the involvement of families

6. Ensure teacher modification of early childhood content to create supportive environments for children with special needs, including those children who were English-language learners

Early SUCCESS

Early SUCCESS provided 80 total hours of professional development in oral language, literacy, and social skills to 137 teachers from the Chattanooga, Tennessee, area. Teachers worked with children from birth to age 5; were predominantly high school graduates (or received their GED) or had completed only some college coursework (58% of participants) but were not certified teachers; and worked in informal home, family group, and center-based care settings.

Tennessee requires only 12 hours of professional development annually, and no early childhood training is mandated prior to beginning work with young children. The teachers participated in an intensive program over 1 year that included 32 hours of training workshops (weekly 2-hour sessions for 16 weeks), 16 hours of observations of master teachers at early childhood model sites, 26 or more hours of individualized coaching in the participants' classrooms, 4 hours of guided viewing of videotapes showing best practices in teaching young children, an extensive 147-page workshop manual, and a 2-hour "Celebration of Learning" to showcase their growth. As an incentive, each teacher received $1,000 toward the purchase of children's books and other educational materials for his or her setting. Supervisors and directors were required to participate to ensure their understanding and support of the teachers' implementation of new strategies with the children in that setting.

Coaching in SUCCESS began at the workshop level. At the sixteen 2-hour training workshops, the teachers spent the first half hour in small, age-specific groups (e.g., infants, young toddlers, older toddlers) led by their coaches. They shared with the group their successes and challenges in implementing the social skills and language/literacy strategies from the previous week's session. Then, with the coaches, they attended the 1-hour whole-group training on a particular topic (e.g., modeling strategies for challenging behaviors, room arrangement, phonological awareness, concepts about print, alphabet knowledge). The teachers then rejoined their small groups for the last 30 minutes, during which their coaches helped them to select specific strategies (in-classroom management, oral language, and/or literacy) from that night's workshop and make plans for implementing them in their settings the following week.

Approximately 8–12 teachers working in similar settings were assigned a coach whose own experience with young children matched that of the teachers. These coaches completed between 20 and 25 hours of individualized support in teachers' settings that began during the 16-week workshop training and continued on a weekly or every-other-week schedule, depending upon the needs expressed by the teacher or observed by the coach. Coaches individualized workshop strategies for their teachers by planning curriculum, supporting goal setting, suggesting improvements, modeling strategies, and celebrating improvements in the settings that supported social skills development, rich oral language, and integration of positive literacy experiences for the children. The teachers in SUCCESS reported that they learned from the workshops and appreciated the opportunities to observe at the model sites, but they *loved* their coaches and the mentoring they received in their classrooms. At the conclusion of the grant period, the teachers' program evaluation responses to the statement, "My coach helped me understand and use the strategies presented in the workshops," received an average of 4.55 on a 5-point Likert scale ranging from "strongly disagree" (1) to "strongly agree" (5).

SUCCESS participants were not randomly assigned in a controlled experiment; thus, we cannot causally attribute their improvements to the training we provided. However, teachers significantly improved on multiple measures that assessed their knowledge and use of strategies to support children's language and literacy development, and their settings were significantly enhanced with literacy materials. For example, over the course of the project, teachers of infants and toddlers tripled their use of strategies supporting language and literacy (from 12% to 42%) and social skills development (from 21% to 69%). Teachers of older children doubled their use of strategies supporting language and literacy (from 31% to 61%) and significantly increased their use of strategies supporting social/emotional development (58% to 79%; see Chapter 12). Importantly, teachers improved regardless of their prior education level and sustained their improvements 1 year after formal training had ended. The convergence of evidence strongly suggests that our professional development model was effective with two cohorts of early childhood educators, and we concluded that was largely based on the integral collaboration of the coaches.

Project REEL

Project REEL, a quasi-experimental delayed-treatment design, revised and extended the SUCCESS model into a statewide project across the 11 Child Care Resource & Referral Network (the Network) regions in Tennessee. The Network is responsible for delivering professional development for the state of Tennessee to child care providers. REEL expanded the SUCCESS professional development design in several ways: 1) professional development was increased from 80 to 120 hours, 2) on-site coaching was increased from 26 to approximately 78 hours, and 3) an additional module on early mathematics was included. In the first and second year, 165 teachers from 85 different programs across the state first received training as necessary in the foundation curriculum (*The Creative Curriculum for Family Child Care* [Dodge, 1991]; *The Creative Curriculum for Infants, Toddlers, and Twos* [Dodge, Rudick, & Berke, 2006]; *The Creative Curriculum for Preschool* [Dodge, Colker, & Heroman, 2002]; and *Literacy: The Creative Curriculum Approach* [Heroman & Jones, 2004]). The Tennessee Child Care Evaluation and Report Card Program, or Star-Quality rating, was chosen to rate the potential participants. The Star-Quality rating is based on director qualifications, professional development, compliance history, parent/family involvement, ratio-group size, staff compensation, and program assessment (Early Childhood Environment Rating Scale [**ECERS**], Infant/Toddler Environment Rating Scale [ITERS], and

Family Day Care Rating Scale [**FDCRS**]) scores. Programs with three star ratings were selected to participate; REEL recruited programs with three star ratings under the assumption that these programs would have sufficient professional development experience, resources, and commitment to benefit from our additional training. Participating teachers had a wide range of educational backgrounds, with approximately 33% having some credential or degree—from a child development associate (CDA) credential to a master's degree—and 67% with a high school diploma only or some college coursework. The teachers also worked in diverse settings and included 30 family providers, 100 infant-toddler teachers, and 97 preschool/pre-K teachers.

Teachers and their program directors received 28 hours of formal workshops (fourteen 2-hour sessions) on 10 modules addressing social-emotional development, oral language development, phonological awareness, concepts about books, concepts about print, **alphabetic principle,** comprehension and motivation, emergent writing, early mathematics, and embedding literacy into center activities; 44 hours of on-site intensive coaching (to support the implementation of the curriculum); and 34 hours of on-site supportive coaching (in response to teacher needs and requests). In addition to the training and coaching, all teachers received a 243-page REEL strategies manual, $1,000 in books and materials, books/training in *The Creative Curriculum,* training in goal setting and self-assessment, and training in assessment instruments to measure children's progress.

REEL used a train-the-trainer model to deliver the project elements to the teachers via their coaches. The coaches were hired and employed by the Network in each of the 11 regions across the state. The REEL co-directors and project manager conducted multiple intensive workshops with pre/posttests to prepare the 11 coaches for working with their mentees and to ensure implementation fidelity.

The coaches were assigned a cohort of 10 teachers from various settings in the region as defined by the Network. Coaching began in the teachers' settings as soon as the fourteen 2-hour workshops were underway. The first 44 hours of intensive coaching were designed to model for and support the teacher in enacting the curriculum from the REEL content modules. Coaches were sensitive to teacher schedules, often offering make-up sessions for those who had to be absent from a regularly scheduled workshop or coaching session. During the next 34 hours of supportive coaching, the coach and the teacher collaborated to address the addition, revision, or refinement of teaching strategies that the teacher was implementing. The coaches worked with up to 10 teachers in the first treatment group, and then up to 10 new teachers in the delayed treatment group, which began approximately 6 months after the initial group began their training.

The bulk of the professional development (98 hours of 120) was provided during the first 2 years for both treatment groups. The third year was considered the maintenance phase, with teacher support considerably reduced, consisting of an additional 10 hours of topical seminars (one 2-hour session each month for

5 months) selected by either coaches and/or teachers to meet ongoing needs, and 12 hours of peer support groups called "Circle of Friends," initially led by the coach and then by the teachers for ongoing collaboration and professional growth after the grant project ended.

All teachers were observed each spring and fall of the grant period by REEL coaches using several different instruments. Teachers improved significantly on all measures of knowledge, practice, and environment. For example, classroom quality as measured by the Early Language and Literacy Classroom Observation Tool (ELLCO) Pre-K (Smith, Brady, & Anatasopoulos, 2008) improved significantly, and improvements were maintained even after support had been reduced (in the third year). At baseline, only 31% of the classrooms were rated as providing high-quality language and literacy support. That figure increased to 64% during the second year of training, and 89% at the end of the project. In addition, the number of classrooms rated as providing low-quality support decreased from 19% initially to zero by the third year.

The REEL model of professional development increased teachers' knowledge and strategies in children's social-emotional, language, literacy, and early mathematics development through the use of small-group training, individual coaching, and an infusion of books/materials in the setting. REEL's professional development was effective in improving the knowledge and skills of teachers in diverse settings and from diverse backgrounds. The majority of the teachers in the sample did not have college degrees, yet they were able to benefit from professional development to the same extent as more highly educated teachers. Several components likely contributed to REEL's success. For instance, participating programs had prior professional development, and directors were willing to attend training and provide support for the teachers to implement new practices. Most importantly, more than half of all of the professional development hours in REEL involved on-site individualized support that included modeling, observation, and feedback. Both the teachers and the coaches felt that on-site support, whether deemed coaching or targeted technical assistance, was critical to their success in applying and adapting the practices taught in formal workshops to their settings. Another important feature of REEL, in particular, was that the teachers had been provided the same books and materials that their coaches were using in the modeling of strategies; coaches then helped teachers transfer the strategies to other appropriate texts. However, future research is necessary to examine the unique effect of coaching; our evaluation design did not allow us to separate it from the effects of the workshops or other components of the professional development provided.

What Did SUCCESS and REEL Teach Us About Coaching?

The research on teacher quality supports the premise that high-quality professional development can contribute to effective teacher practice and children's social and academic outcomes. Our experiences in SUCCESS and REEL revealed valuable information about the qualities of coaches and the value of coaching as an essential element of professional development. This section details some of our successes, challenges, and the revisions we would make to our coaching plans within the larger professional development design.

In broad terms, coaches in SUCCESS and REEL who were particularly successful were those who

1. Had greater knowledge about child development and **developmentally appropriate practices**

2. Were former teachers themselves with setting/classroom experiences that were applicable to problem-solving strategies for and with the teacher

3. Had prior training experience with adults and understood the unique characteristics of the adult learner

4. Understood the organizational structure, schedule, and culture of the setting

5. Acknowledged that trust was key to a successful coach–teacher relationship

6. Entered the teacher's setting with a sense of respect for what the teacher was already doing and a collaborative attitude about adding to the quality of instruction

7. Allowed the teacher to drive the process while still meeting project objectives

8. Offered make-up sessions and other alternative scheduling for workshop training and coaching

9. Were aware of the need for implementation fidelity of the project objectives/goals while simultaneously addressing the concerns expressed by the teacher about a specific setting

Although the professional development *workshop* instruction may not have been easily modified for the varying educational and experiential levels of teachers, the element of *coaching* was more easily differentiated to meet teachers' specific needs.

It was essential for REEL to have coaches embedded in and later absorbed by the Network across the state when the grant period ended. The REEL coaches were to be indistinguishable from the Network specialists, who were already established as consultants delivering professional development sessions in the region for teachers. These specialists were already perceived as possessing a wealth of information and resources to improve the early childhood setting and child outcomes. The Network also proved to be as supportive for coaches as for teachers: Coaches received support from more experienced trainers in their regional centers, borrowed materials to show teachers the resources available to them, and were provided training tips such as workshop ice-breakers and closing strategies. Concurrent with the implementation of REEL in 85 diverse programs across Tennessee, the Network revised its delivery of professional development to the 5,034 child care centers and family providers across the state. In 2005, when REEL began, the Network was using a workshop model in which PowerPoint presentations with handouts were the primary element. In 2008, the Network began using a workshop plus targeted technical assistance model of delivery in which teachers are individually coached to improve their instructional support for young children. This important shift in professional development design by the Network contributed to our expectation that the advances in REEL teachers' professional growth will be sustained by the Network in the future.

There are elements of coaching in the REEL professional development design that we would now revise or include if we were to repeat the project.

1. Project directors/investigators need an intensive 3- to 5-day workshop with the coaches prior to delivering the project content. This time should focus on building relationships between the co-directors and coaches, delving deeply into adult learner characteristics and valuable teaching strategies, learning about the evaluation plan, and practicing using measures of teacher and child assessment.

2. Project directors/investigators should network with program directors/administrators before beginning the professional development with teachers, perhaps even training the directors *prior to* working with the teachers, to assure administrative buy-in for the project, the ongoing role of the coaches, and teacher changes in practice.

3. In addition to utilizing a coach coordinator for large projects, directors/investigators should establish weekly teleconferences to check progress, success, and challenges of coaches in their work with teachers.

4. Directors/investigators should work closely with coaches to create a workshop manual with careful consideration for the teachers with low levels of education by making modules easy to read, with more sequenced photos of good practice in action.

5. Directors/investigators should involve coaches in creating instructional videos in which teachers can see demonstrations of the target strategies.

6. Directors/investigators should arrange more opportunities for coaches and their teachers to view master teachers at work with children in the age groups that match the observers' experiences.

7. Coaches should deliver separate workshops for teachers who work with infants/toddlers, as these participants in SUCCESS and REEL seemed to have frequent challenges modifying strategies for younger children.

8. The time during which coaches deliver the workshop element of the professional development design should be extensive, as 14–16 weeks of 2-hour

sessions were perceived by some coaches as "too much too fast" for the teachers to absorb.

We offer that professional development designs must necessarily involve some version of individualized classroom coaching similar to that teachers received in the SUCCESS and REEL projects. Their relationships with coaches were consistently positive and were critical to implementation of the project elements. The intensive coaching (44 hours) was directed at project implementation, but the additional supportive coaching (34 hours) was tailored to the individual teacher's needs. Coaching was more favorably perceived by the teachers than were the workshops, and both teachers and coaches reported the benefits of immediate application of new strategies to their settings. It is important to note that teachers improved at equivalent rates regardless of their educational levels and backgrounds. The involvement and support of the directors was crucial to creating a setting where teachers could take risks in their practice to benefit the children learning. Teachers improved on all measures, indicating the REEL model of professional development increased the knowledge and strategies of teachers in children's social-emotional, language, literacy, and early mathematics development through the use of small-group training, individual coaching, and an infusion of books/materials in the setting.

WHAT QUESTIONS ABOUT COACHING REMAIN?

Although one meta-analysis suggested that student achievement can be improved with as little as 14 hours of teacher professional development (Yoon et al., 2007), it is more likely that individualized, intensive, in-classroom support of substantial duration provided by knowledgeable coaches will affect teacher quality in order to increase student achievement (Neuman & Cunningham, 2009). What we do not yet know is the threshold for the amount of coaching and whether it differs by area (early childhood language, literacy, mathematics, and social-emotional development) and teacher characteristics. How does coaching for infant-toddler teachers differ from coaching designed for teachers of preschoolers? Our teachers' lowest scores in knowledge and skills (as measured by workshop posttests and grant-specific Strategy Checklists) in both SUCCESS and REEL were in the areas of emergent writing and alphabetic principle. How much more coaching in areas of particular challenge for teachers would be required to see a significant increase in classroom performance? How can we create more sensitive measures of teacher behaviors that would target progress within his or her zone of proximal development? Does a more intensive coaching focus on child development and how children learn (in addition to the emphasis on teacher behaviors) improve the teacher's instructional quality? How can teachers continue to add to their knowledge and skills when the workshops are over and the coaches are gone? We need more controlled studies in varied settings to answer this and other questions.

WHAT IS COACHING'S CONTRIBUTION TO PROFESSIONALIZING THE TEACHER WORK FORCE?

The REEL coach coordinator suggested that coaches must hold a foundational belief that "teachers want to do it right, even if they are currently doing it wrong." If some teachers have been "doing it wrong," then it is likely attributable to the generally low level of education of the early childhood work force and the scant amount of professional training provided to them in child development and language, literacy, and early mathematical teaching strategies. Teachers have struggled to recognize their role of blazing the learning trail for children's later academic success, instead viewing themselves as babysitters allowing parents to work. But the results from SUCCESS and REEL suggested that even when teachers in a professional development project have only high school diplomas/GEDs or some college coursework, with as little as 12 hours of training in early childhood health and safety in their first year, they can come to see themselves as agents of change for children's lives and improve their social-emotional support of young children and their language, literacy, and early mathematics instruction. It is also important to note that, in contrast to other studies of professional development in early childhood settings that were undertaken in public schools with certified teachers, the vast majority of the SUCCESS and REEL teachers were working in informal home, family group, and center-based care. We can report with relative confidence that coaching was the variable that bridged the gap between the workshops (theory) and classroom application (practice) and that ultimately improved the quality of the teachers in those settings.

REFERENCES

Bowman, B.T., Donovan, M.S., & Burns, M.S. (Eds.). (2001). *Eager to learn: Educating our preschoolers.* Washington, DC: National Academies Press.

Burchinal, M.R., Roberts, J.E., Riggins, R., Zeisel, S.A., Neebe, E., & Brant, D. (2000). Relating quality of center-based child care to early cognitive and language development longitudinally. *Child Development, 71*(2), 339–357.

Darling-Hammond, L., & McLaughlin, M.W. (1995). Policies that support professional development in an era of reform. *Phi Delta Kappan, 76*(8), 597–604.

Deussen, T., Coskie, T., Robinson, L., & Autio, E. (2007). *"Coach" can mean many things: Five categories of literacy coaches in Reading First* (Issues & Answers Report, REL 2007-No. 005). Washington, DC: U.S. Department of Education, Institute of Education Sciences, National Center for Education Evaluation and Regional Assistance. Retrieved September 15, 2008, from http://ies.ed.gov/ncee/edlabs/regions/northwest/pdf/REL_2007005.pdf

Dickinson, D.K., & Brady, J.P. (2006). Toward effective support for language and literacy through professional development. In M. Zaslow & I. Martinez-Beck (Eds.), *Critical issues in early childhood professional development* (pp. 141–170). Baltimore: Paul H. Brookes Publishing Co.

Dickinson, D.K., & Caswell, L. (2007). Building support for language and early literacy in preschool classrooms through in-service professional development: Effects of the

Literacy Environment Enrichment Program (LEEP). *Early Childhood Research Quarterly, 22,* 243–260.

Dodge, D.T. (1991). *The Creative Curriculum for Family Child Care* (2nd ed.). Silver Spring, MD: Gryphon House.

Dodge, D.T., Colker, L.J., & Heroman, C. (2002). *The Creative Curriculum for Preschool* (4th ed.). Washington, DC: Teaching Strategies.

Dodge, D.T., Rudick, S., & Berke, K.L. (2006). *The Creative Curriculum for Infants, Toddlers, and Twos* (2nd ed.). Washington, DC: Teaching Strategies.

Dole, J.A. (2004). The changing role of the reading specialist in school reform. *The Reading Teacher, 57*(5), 462–471.

Early, D.M., Maxwell, K.L., Burchinal, M., Alva, S., Bender, R.H., Bryant, D., et al. (2007). Teachers' educations, classroom quality, and young children's academic skills: Results from seven studies of preschool programs. *Child Development, 78*(2), 558–580.

Fukkink, R.G., & Lont, A. (2007). Does training matter? A meta-analysis and review of caregiver training studies. *Early Childhood Research Quarterly, 22,* 294–311.

Garet, M.S., Porter, A.C., Desimone, L., Birman, B.F., & Yoon, K.S. (2001). What makes professional development effective? Results from a national sample of teachers. *American Educational Research Journal, 38*(4), 915–945.

Guskey, T.R. (2003). What makes professional development effective? *Phi Delta Kappan, 84*(10), 748–750.

Gutierrez, K., Crosland, K., & Berlin, D. (2001, April). *Reconsidering coaching: Assisting teachers' literacy practices in the zone of proximal development.* Paper presented at the annual meeting of the American Educational Research Association, Seattle, WA.

Heroman, C., & Jones, C. (2004). *Literacy: The Creative Curriculum Approach.* Florence, KY: Delmar Cengage Learning.

International Reading Association. (2004). *The role and qualifications of the reading coach in the United States: A position statement of the International Reading Association.* Retrieved May 13, 2009, from http://www.reading.org/downloads/positions/ps1065_reading_coach.pdf

Jackson, B., Larzelere, R., St. Clair, L., Corr, M., Fichter, C., & Egertson, H. (2006). The impact of *HeadsUp! Reading* on early childhood educators' literacy practices and preschool children's literacy skills. *Early Childhood Research Quarterly, 21,* 213–236.

Justice, L.M., Mashburn, A.J., Hamre, B.K, & Pianta, R.C. (2008). Quality of language and literacy instruction in pre-kindergarten programs serving at-risk pupils. *Early Childhood Research Quarterly, 21*(1), 51–68.

National Staff Development Council. (2001). *NSDC's standards for staff development.* Retrieved March 19, 2008, from http://www.nsdc.org/standards/index.cfm

Neufeld, B., & Roper, D. (2003). *Coaching: A strategy for developing instructional capacity: Promises and practicalities.* Retrieved August 29, 2008, from http://www.annenberginstitute.org/pdf/Coaching.pdf

Neuman, S.B., & Cunningham, L. (2009). The impact of professional development and coaching on early language and literacy instructional practices. *American Educational Research Journal, 46*(2), 322–353.

No Child Left Behind Act of 2001, PL 107-110, 115 Stat. 1425, 20 U.S.C. §§ 6301 *et seq.*

Phillips, D., Mekos, D., Scarr, S., McCartney, K., & Abbott-Shim, M. (2000). Within and beyond the classroom door: Assessing quality in child care centers. *Early Childhood Research Quarterly, 15*(4), 475–496.

Phillipsen, L.C., Burchinal, M.R., Howes, C., & Cryer, D. (1997). The prediction of process quality from structural features of child care. *Early Childhood Research Quarterly, 12,* 281–303.

Podhajski, B., & Nathan, J. (2005). Promoting early literacy through professional development for childcare providers. *Early Education & Development, 16*(1), 23–41.

Poglinco, S.M., & Bach, A.J. (2004). The heart of the matter: Coaching as a vehicle for professional development. *Phi Delta Kappan, 85*(5), 398–402.

Showers, B., & Joyce, B. (1996). The evolution of peer coaching. *Educational Leadership, 53*(6), 12–16.

Smith, M.W., Brady, J.P., & Anatasopoulos, L. (2008). *Early Language and Literacy Classroom Observation Tool (ELLCO) Pre-K.* Baltimore: Paul H. Brookes Publishing Co.

Tout, K., Zaslow, M., & Berry, D. (2006). Quality and qualifications: Links between professional development and quality in early care and education settings. In M. Zaslow & I. Martinez-Beck (Eds.), *Critical issues in early childhood professional development* (pp. 77–110). Baltimore: Paul H. Brookes Publishing Co.

Veenman, S., Denessen, E., Gerrits, J., & Kenter, J. (2001). Evaluation of a coaching programme for cooperating teachers. *Educational Studies, 27*(3), 317–340.

Wei, R.C., Darling-Hammond, L., Andree, A., Richardson, N., & Orphanos, S. (2009). *Professional learning in the learning profession: A status report on teacher development in the United States and abroad.* Dallas, TX: National Staff Development Council.

Welch-Ross, M., Wolf, A., Moorehouse, M., & Rathgeb, C. (2006). Improving connections between professional development research and early childhood policies. In M. Zaslow & I. Martinez-Beck (Eds.), *Critical issues in early childhood professional development* (pp. 369–394). Baltimore: Paul H. Brookes Publishing Co.

West, L. (2009). Content coaching: Transforming the teaching profession. In J. Knight (Ed.), *Coaching: Approaches and perspectives* (pp. 113–144). Thousand Oaks, CA: Corwin.

Yoon, K.S., Duncan, T., Lee, S.W.-Y., Scarloss, B., & Shapley, K. (2007). *Reviewing the evidence on how teacher professional development affects student achievement* (Issues & Answers Report, REL 2007-No. 033). Washington, DC: U.S. Department of Education, Institute of Education Sciences, National Center for Education Evaluation and Regional Assistance. Retrieved May 13, 2009, from http://ies.ed.gov/ncee/edlabs/regions/southwest/pdf/REL_2007033.pdf

6

Mentoring

More Than a Promising Strategy

Annette Sibley, Robert Lawrence, and Richard G. Lambert

The strongest predictor of children's school readiness is the quality of teaching practices (Howes, 1997; Neuman & Cunningham, 2009; Phillepsen, Burchinal, Howes, & Cryer, 1997). Accumulating evidence indicates that teachers with more education and specialized training in early childhood development have classrooms of higher quality and demonstrate more effective teaching practices (Fukkink & Lont, 2007). Since the late 1990s, both state and federal programs have continued to establish higher standards for early childhood teachers, under-scoring the influence of the growing body of research that shows significant rela-tionships among teacher qualifications, classroom quality, and child outcomes. It is widely believed that quality teaching practices include a complex set of skills, content knowledge, and disposition. It is also widely believed that high-quality teachers are self-motivated and demonstrate ongoing learning, collaboration, and reflective thinking in their role as early childhood professionals (National Association for the Education of Young Children, 2009; Tarrant, Greenberg, Kagan, & Kauerz, 2009).

Although most professions require formal academic preparation prior to entering the work force, professional preparation in early childhood education is commonly obtained through on-the-job training. Historically, professional devel-opment for early childhood teachers has consisted of an informal and episodic workshop approach that lacks depth and continuity of content and has most often been intended to satisfy basic state child care licensing requirements. Federal and state mandates, however, have begun placing increased emphasis on traditional academic credentials (i.e., postsecondary degrees). Neither approach fully addresses the needs of the early childhood work force. Preparation of highly skilled early childhood educators requires a knowledge and understanding of the characteristics of the existing work force, clarity of content, and innovative pro-fessional development strategies that are appropriate for teachers already practic-ing in the field.

According to the National Staff Development Council, mentoring and coaching are the fastest growing and most promising strategies for professional development; however, although these high-intensity, job-embedded collaborative learning approaches are highly effective, they are not yet universally adopted across states or early childhood settings (Darling-Hammond, Chung Wei, Andree, Richardson, & Orphanos, 2009). Among those initiatives that use mentoring, there is considerable variation in the definitions, activities, and objectives of mentoring and very little descriptive information regarding the qualifications and essential competencies for effective mentoring. The terms *mentoring, coaching, technical assistance,* and *training* are used interchangeably throughout the early childhood literature. Just as there is a lack of uniform definition about what mentors *should* do and who they are, there is little documentation of what mentors *actually* do.

There are differences between mentoring and coaching (Sweeny, 2008). Coaches provide technical support to develop specific job-related skills. A coach, for example, uses observation, data collection, reflective questioning, nonjudgmental feedback on specific behaviors and techniques, and goal setting. This coaching description is consistent with the directive coaching model described in Chapter 5.

In contrast, mentoring provides a more inclusive relationship and process. A mentor is both a tutor and a guide who strives to integrate and extend the teaching techniques and knowledge of her or his protégé. There is often a status differential between mentor and protégé, with the mentor often facilitating learning opportunities for someone new to the field or returning for additional learning. Although mentorship, like coaching, is a joint venture that promotes intentional learning and shared responsibility, generally mentors will guide their colleagues through their educational or professional development program whereas coaches focus on specific job-related skills. To optimize learning and professional development, therefore, mentoring and coaching are both critically important.

This chapter sets mentoring in historical context, develops a definition and description of mentoring as a professional development approach that uniquely addresses the early childhood work force needs, and pinpoints the distinguishing elements of mentoring. Mentoring is distinctive when it reveals the experiences, beliefs, and values of the protégé teacher; draws out contrasts with cutting-edge knowledge of the field; and then guides alignment and integration to transform classroom practices. Therefore, this chapter also examines the critical role and contribution of the mentor's knowledge, skills, and disposition as related to adult learning and facilitating change.

HISTORICAL CONTEXT OF MENTORING IN EARLY CHILDHOOD SETTINGS

Mentoring emerged in the 1970s as an innovative business strategy that was perceived to be a cost-effective method for work force development, knowledge transfer, and employee retention (Murray & Owens, 1991; Odiorne, 1985). By 2002, 77% of the top U.S. companies were implementing mentoring programs (Galvin, 2002, as cited in Onchwari & Keengwe, 2008). In addition to their roles as teacher and guide, mentors were meant to be supportive, trusted friends and professional advisors. Typically, mentors were older, more experienced individuals who shaped the professional development of younger, aspiring professionals (Shea, 1994; Whitaker, 2002).

During the late 1980s, mentoring programs emerged as a promising strategy within the early childhood field. The emphasis was on peer-to-peer mentoring that was nonsupervisory in nature and job-embedded; it relied on mentors who were highly accomplished teachers, and it was thought of as a strategy to raise the overall quality of the protégé's classroom practices while promoting retention among novice teachers as well as veterans. The hope was that mentoring would become an integral component of a national career and compensation lattice.

During the 1990s, locally designed and implemented mentoring programs appeared across the country. However, due to unstable funding and inadequate infrastructure supports, many of these programs were short lived. The proliferation of early childhood mentoring programs also produced variation in purpose and design and limited empirical evidence about the affect of mentoring in early childhood programs.

The California Early Childhood Mentor Program is the largest and most established early childhood program of its kind in the United States. It was initiated with private funding in 1988 by Chabot College and the National Center for the Child Care Workforce (previously known as the Child Care Employee Project). The purpose of the program is to support supervised practicum experiences for a certificate or an associate's degree, provide guidance for inexperienced teachers, and improve the quality of child care. The California program established mentoring in the context of supervision and practicum experiences.

By 2008, the California Early Childhood Mentor Program was embedded in 95 of California's community colleges and funded with Child Care Development Block Grant funds through the California Department of Education. In their 2007–2008 annual report, the California Early Childhood Mentor Program (n.d.) reported a substantially lower turnover rate (11.7%) among mentor teachers than the national average (30%). It also reported that mentor teachers were likely to seek continuing education opportunities and establish career advancement goals.

In response to the No Child Left Behind Act of 2001 (PL 107-110), the Head Start Bureau initiated a national effort to increase teachers' knowledge and skills in early language and literacy development through the Strategic Teacher Education Program (STEP). The intent of STEP was to train teachers in research-based literacy practices that would lead to positive child outcomes and school readiness using a mentor model for professional development. The STEP program initially appeared to be an innovative approach for creating a national mentor model. However, implementation of the program more closely resembled a conventional train-the-trainer approach.

As national attention has increasingly focused on the critical importance of early language development and reading in the preschool years, mentoring and coaching are being used as professional development strategies within numerous federally funded Early Reading First and Early Childhood Educator Professional Development initiatives. As a result, mentor and coach job positions have emerged within the early childhood field. In some instances mentoring or coaching is an added job responsibility; in other cases, a mentor or coach is a specialized position in and of itself.

Today, mentoring occurs in many formats. A mentor may be a classroom teacher who has assumed additional responsibility within a practicum placement site as a supervisor (as in the California Early Childhood Mentor Program), or a mentor may be a classroom teacher who provides peer-to-peer support within or across program auspices. Mentors are also referred to as *literacy mentors* or *literacy mentor-coaches*. As external agents, mentors provide in-classroom support and guidance, as is the case with Early Reading First and Early Childhood Educator Professional Development projects.

WHO IS A MENTOR?

For the purposes of this discussion, the term *mentor* refers to an experienced and skilled professional who provides guidance and support to a less experienced or less skilled teacher, or *protégé*. The emphasis of mentoring is on deepening the protégé's knowledge and conceptual understanding, promoting a sense of self and purposefulness, and increasing intentional application of newly acquired knowledge to teaching skills. Mentors promote the protégé's professional growth and personal efficacy. Mentors use a variety of strategies including observation and assessment of practices, modeling demonstration lessons, coaching, dialogic conversation, and skillful questioning to promote self-analysis and reflection. Mentors engage protégés in joint problem solving; they are guides and role models. The subject and focus of mentoring activities are based on the protégé's needs and are therefore protégé centered. An effective mentor–protégé relationship is grounded in mutual trust and respect; it is confidential and nonsupervisory in nature to allow the protégé to reveal mistakes and confusion and to freely experiment through trial and error. A mentor brings extensive experience and expertise and may be an accomplished peer who can convey the message, "I understand because I do what you do, and I have personally experienced your challenges," or he or she may be an older, more experienced professional who can convey the message, "I've been there, done that, and together we can find solutions to your challenges."

Skilled mentors create safe and supportive environments; actively and attentively listen to gain a deeper understanding of the protégé's frame of reference; engage in powerful questioning and reflection to uncover beliefs, values, and conceptual understanding; use direct and explicit communication; create aware-ness and scaffold experience, beliefs, and knowledge; set individual goals; and jointly design action plans with their protégés. Mentors maintain mutual accountability for follow through, and they track progress. Effective mentoring requires fluid movement among these elements and represents the art and science of facilitating meaningful and sustained change.

If mentors have limited experience and lack clarity and preparation for their role, however, there is likely to be a disparity between what mentors should do and what they actually do (Feiman-Nemser, 1996). Literacy mentors themselves have reported that they struggled with classroom demands that often supplanted their ability to focus on literacy instruction, and at other times they became the teacher's assistant rather than a model for literacy instruction. Although literacy mentors may receive extensive training, they are most often learning about early language and literacy development concurrently with the protégé teachers, and equally important, they are not trained in the "art of working with adults, adult education, or managing relationships" (Romo, Elmer, & Casso, 2007).

There is very little reference in the literature to the qualifications and prepa-ration of mentors. Information about the credentials and background of mentors is incomplete and reveals a wide variability in mentor qualifications. For example, mentors are described as experienced teachers (Onchwari & Keengwe, 2008) or senior-level trainers (Assel, Landry, Swank, & Gunnewig, 2007). In other cases, mentors are described as early childhood specialists with education ranging from Child Development Associate (CDA) credentials to associate's, bachelor's, or mas-ter's degrees (Grace et al., 2008; Whitebook & Sakai, 1995). Descriptions of mentor preparation are also uneven and variable. Mentors from the California Early Childhood Mentor Program participate in a formal course and receive training in adult supervision and principles of adult learning. In other cases, men-tor training focuses on a target curriculum such as the Head Start CIRCLE train-ing program or HighScope Literacy Curriculum (Assel et al., 2007; Onchwari & Keengwe, 2008; Romo et al., 2007).

There appears to be implicit assumptions about the content knowledge, experiential knowledge, and disposition of mentors. Do mentors themselves have substantive content knowledge about child development and more specifically the most current understanding of scientifically based practices in promoting early language and literacy development? There is little research investigating the pos-sible negative effects of mentoring that may occur if mentors simply pass along their own teaching practices whether or not they are effective (Ingersol & Kralick, 2004). The U.S. Department of Education's Institute for Education Sciences eval-uated the Early Reading First program, and their findings were inconclusive due to the variability in the expertise of the coaches, content, and implementation of coaching that confounded results (Duessen, Coskie, Robinson, & Autio, 2007). Head Start's STEP/CIRCLE initiative, as well as the authors' experiences support-ing numerous Early Reading First projects, reveals that literacy mentors are often learning both child development and scientifically based language and literacy content concurrently with their protégés.

In addition to content knowledge, mentors must have experiential knowledge of best classroom practices. The California Early Childhood Mentor Program demonstrated that it is beneficial for mentors to have experience with a wide range of quality in classroom practices. Although it is important for mentors to know and implement best practices, experience with lower levels of classroom quality deepens understanding of the protégé's frame of reference and broadens the mentor's ability to facilitate change in practices. Broad experience that is specific to the field of early childhood provides an authentic understanding and appreciation of the program culture, the classroom context in which teachers work, and individual backgrounds and experiences that guide teachers' practices. This experiential frame of reference is essential when establishing credibility with protégé teachers and realistic and feasible instructional approaches and learning goals.

Mentors also need to be knowledgeable in the principles of adult learning and skilled in facilitating change, observation, communication, assessment, goal setting, joint problem solving, reflective practice, and much more. Finally, it is reasonable to assume that, even if content knowledge and experience is comparable, not all mentors are equal in skill or disposition. The disposition of a mentor has been undervalued and overlooked. Combs and colleagues (1969) defined effective teaching as a "helping relationship," and effective helpers have the ability to facilitate positive change in others. Effective versus ineffective helpers can be distinguished on the basis of their perceptual orientation to subject matter, self, other people, the teaching task, and general frame of reference. Based on Comb's humanistic theory, Wasicsko (2002) has done some preliminary work to develop an assessment system to determine if certain dispositions are more suited to facilitating change than others. Although this research has not extended specifically to mentors, it does suggest that there is much more to learn about the contribution of the mentor's disposition.

The NEA Foundation for the Improvement of Education (1999) identified four qualities of effective mentors: 1) attitude and character, 2) professional competence and experience, 3) communication skills, and 4) interpersonal skills. Gallacher also described the qualities of effective mentors as "encouraging and supportive, committed to their protégé, sensitive, helpful but not authoritative, flexible, respectful, enthusiastic about the profession, diplomatic, patient, willing to share information, willing to share credit or recognition, and willing to take risks" (1997, p. 198).

MENTOR–PROTÉGÉ RELATIONSHIP

Martin and Trueax (1997) have proposed five periods in the formation of a mentor–protégé relationship: 1) relationship building, 2) agenda building, 3) information exchange, 4) groundwork for change, and 5) moving to transformation. The *relationship building* period is characterized as time to establish trust, openness, acceptance, support, encouragement, and comfort. During the *agenda building* period, the emphasis is on the mentor's knowledge (e.g., child development, instructional strategies, resources) and expertise (e.g., wisdom derived from experience and breadth of problem-solving strategies). During the *information exchange* period, the emphasis is on the processes of communication, feedback, and reflection. The *groundwork for change* period begins to resemble a collegial, less dependent, relationship. The *moving to transformation* period occurs as the mentor–protégé relationship changes from that of teacher and student to trusted colleagues with mutual benefits.

The mentor–protégé relationship, however, has complexities that emerge when the relationship is not protégé-initiated and therefore involuntary. The movement to provide professional development for early childhood teachers has been a top-down approach, with policy makers and administrators initiating and mandating changes that have a profound impact on the day-to-day lives of teachers. There is evidence that a bottom-up model (i.e., initiated by teachers) is more responsive to how teachers learn and is more likely to produce changes in teaching practices (Vaughn & Coleman, 2004). Teachers ultimately have the responsibility to implement mandates and policies, embrace learning and new ways of thinking, develop new and unfamiliar skills, and change the familiar classroom practices that they believe are "tried and true" and represent their years of experience. Effective mentors take into consideration *who* is initiating the change. When change emanates from external sources (e.g., mentor, administrator, trainer), it is most likely to produce only short-term compliance. The task of the mentor is to understand and elicit a protégé teacher's intrinsic motivation and commitment to professional development and to make meaningful changes in classroom practices. If the desire for change resides with the protégé teacher, learning will be meaningful and is more likely to result in sustained changes.

TRANSTHEORETICAL MODEL OF CHANGE

The Transtheoretical Model of Change (DiClemente & Prochaska, 1982) is particularly applicable to the mentor–protégé relationship and the challenges of guiding the protégé through behavioral changes in classroom practices. The model describes six characteristic stages of behavior change: 1) precontemplation, 2) contemplation, 3) preparation, 4) action, 5) maintenance, and 6) relapse. Although the model emerged from research to identify effective interventions that produce behavioral health changes (e.g., smoking, addiction), it has particular relevance to professional development intervention programs (such as Early Reading First and Early Childhood Educator Professional Development programs) that are externally initiated.

The Transtheoretical Model of Change makes no assumption about the individual's readiness or willingness to change behavior in the short-term or about an individual's willingness to make permanent changes. In fact, the model proposes that the behavioral change is an intentional and individual decision. In contrast, most professional development intervention approaches rely on an implicit assumption that increased knowledge will lead to immediate, long-term change in the teacher's classroom practices.

Each stage in the model has implications for mentoring and the professional development process. Teachers in the *precontemplation* stage are not aware of the need to change their teaching practices; they generally believe that they are knowledgeable and have an expertise based on their years of experience and/or formal education. Teachers at the *contemplation* stage are ambivalent about changing their practices. At this stage, teachers may attend training and consider new information, but they are not ready to incorporate the information in a manner that changes their classroom practices. Teachers who are in the precontemplation and contemplation stages are not ready for change and will most likely be resistant to mentoring. During these stages, teachers typically offer a variety of reasons to justify why it is not necessary or timely to change their classroom practices (e.g., their approach works, the children in the class have special needs, time of year is not good, too many administrative requirements, changes would conflict with other standards).

In order to develop receptiveness to learning and change, a mentor must establish a mutually respectful and trusting relationship with the protégé teacher. To avoid raising defensiveness, it is important for the mentor to know the protégé teacher, his or her practices, and the classroom context in which he or she works. A mentor must genuinely respect the protégé's years of experience and knowledge. A skillful mentor will acknowledge the protégé's lack of readiness to change classroom practices, encourage exploration of new ideas and instructional approaches, and affirm the protégé's decisions whether or not to modify his or her practices. For professional development programs, this juncture is exceptionally challenging because the expectation of results within a predetermined timeframe pressures mentors to overlook these stages and/or to power through them at the risk of getting immediate but short-term changes in instructional practices.

At the *preparation* stage, teachers have begun to experiment with some changes as if "testing the water." The teacher is cautiously open to considering change and reviews his or her skills and gathers resources. During the *action* stage, teachers are engaged in practicing new skills and implementing changes in classroom practice. The mentor is instrumental in joint problem solving, guiding the protégé teacher in skill development, translating new knowledge into appropriate applications, and transforming unsuccessful trials into new learning. At this time it is important for protégés to feel comfortable with revealing mistakes and to become an active partner in joint problem solving. Pearson and Gallagher's (1983) Gradual Release of Responsibility Model is useful during the preparation and action stages because it scaffolds classroom experiences using a progression from high support demonstration lessons (I do, you watch), to medium support of collaborative lessons (You do, I help), to low support of teacher independent lessons (You do, I watch).

During the *maintenance* stage, the teacher has modified his or her classroom practices and continues to incorporate new learning into daily routines. At this stage, the teacher's self-reliance and independence, self-directed learning and resourcefulness, personal commitment, and purposefulness will all influence the sustainability and progression of professional development. It is also at this stage in which contextual support makes a difference; teachers may find that without peer and/or administrative support they lapse into familiar habits and old practices. Once the external professional development program has concluded, the teacher assumes full responsibility for sustaining the quality and intentionality of instructional practices. However, as the National Staff Development Council noted, "If…new practices are not supported and reinforced [by larger school reform efforts, rather than isolated efforts], then professional development tends to have little impact" (Darling-Hammond et al., 2009, p. 10).

Evidence of the *relapse* stage includes abandonment of the recently acquired skills and instructional approaches, reversion to old habits and routines, and failure to initiate on-going self-directed learning to remain current with advances in the field and to deepen understanding and refine skills. For example, at this stage, teachers may abandon or change the newly acquired early language and literacy curriculum and instructional approaches, eliminate assessment strategies, or fail to maintain the literacy rich elements of the environment.

The Transtheoretical Model of Change is particularly applicable to mentoring because it emphasizes that change is an individual choice, and it makes no assumptions about a protégé teacher's readiness or willingness to change. As a professional development strategy, mentoring is an individualized approach to change based on an understanding of teachers' beliefs and behaviors in the context of the classrooms in which they work. As Grace and colleagues (2008) noted, professional development supports must continue long enough for teachers to embrace new concepts and take ownership of them. "Long enough" involves movement from precontemplation to maintenance, and each stage of the process has distinct implications for mentoring.

INTEGRATING MENTORING INTO A MULTIDIMENSIONAL PROFESSIONAL DEVELOPMENT PROGRAM

Based on their comprehensive review of professional development approaches, the National Staff Development Council identified four basic principles of effective learning experiences (Darling-Hammond et al., 2009). Professional development for teachers produces meaningful results when it is

1. Intensive, ongoing, and connected to practice and ranges from 30 to 100 hours over 6–12 months— (These experiences are even more powerful when based on individualized knowledge of the teachers' practices.)

2. Focused on specific curriculum content and how new practices are modeled

3. Aligned with larger system improvement priorities and goals and, therefore, accompanied with ongoing support and system commitment

4. Supported by strong relationships among teachers that form learning networks and provide opportunities for teachers to observe each other, give and get feedback, and foster reflective analysis of practices

Mentoring aligns with these principles and is further strengthened when it is embedded in a multidimensional professional development program. Professional development that is multidimensional (e.g., mentor-coaching, group training seminars, peer networks) results in greater gains in teacher knowledge, improved classroom practices (Foorman & Moats, 2004; Grace et al., 2008; Neuman & Cunningham, 2009), and child language and early literacy skills (Abbott-Shim & O'Donnell, 2009; Lambert, O'Donnell, Abbott-Shim, & Kusherman, 2006).

Grace and colleagues (2008) evaluated a comprehensive Early Reading First professional development program over 3 years that included treatment and nontreatment comparison groups. Over the 3 years, there were significant improvements within the treatment classrooms in literacy environments, as measured by the Early Language and Literacy Classroom Observation Tool (ELLCO) Pre-K (Smith, Brady, & Anastasopoulus, 2008), and instructional practices, as measured on the Literacy Activities Rating Scale (LARS; Dickenson & Anastasopoloulos, 2002). The professional development program included 1) literacy mentors who modeled and gave feedback to teachers based on classroom observations, 2) high-quality monthly workshops based on teacher-identified needs, 3) feedback from environmental assessments and the provision of literacy materials, and 4) equipment and instruction on how to use it. Administrative support; teachers' personal commitment; and the collegial network among the teachers, mentors, administration, and workshop leaders also contributed to positive changes.

Multidimensional professional development programs improve classroom practices when they continue long enough for teachers to embrace new concepts and instructional practices. The program must be sustained until it is evident that teaching staff have taken ownership, and it must be linked to needs identified through classroom observation and teacher reported concerns (Grace et al., 2008).

The Partners in Quality mentoring program was developed in 1995 by Quality Assist, Inc., in response to several factors, including the findings of a statewide evaluation of Head Start programs preparing for national accreditation, a keen awareness of the limited academic and literacy proficiency of early childhood teachers, and recurring reports from administrators that teacher training failed to produce observable and sustained changes in classroom practices. The mentoring model was designed to

•   Address the specific characteristics and contexts within which the protégé teachers work (i.e., who)

- Work collaboratively with protégés to determine what knowledge and skills are needed to achieve positive learning outcomes for children (i.e., what)

- Promote self-directed, reflective, and experientially oriented learning that is relevant for and transformed into classroom practices (i.e., how)

The Partners in Quality mentor model has subsequently been implemented in numerous projects, including Head Start Quality Initiatives, Early Reading First, and Early Childhood Educator Professional Development Program, and embedded in a multidimensional approach to professional development. In some projects, mentors were teachers who completed the Partners in Quality 50-hour mentor preparation course. In other projects, mentors were early childhood professionals who were external agents to the protégés' program. Across the projects the professional development and mentoring program extended for 1–3 years.

Mentoring in the Partners in Quality model was supported by and integrated into a multidimensional approach to professional development that involved peer networks, on-site study groups, short courses, and intensive study during a weeklong Challenging Teachers Institute. The focused content of study groups, short courses, Challenging Teachers Institute, and classroom-based mentoring was coordinated and reinforced so that conceptual learning was directly linked to classroom practices. Mentoring served as the catalyst for individualizing and integrating protégé teachers' conceptual learning with their beliefs and values and subsequently with their instructional methods and techniques.

The mentoring model focused on establishing a mutually respectful relationship with the intent of facilitating change. Mentoring was grounded in principles of adult learning, and mentors were active listeners. They engaged in powerful questioning to create awareness and promote reflective practice. Mentors used direct communication and dialogic conversations in addition to a variety of mentoring techniques (e.g., modeling, side-by-side mentor-coaching, collaborative lessons, structured observations, action research). Working closely with the protégé teachers, they jointly set goals and designed appropriate and meaningful action, holding accountability in a safe and supportive relationship.

Mentoring focused on helping teachers establish integrity and congruence among knowledge, values, and behaviors. Both the Challenging Teachers Institute and the Partners in Quality mentor approach are built on a strong theoretical and experiential foundation of adult, self-directed learning and collaborative support for others. The core values and approach of mentoring and the Challenging Teachers Institute are grounded in the *Rights of the Learner*:

> We believe that all learners construct their knowledge through interactions with physical and social environments. Therefore, learners have the right to explore the environment. Learners have the right to formulate and test hypotheses, invent strategies, seek multiple plausible solutions, pose new questions, and revise beliefs. In recognition of the rights of the learner, we approach learning through rigorous, inquiry-based reflection. This involves drawing on the experiences that you bring

and those that we create together. We value uncertainty in the learning process and see it as a time of infinite possibilities. We believe that learning is authentic when it is learner-centered and results in changes in your daily practices. Learning is enduring when feelings, knowledge, and actions are synergistic. The educational process is successful when it inspires the learner to be a life-long investigator. (Sibley, 1999)

In their 5-year study, Abbott-Shim and O'Donnell (2009) examined the impact of a professional development program across four Head Start agencies. The program was based on a combination of job-embedded peer-to-peer mentoring and the Challenging Teachers Institute. Mentor teachers were screened through observation, interviews, reflective writing samples, and professional references. A rigorous screening process was implemented to ensure that mentor teachers were knowledgeable and that they demonstrated high-quality practices and, therefore, were qualified to assist protégés in developing appropriate, high-quality classroom practices. Mentor candidate classrooms scored a full standard deviation higher than the mean on the Learning Environment, Scheduling, and Individualizing subscales of the Assessment Profile for Early Childhood Programs: Research Edition II (Abbott-Shim & Sibley, 1998), and they scored at the mean on the Curriculum and Interacting subscales. Children in the protégés' classrooms also made greater gains than control children on the Peabody Picture Vocabulary Test, Third Edition (Dunn & Dunn, 1997); the Woodcock Johnson Letter-Word Identification assessment (Woodcock, McGrew, & Mather, 2001); and the Language and Emergent Literacy Assessment (LELA; Cunningham, Hicks, & Williams, 2002). In addition, the protégé treatment children scored higher than control children on the Woodcock Johnson Diction and Book Knowledge assessments.

CONCLUSION

Transforming the professional qualifications of the early childhood work force presents unique challenges. A majority of the work force is characterized by women in their late 30s and early 40s who have years of on-the-job experience, fragmented professional training, and limited formal education (Tarrant et al., 2009). It is estimated that only one third of early childhood teachers have formal education at the bachelor's level or higher, one third have associate's degrees, and one third have high school diplomas (Herzenberg, Price, & Bradley, 2005). Teachers in the early childhood work force are typically employed full time but earn wages at or below the poverty level. Low compensation and the absence of a career lattice contribute to high turnover (Cost, Quality, and Child Outcomes Study Team, 1995) and an inability to attract and retain educated, young teachers (Herzenberg et al., 2005).

Although the episodic workshop approach to professional development has inadequately prepared early childhood teachers, traditional formal education presents obstacles of a different nature. Early childhood teachers generally lack both the economic resources and the academic prerequisites for institutions of higher learning. There is evidence that the language and literacy skills of a substantial portion of early childhood teachers tend to be at the most basic levels. For example, the National Adult Literacy Survey reported that nearly half (44%) of the early childhood teachers they surveyed had difficulty understanding written material; more than half (57%) of the teachers had difficulty locating and using information from written materials or applying arithmetic operations using numbers embedded in printed material (Kaestle, Campbell, Finn, Johnson, & Mikulecky, 2001).

These findings are consistent with our own experience. We assessed the vocabulary, reading comprehension and reading efficiency of 37 early childhood teachers participating in an Early Childhood Educator Professional Development program. A majority of the teachers scored below the 30th percentile in reading efficiency and comprehension. Approximately 74% of the teachers with high school diplomas scored below the 30th percentile for reading efficiency, and 35% scored at the 1st percentile. In addition, 87% of the teachers scored below the 30th percentile in reading comprehension. Teachers with associate's degrees did slightly better—38% of the teachers scored below the 30th percentile for reading efficiency; however, 71% scored below the 30th percentile for reading comprehension. The most surprising results were related to teachers with bachelor's degrees—65% of the teachers scored below the 30th percentile in reading efficiency, and 77% scored below the 30th percentile in reading comprehension (Lambert, Sibley, & Lawrence, 2009).

Despite federal and state efforts to improve the qualifications of teachers, and therefore the quality of early childhood programs, there is evidence that formal education alone is insufficient to raise the quality of teaching practices. Neuman and Cunningham (2009) compared the teaching practices of three groups of teachers. One group attended a 45-hour language and literacy college course and received 64 hours of practice-based coaching. The second group participated in the course but did not receive coaching support, and the third group received no professional development support. Although the course involved 45 hours of instruction, it produced modest growth in teacher knowledge and limited change in teaching practices. There were no differences in the quality of teaching practices between teachers who participated in the course but did not receive coaching and those who received no professional development support. In contrast, teachers that participated in the course and received practice-based coaching demonstrated higher quality in language and literacy practices. These findings provide support for job-embedded, practice-based professional development in combination with coursework.

Public investment in professional development for early childhood teachers has significantly increased through Head Start, Early Reading First, and Early Childhood Educator Professional Development initiatives. These investments have the potential to reshape the patchwork approach of community-based workshops into a systematic approach to professional development that is responsive to the existing work force needs and that moves the field forward. As investments increase, policy makers are turning to researchers and professional development providers to identify the most effective professional development approaches. Yet, there is little conclusive empirical research available to guide the development of approaches that will most likely increase the knowledge and skills of early childhood teachers and subsequently produce positive learning outcomes for young children.

Comprehensive professional development systems require substantial investments of resources at the program and classroom level and significant allocations of state and/or federal resources at public and private institutional and agency levels. Systematic evaluation of the effectiveness of professional development systems can offer program administrators and policy makers specific guidance regarding the potential for a return on their investments. The research literature in the field of early childhood, however, contains surprisingly little guidance regarding specific professional development strategies that lead to enhanced teaching practices and improved child outcomes (Zaslow & Martinez-Beck, 2006). And yet, the consequences of inadequate professional preparation for early childhood teachers, particularly for new teachers, can result in poor developmental outcomes for children, high turnover among teachers, and teachers who leave the profession. Rigorous evaluation can guide public policy and investment, particularly for investment in large scale professional development initiatives, if it is sensitive to the conditions of field settings and approaches professional development as a complex system of interrelated strategies.

Although a consensus does not currently exist as to the meaning of the terms and strategies of early childhood professional development, a framework is emerging that can facilitate an understanding of the extant systems of providing support for early childhood teachers (National Professional Development Center on Inclusion, 2008; Zaslow & Martinez-Beck, 2006). Early childhood education takes place in diverse settings with patchwork funding and delivery systems under multitiered standards and governing authorities. In addition, within these diverse contexts, early education is provided by a work force with a wide variation in skills, abilities, experiences, and levels of education. An overall framework is necessary in order to begin to interpret the emerging research and guide future evaluation efforts to determine the efficacy of systems of support for early educators. A professional development framework that focuses on *who* is the target audience, *what* is delivered to the teachers, and *how* it is delivered would allow us to categorize findings into a coherent body of work that can begin to inform the field about what is working for whom and under what conditions.

What is delivered to early childhood teachers and how it is delivered can vary so greatly that we refer to the collective of professional development strategies as a "system of professional development and support," to be inclusive of mentoring, coaching, on-site technical assistance, group training outside the formal education settings, and formal education. Given the magnitude and complexity of the needs of the early childhood work force, and the range of supporting professional development systems that have been proposed to meet these needs, three types of evaluation models are relevant: 1) teacher-centered, 2) administrator-centered, and 3) system-centered. Each of these models contains both formative and summative components and tasks and informs a synthesized model of evaluation strategies that we recommend.

As social, economic, and political conditions place increased pressure on early childhood educational programs to produce better child outcomes, formative evaluation is essential. This process of systematically measuring the quality and effectiveness of a professional development program during its implementation serves as an important guidepost and compass, allowing professional development providers to make timely adjustments to their practices. In effect, formative evaluation is a self-correcting system and is generally context specific.

Evaluators need to document the unique features of the contextual setting in which professional development is delivered and include descriptions of the community settings, program resources, characteristics of the families and children served by the program, characteristics of the teachers including education and experience levels, and the overall policy climate within which the program operates. The qualifications as well as the specialized knowledge and skills of mentors are contextual elements and contribute to the quality and effectiveness of the professional development system. Context evaluation helps tell the complete story of the implementation of a system of professional development and support, from the challenges and barriers encountered to the results obtained, and informs the ultimate summary judgment about both the effectiveness of the system and its applicability and appropriateness for the needs of the teachers in the particular setting under review.

Systems of teacher professional development support vary greatly with respect to their focus and features. Even basic definitions of what constitutes mentoring, coaching, training, and technical assistance have not been consistent in the research literature. Therefore, evaluators need to define exactly what the strategies, dosage, and duration of professional development involve and the exact nature of its features before conclusions regarding the exportability or potential replication of any findings can be addressed.

Mentoring is more than a promising professional development strategy. As a job-embedded strategy, mentoring is uniquely designed to translate conceptual, ideological learning to practical application in real-life contexts. It is context specific and focuses on practices, gaining strength and impact when combined with other modalities of learning (e.g., study group networks, group training, visits to model classrooms, formal education courses) that focus on the acquisition of content knowledge (Abbott-Shim & O'Donnell, 2009; Neuman & Cunningham, 2009). Future research and evaluation that captures the interrelationship of diverse professional development modalities will allow us to design models of professional development that are responsive to teachers' needs, contexts, and learning preferences. Systematic documentation and analysis combined with descriptive information about the mentors, protégé teachers, dosage, and contextual supports will inform future professional development designs, determine the critical features that must be considered when attempting to generalize and scale-up professional development designs, and optimize public and private investments in professional development programs.

In the meantime, the supporting literature, although variable and incomplete, is emerging, and mentoring has a prominent role, making a significant contribution in the early childhood professional development system. The contribution of mentoring derives from the fact that it is job-embedded, builds on the teacher's values and beliefs, and occurs over a period of time. It is essential to take into consideration the knowledge, skills, and disposition of the mentor whose pivotal task is to elicit the protégé teacher's motivation and commitment to professional development and meaningful changes in classroom practices. When the desire for change emerges from the teacher, learning will be meaningful and is more likely to result in sustained changes.

REFERENCES

Abbott-Shim, M., & O'Donnell, M. (2009). The effect of Creative Curriculum training and technical assistance on Head Start classroom quality. In P. Starkey (Ed.), *Preschool curriculum models: Findings from the PCER studies.* Manuscript submitted for publication.

Abbott-Shim, M., & Sibley, A. (1998). *Assessment Profile for Early Childhood Programs: Research Edition II.* Atlanta, GA: Quality Counts.

Assel, M.A., Landry, S., Swank, P.R., & Gunnewig, S. (2007). An evaluation of curriculum, setting, and mentoring on the performance of children enrolled in pre-kindergarten. *Reading and Writing, 20,* 463–494.

California Early Childhood Mentor Program. (n.d.). *California Early Childhood Mentor Program: Annual report 2007–2008.* Retrieved February 26, 2009, from http://www.ecementor.org/annualreport/completeWEB.pdf

Combs, A.W., Soper, D.W., Gooding, C.T., Benton, J.A., Dickman, J.F., & Usher, R.H. (1969). *Florida studies in the helping professions* (Social Science Monograph #37). Gainesville: University of Florida Press.

Cost, Quality and Child Outcomes Study Team. (1995). *Cost, quality, and child outcomes in child care centers.* Denver: University of Colorado, Economics Department.

Cunningham, G., Hicks, D., & Williams, G. (2002). *Language and emergent literacy assessment (LELA).* Birmingham, AL: Jefferson County Committee for Economic Opportunity.

Darling-Hammond, L., Chung Wei, R., Andree, A., Richardson, N., & Orphanos. S. (2009). *Professional learning in the learning profession: A status report on teacher development in the United States and abroad.* Palo Alto, CA: Standford University, National Staff Development Council.

Dickinson, D.K., & Anastasopoulos, L. (2002). *Early Language and Literacy Classroom Observation (ELLCO) Toolkit, Research Edition.* Baltimore: Paul H. Brookes Publishing Co.

DiClemente, R., & Prochaska, J.O. (1982). *Transtheoretical Model/stages of change.* Retrieved January 2009 from http://www.cpe.vt.edu/gttc/presentations/8eStagesofChange.pdf

Duessen, T., Coskie, T., Robinson, L., & Autio, E. (2007). *"Coach" can mean many things: Five categories of literacy coaches in early reading first* (Issues & Answers Report, REL 2007-No. 005). Washington, DC: U.S. Department of Education, Institute of Education Sciences, National Center for Education Evaluation and Regional Assistance, Regional Educational Laboratory Northwest.

Dunn, L.M., & Dunn, L.M. (1997). *Peabody Picture Vocabulary Test* (3rd ed.). Circle Pines, MI: American Guidance System.

Feiman-Nemser, S. (1996). *Teacher mentoring: A critical review.* (ERIC Document Reproduction Service No. ED397060)

Foorman, B.R., & Moats, L.C. (2004). Conditions for sustaining research-based practices in early reading instruction. *Remedial and Special Education, 25*(1), 51–60.

Fukkink, R.G., & Lont, A. (2007). Does training matter? A meta-analysis and review of caregiver training studies. *Early Childhood Research Quarterly, 22,* 294–311.

Gallacher, K.K. (1997). Supervision, mentoring, and coaching. In P.J. Winton, J.A. McCollum, & C. Catlett (Eds.), *Reforming personnel preparation in early intervention: Issues, models, and practical strategies* (pp. 191–214). Baltimore: Paul H. Brooks Publishing Co.

Grace, C., Bordelon, D., Cooper, P., Kazelskis, R., Reeves, C., & Thames, D.G. (2008). Impact of professional development on the literacy environments of preschool. *Journal of Research in Childhood Education, 23*(1), 52–74.

Herzenberg, S., Price, M., & Bradley, D. (2005). *Losing ground in early childhood education: Declining work force qualifications in an expanding industry, 1979–2004.* Washington, DC: Economic Policy Institute.

Howes, C. (1997). Children's experiences in center-based child care as a function of teacher background and adult-child ratio. *Merrill-Palmer Quarterly, 21,* 213–226.

Ingersol, R., & Kralick, J. (2004). *The impact of mentoring on teacher retention: What the research says.* Retrieved March 1, 2009, from http://www.ecs.org/clearinghouse/50/36/5036.htm

Kaestle, C.F., Campbell, A., Finn, J., Johnson, S., & Mikulecky, L. (2001). *Adult literacy and education in America: Four studies based on the national adult literacy survey.* Washington, DC: National Center for Education Statistics.

Lambert, R., O'Donnell, M., Abbott-Shim, M., & Kusherman, J. (2006, April). *The effect of Creative Curriculum training and technical assistance on Head Start classroom quality.* Paper presented at the annual meeting of the American Educational Research Association, San Francisco.

Lambert, R., Sibley, A., & Lawrence, R. (2009, November). *Professional development and mentoring for educators serving at-risk children: The PEACH project in Georgia.* Paper presented at the annual meeting of the National Association for the Education of Young Children, Washington, D.C.

Martin, A., & Trueax, J. (1997). Transformative dimensions of mentoring: Implications for practice in training of early childhood teachers. In China–U.S. Conference on Education, *Collected papers: Beijing, People's Republic of China, July 9–13, 1997.* (ERIC Document Reproduction Service No. ED425405)

Murray, M., & Owens, M.A. (1991). *Beyond the myths and magic of mentoring.* San Francisco: Jossey-Bass.

National Association for the Education of Young Children. (2009). *Where we stand on standards for programs to prepare early childhood professionals.* Available online at http://www.naeyc.org/positionstatements/ppp

National Professional Development Center on Inclusion. (2008). *What do we mean by professional development in the early childhood field?* Chapel Hill: The University of North Carolina, FPG Child Development Institute.

NEA Foundation for the Improvement of Education. (1999). *Creating a teacher mentoring program.* Paper based on the proceedings of NFIE's Teacher Mentoring Symposium, Los Angeles.

Neuman, S.B., & Cunningham, L. (2009). The impact of professional development and coaching on early language and literacy instructional practices. *American Educational Research Journal, 46*(2), 322–353.

No Child Left Behind Act of 2001, PL 107-110, 115 Stat. 1425, 20 U.S.C. §§ 6301 *et seq.*

Odiorne, G.S. (1985). *Mentoring: An American management innovation.* Alexandria, VA: American Society for Personnel Administration.

Onchwari, G., & Keengwe, J. (2008). The impact of a mentor-coaching model on teacher professional development. *Early Childhood Education Journal, 36,* 19–24.

Pearson, P.E., & Gallagher, M. (1983). The instruction of reading comprehension. *Contemporary Educational Psychology, 8*(3), 317–344.

Phillepsen, L., Burchinal, M., Howes, C., & Cryer, D. (1997). The prediction of process quality from structural features of child care. *Early Childhood Research Quarterly, 12,* 281–303.

Romo, H.D., Elmer, A., & Casso, T. (2007, November). *Mentoring as a strategy for implementing change in teaching ideology: Promoting early literacy instruction.* Presentation at the annual meeting of the American Sociological Association, New York. Retrieved March 4, 2007, from http://www.allacademic.com/meta/p185072_index.html

Shea, G.F. (1994). *Mentoring: Helping employees reach their full potential.* New York: American Management Association.

Sibley, A. (1999). *Rights of the learner.* Atlanta, GA: Quality Assist.

Smith, M.W., Brady, J.P., & Anastasopoulos, L. (2008). *Early Language and Literacy Classroom Observation Tool (ELLCO) Pre-K.* Baltimore: Paul H. Brookes Publishing Co

Sweeny, B. (2008). *Defining the distinctions between mentoring and coaching.* Retrieved January 1, 2009 from http://mentoring-association.org/DefM&Coach.html#HOW

Tarrant, K., Greenberg, E., Kagan, S.L., & Kauerz, K. (2009). The early childhood work force. In S. Feeney, A. Galpar, & C. Seefeldt (Eds.), *Continuing issues in early childhood education* (3rd ed., pp. 134–157). Upper Saddle River, NJ: Reason Education.

Vaughn, S., & Coleman, M. (2004). The role of mentoring in promoting use of research-based practices in reading. *Remedial and Special Education, 25,* 25–38.

Wasicsko, M. (2002). *Assessing educator dispositions: A perceptual psychological approach.* Retrieved June 15, 2008, from http://www.education.eku.edu-Dean-DispositionsManual.pdf

Whitebook, M., & Sakai, L. (1995). *The potential of mentoring: An assessment of the California Early Childhood Mentor Teacher Program: A report by the National Center for the Early Childhood Work Force.* Washington DC: National Center for the Early Childhood Work force.

Whitaker, S.D. (2002). Mentoring beginning special education teachers and the relationship to attrition. *Teaching Exceptional Children, 66*(4), 546–556.

Woodcock, R.W., McGrew, K.S., & Mather, N. (2001). *Woodcock-Johnson III Tests of Achievement.* Itasca, IL Riverside Publishing.

Zaslow, M., & Martinez-Beck, I. (Eds.). (2006). *Critical issues in early childhood professional development.* Baltimore: Paul H. Brookes Publishing Co.

7

Participatory Action Research

An Effective Methodology for Promoting Community-Based Professional Development

Amy C. Baker and Shira M. Peterson

Increasingly, policy makers have begun to prioritize evidence-based programs (those supported by scientific evaluations, such as randomized experiments), and for good reason. Experimental research relies on a rigorous methodology using carefully constructed designs and standardized instruments to measure the outcomes. It is designed to assess a program's effectiveness objectively, with a minimum of bias. Experimental research gives us confidence: If we replicate an evidence-based program with fidelity, we can be confident about our outcomes.

But the rigor of experimental research is also its weakness. Fidelity to a program design prohibits major mid-course adjustments or corrections, and real life can be complicated. Midway into an experiment, it can become apparent that a strategy is not working, a different management structure needs to be implemented, or logistical factors are preventing the program from operating as intended. Factors such as these can have a significant impact on the study design and its findings, but rigorous experimental research often cannot make modifications to account for these kinds of changes. At best, it can create a follow-up study, and that takes more time.

This chapter describes the benefits of using *participatory action research* as an alternative methodology to evaluate the success of community-based professional development initiatives. It begins with an overview of this approach and then describes its use in a program funded by an Early Childhood Educator Professional Development (ECEPD) grant in Rochester, New York. The chapter closes with a summary of key take-home lessons for practitioners and policy makers.

PRINCIPLES OF PARTICIPATORY ACTION RESEARCH

Participatory action research, which has its roots in social psychology, is based on social models developed in the early and mid-1900s by Kurt Lewin. It focuses on relationships among individuals, within networks and groups, and among networks and communities. The approach is undertaken by a group of people who face a real-life problem and are invested in finding a solution. For example, a child care center needs to enrich its classroom literacy environment in order to become nationally accredited; infant-toddler caregivers need updated information on attachment theory and brain development; preschool teachers at a Head Start program need access to courses that will lead to an associate's degree in early childhood education. In participatory action research, the relevant stakeholders identify a problem and take action to correct it (Kemmis & McTaggart, 1988; Reason & Bradbury, 2001; Wadsworth, 1998).

The methodology follows a cycle of *reflection, planning, action,* and *observation.* The period of reflection takes place when the group of stakeholders identifies a concern and, through inquiry and data gathering, defines a goal and then a plan to achieve it. Action is the moment when the plan is implemented and hoped-for improvements begin to emerge. Observation occurs when the group analyzes the data and evaluates the outcomes (Kemmis & McTaggart, 1988). The process is cyclical because it may be repeated until the original goal—or a new one—is reached.

If the key to experimental research is fidelity to the program design, the key to participatory action research is *collaboration,* or the group's ability to maintain cohesion throughout the research process. Relevant stakeholders, who share broad goals, address the challenges that confront them by putting aside differences in style, culture, and social context for the sake of the common mission. In other words, the group's success depends on its ability to generate and maintain its *social capital,* or the interpersonal connections within and among social networks. The value of social capital is that it makes it possible for stakeholders to reach goals they could not reach on their own (Putnam & Feldstein, 2003). Building social capital takes a willingness to invest time and effort into relationships, usually through simple social routines as lunch meetings, friendly telephone calls and e-mail, or casual exchanges about life outside of work. It depends on mutual respect, assistance, trustworthiness, the ability to listen actively, and the willingness to be assertive rather than confrontational in the face of conflict.

In participatory action research, two types of social capital are important: *bonding* social capital and *bridging* social capital. Bonding social capital is the connection that forms among like-minded people who have similar values, styles of interacting, missions, and goals. Networks that work with the same population, offer similar services, and have similar expectations have the basis for bonding social capital. Bridging social capital refers to the capacity to build ties among groups that have different kinds of experience, styles of interacting, and different social or cultural contexts (Putnam & Feldstein, 2003). Bridging social capital takes a willingness to clarify and disagree respectfully. It begins with the belief that every voice counts (Straus, 2002).

THE ROCHESTER EARLY CHILDHOOD COMMUNITY

A group of five early childhood agencies in Rochester, New York, collaborated to apply to the U.S. Department of Education for an ECEPD grant in 2002. The proposal was one step in a long history of community-based planning and assessment. Rochester's early childhood stakeholders had been assessing the quality of their child care programs and the need for professional development since 1986, when the mayor appointed the first Early Childhood Task Force to deal with issues that were receiving urgent public attention. The task force, composed of representation from the County Department of Social Services, the United Way, the Community Foundation, the City School District's office of Early Childhood, and representatives from the business community, was tasked with the responsibility of outlining a strategy that addressed those issues.

Over the next 4 years, the group morphed into a loosely knit voluntary collaborative that included stakeholders from 20–25 early childhood networks. The Early Childhood Direction Initiative, as it was called, defined a broad vision: Every child will have the foundation needed to succeed in school and in life. Its focus was on children, prenatal through age 5 (until school entry) and their families. Families with few resources and supports were the highest priority.

Each member of the collaborative represented a network that offered an array of early childhood services, including the family resource centers, the Child Care Resource and Referral agency, the family child care satellite network, and the county early intervention program. Membership was inclusive, open to anyone who wanted to take part. The group was headed by an unaffiliated, unpaid retiree who supported the vision, understood the collaborative process, and had the ability to look at the challenges to the service delivery system overall. The group met monthly to share news and discuss current challenges and concerns.

Using the Participatory Action Research Cycle Framework

The Early Childhood Direction Initiative was committed to finding solutions to achieve the goal of providing every child a foundation to succeed in school and life. In order to do this effectively, the collaborative followed the participatory action research cycle framework of reflection, planning, action, and observation.

Reflection/Planning In 2000, the collaborative convened a working conference for early childhood professionals (e.g., caregivers, directors, educators, university faculty, researchers, advocates) for the purpose of identifying gaps and barriers to professional development. The areas of greatest need that were identified were professional development and technical assistance for center directors, an associate's degree in higher education, parent education, coursework that focused on the needs of infants and toddlers, and education to support practitioners working with children with challenging behaviors.

Once these challenges were identified, participants broke into small groups to discuss strategies to address them. Participants were charged to answer these questions: What would you do to improve the professional development system if you had the resources you needed? How would you address the gaps and overcome the barriers? How much would it cost?

The small groups formed committees that continued to meet for 1 year. They collected data in the form of formal needs assessments, demographic information, and documentation of strategies that had proved successful in other communities. Based on this information, they created detailed action plans including the cost for implementation.

Action   When the opportunity for federal funding arose, the collaborative was ready with a research-based plan and strategies to support it. The proposal's overriding goal was to create an integrated professional development system from entry level through the completion of a bachelor's degree. The major components of the grant included 1) implementing classroom-based mentoring for infant-toddler and preschool practitioners, 2) creating an associate's degree program in early childhood education (including research-based courses on early literacy, infant-toddler development, and observing and assessing young children), 3) disseminating information about professional development opportunities to educators, 4) creating a model infant-toddler child care program, and 5) operating an interactive multifaceted communication network for parents and early childhood educators.

Observation   The ECEPD project was led by a management team that included representatives from five key partner organizations. Working groups responsible for each of the grant's components continually observed the process and analyzed data on the outcomes. Data were collected using multiple methods including participant surveys, focus groups, mentor logs, and student records. The management team met monthly to reflect on its progress and discuss areas of concern. When small problems arose, the group proposed solutions. If a strategy proved to be unrealistic or ineffective, the management team made a mid-course correction.

Significant new strategies came out of this evaluative process. After mentors observed that many protégées were not ready to change or modify their practices, the management team hired a consultant to train mentors on the change process. A "stage of change" tool was developed to understand and measure protégées' receptivity to professional development. (See Chapter 3 for a description.) Another mid-course correction occurred when a focus group of center directors revealed that they were not able to fully support their staff members' professional growth because the mentoring program did not have a formal way of involving administrators. The management team responded by reviewing the literature on systems change and subsequently committed to a centerwide mentoring approach that included administrative staff.

Reviewing Outcomes and Repeating the Cycle

One of the goals of the early childhood collaborative was to create an Early Educator Professional Development Institute, which would become a one-stop resource for information. Its purpose would be twofold: 1) to make it easier for directors and caregivers to find the coursework they wanted, and 2) to make gaps in training visible to educators and policy makers. The Institute hoped to accomplish these goals by posting course offerings on its web site, conducting electronic surveys, and tracking web-site inquiries.

An advisory group from the early childhood collaborative volunteered to create the web site, promote it, update it, and monitor its uses. They projected that by the end of 6 months, 300 people would access the site (50 per month). But at the end of 6 months, only 15 people had accessed the site, and that figure included members of the advisory committee. Uncertain how to explain the data, the group surveyed potential users including directors, classroom teachers, and family child care providers. The responses were revealing. Classroom teachers had little interest in professional development opportunities other than those that were mandated by their directors. Family child care providers preferred to attend classes offered by the agencies that administered their Child and Adult Care Food Programs.

The advisory committee reflected on their original objective of giving practitioners more information about professional development opportunities. The committee then developed a new strategy to pursue this goal: The community college developed a new one-credit course, Seminar for Early Childhood Practitioners, which was designed to help students understand career paths in early childhood. The advisory committee tracked attendance to see if the course was meeting its goal of reaching the early educator community. During 2004, the first year of the grant, the course was offered twice, with 14 participants. In 2005, the course was offered three times, with a total of 53 participants. Based on this information, the committee made the strategic decision to take down the web site and market the course instead. Over the 3 years of the grant (counting the 1-year extension), course attendance held steady. By the end of the grant period, a total of 118 early childhood educators had assessed their strengths and interests and written 5-year professional development plans. The course continues to be offered on campus and at child care centers throughout the community.

Another goal the collaborative pursued was educating practitioners, directors, and the community at large about infant and toddler development. Local agencies and funders had invested significant time and resources developing high-quality center-based child care programs for preschool children, but little attention had been paid to infant-toddler care. Few educators were familiar with research on attachment and brain development and their implications for programs serving children from birth to age 3.

The bonding social capital among members of the infant-toddler committee enabled them to work together to address the problem quickly and effectively. The infant-toddler committee created three strategies to address this challenge: 1) train a group of trainers who could teach attachment theory and best practices for group care, 2) develop a cadre of mentors who could go into centers and offer practical suggestions to classroom-based caregivers, and 3) create a model infant-toddler child care program where directors, caregivers, students, and policy makers could observe best practices and talk with knowledgeable early childhood professionals.

The ECEPD grant enabled Rochester's early childhood collaborative to send a group of 14 educators to WestEd's Program for Infant/Toddler Caregiver training. From that group, 10 participants became infant-toddler mentors, and 5 became certified trainers. The trainers developed a 32-hour course that focused on attachment theory, brain development, and the importance of early relationships. The mentors took the information into the classroom to help practitioners translate theory into practice. An infant-toddler specialist helped one of the child care centers become a model program where directors, caregivers, policy makers, and students could observe best practices. By the end of the grant period, 77 center-based infant-toddler caregivers had received mentoring services. A total of 214 staff members from 28 centers had taken 32 hours of infant-toddler training, and 196 visitors toured the model infant-toddler child care program.

The infant-toddler committee reviewed the outcomes of the training. Although they found that center-based child care staff members were better educated about infant-toddler development, other delivery systems had little understanding of attachment theory, brain development, and their implications. The committee decided to create a simple message that would appeal to a broad audience: Every child should have a secure attachment to at least one nurturing adult who is committed to the well-being of that child. Because bonding social capital was so high among the stakeholders in the early childhood collaborative, the message spread quickly. Thirty perinatal and preschool home visitors agreed to take a refresher course in attachment theory and brain development. Four videos on attachment were broadcast to 200,000 homes via the community college education channel on cable TV. The message became the core vision of a broad initiative involving home visitors, pediatricians, grandparents, and family child care providers.

The Positive Effects of Bridging Social Capital

Bridging social capital is important when stakeholders do not share the same experience, culture, context, or expectations. Members of Rochester's early childhood collaborative had a cordial relationship with the community college, but it was formal, without personal ties or a working history. The two organizations had a similar mission—professional development—but little understanding of one another's processes or constituencies. The collaborative represented a population that worked for a minimal wage, with few avenues for economic advancement. Caregivers typically attended in-service workshops on mandated topics. Although some had a high school degree, many did not. Few were motivated to pursue other professional development opportunities. In contrast, the community college worked with men and women who had a high school diploma or a GED and were motivated to further their education. Faculty held students accountable to academic standards, expecting them to attend classes, read assigned texts, and complete written assignments.

When the federal government mandated that Head Start teachers at minimum have an associate's degree or be enrolled in an associate's degree program, the early childhood collaborative asked to meet with representatives from the community college. The collaborative wanted the college to 1) develop coursework leading to a New York State infant-toddler credential, 2) create an associate's degree in early care and education, and 3) create articulation agreements with 4-year colleges that would enable students to move up the education, and hopefully career, ladder.

From the community college's perspective, these demands were unrealistic. The college's measure of success in developing new coursework was the number of full-time students interested in enrollment. It was willing to create coursework and a degree program if there was a need, but in its view, the demand had yet to be demonstrated. The college agreed that articulation agreements were important but cautioned that it was impossible to create them without support from the State Department of Education. Frustration on both sides ran high.

The person who brought the two groups together had a degree in elementary education and more than 20 years of experience at the college teaching interpersonal communication skills. His familiarity with the college and his skill as a facilitator made him an ideal liaison. As a result of his efforts to forge relationships among these diverse constituencies, the college created an associate's degree in liberal arts with a concentration in early childhood and created the courses leading to an infant-toddler credential. By the end of the grant period, 243 practitioners had completed at least one college-level course in early care and education.

The liaison also persuaded the college to provide support for an interactive communication network designed to give parents and early childhood educators—especially nonreaders—access to up-to-date information related to the care of children. This system is still in use and delivers information via cable TV 5 days per week, from 10:00 a.m. to 11:00 a.m. and from 8:00 p.m. to 10:00 p.m. To date, the network has produced more than 100 videos on diverse topics including breastfeeding, diaper rash, colic, obesity, attachment, brain development, adoption, and lead poisoning—all of which can be downloaded from its web site, http://www.292baby.org. The network is connected to a call center that enables parents and early childhood educators to call pediatric nurses 17 hours per day with nonemergency questions. The health nurses field between 125–150 calls per month. The network also hosts a TV show, *News from Early Childhood*, which provides early educators with information about current issues and upcoming events.

Tracking Outcomes

The major goal of the Rochester ECEPD project was to raise the quality of care in infant-toddler and preschool classrooms through a cohesive system of professional development, including access to state-of-the-art coursework, consistent research-based messages about best practices disseminated across constituencies, and mentoring to support integration of new knowledge into practice. The collaborative collected multiple forms of data on the project's outcomes. Mentor logs and participant survey data demonstrated the positive impact of the project on early educators' professional beliefs and practices. Mentors shared numerous stories of caregivers who experienced increased learning opportunities through the combination of research-based coursework and mentoring. One educator who initially was skeptical of her mentor's suggestions experienced an epiphany after attending the community college infant-toddler development class. The mentor observed, "The next time [the educator] saw me she said excitedly, '[The instructor] said the same thing that you told me!' Then she went on telling me other things that [the instructor] had said." Other mentors had similar stories of mentees who made connections across their multiple professional development experiences.

Mentor logs and observations also documented evidence of widespread growth in educators' professional identity. For example, a positive change occurred in educators' outlook on the use of the observation assessments for informing their own practices. The assessments became a source of discussion and goal-setting between the educator and mentor. Many educators expressed a great deal of pride when they were successful in meeting their goals to implement positive changes. This experience also enabled educators to become more confident and open to pursuing other forms of professional development and enrolling in community college courses.

The project tracked the quality of preschool and infant-toddler classrooms using standardized observational assessments: the Early Childhood Environment Rating Scale–Revised (ECERS-R; Harms, Clifford, & Cryer, 1998), the Early Language and Literacy Classroom Observation Tool (ELLCO) Pre-K (Smith, Brady, & Anatasopoulos, 2008), and the Infant/Toddler Environment Rating Scale–Revised (ITERS-R; Harms, Cryer, & Clifford, 2003). Over the course of the grant period, there was improvement in classroom quality in mentored classrooms on all three measures. After 2 years of mentoring, classrooms showed significant positive changes on the ITERS-R and ELLCO Pre-K. Classrooms were assessed twice per year, and although there was continual growth across time, the greatest amount of growth occurred between the last two assessments. Thus, it appeared to take an investment of time to create and observe systematic changes in quality.

The significant positive changes on the literacy environment scale illustrate the impact of the strong literacy focus of the mentoring program. Mentor logs indicated that literacy was one of the most frequently identified goals on which mentors and mentees focused. This supports the widely accepted notion that significant changes occur when professional development interventions are focused on making specific changes (Garet, Porter, Desimone, Birman, & Yoon, 2001). Likewise, the significant changes on the infant-toddler rating scale reflect the project's intensive focus on raising the quality of infant-toddler care in the community. In addition to mentoring, infant-toddler caregivers now had multiple supports for learning about and implementing best practices: research-based coursework, a model infant-toddler child care program to observe, videos on cable TV, and a consistent message about attachment permeating across the community.

Ultimately, it was the young children in the community who benefitted most from the work accomplished by the project. Mentors observed numerous improvements in children's classroom experiences in terms of their interactions with educators, activities, and daily routines. For example, before participating in the project, many toddler educators ran their classrooms much like they would a preschool room. However, after hearing consistent messages about attachment and developmentally appropriate practices, infant-toddler caregivers became more confident of their unique role as a nurturer as well as educator of very young children. As one participant in the mentoring program commented, "[I had to get] used to not having a schedule, so to speak. 'Cause you know with toddlers you're going at their pace. You're not going at the 4-year-old pace of 'half an hour for this, 20 minutes for that.' [You're] adjusting to their needs."

Standardized assessments were used to measure preschool children's developmental growth, especially in the area of early literacy. By the end of the project, classrooms that received 2 years of mentoring had students who performed better on the Language/Literacy subscale of the **Child Observation Record** (**COR**; High/Scope Educational Research Foundation, 1992) and on the Meaning subscale of the Test of Early Reading Achievement (**TERA;** Reid, Hresko, & Hamill, 2001), compared with classrooms that did not receive mentoring.

KEY TAKE-HOME LESSONS

Rochester's experience has shown that participatory action research can be an effective methodology for raising the quality of early care and education through community-based professional development. This approach employs a cyclical process of continual reflection, planning, action, and observation to inform its course of action and evaluate its outcomes. One of its main advantages is its ability to make mid-course corrections when change is warranted. This flexibility permits stakeholders to make strategic adjustments without a significant delay.

Key take-home lessons for conducting participatory action research include the following:

• **Understand change as a cyclical process.**

Plan your intervention around the four moments of change: reflection (defining your goal, gathering data, understanding the challenges), planning (deciding on solutions to problems and tools for measuring outcomes), action (implementing new strategies), and observation (gathering data, comparing data with expected outcomes, and returning to reflection). Plan for success but expect complications, confusion, and unintended consequences. Be prepared to make mid-course corrections when they are warranted.

• **Make use of data and research.**

Use data from multiple sources such as standardized assessments, surveys, focus groups, attendance records, logs, and anecdotal information when you reflect on the problem and its challenges. Before designing an action plan, review the relevant research literature. Monitor the success of your program using data about the participants' experiences. Participatory action research has the advantage of flexibility, but its strength lies in careful use of data and analysis.

• **Collaboration is critical.**

For participatory action research to be an effective approach to improving community-based early childhood professional development, the collaborative must be open to all the relevant stakeholders. Every organization or network that shares the vision and has a wish to participate must be included as a valuable contributor. Each stakeholder should have a role at each step of the process.

• **Build social capital.**

Social capital makes it possible for stakeholders to reach goals they could not reach on their own. Bonding social capital, or connections among individuals who share values and ideals, allows motivated groups of people to unite their resources in pursuit of a common goal. Bridging social capital becomes important when collaboration is necessary among stakeholders with different constituencies and missions. Although it takes time and intentionality for groups to build relationships when they have a common mission, an even greater effort is needed when stakeholders have to bridge differences in mission, style, outlook, or expectations. When differences threaten to divide the group, return to the vision and the reason for the collaboration. Remind stakeholders of the goal and its importance. Keep in mind that relationships develop more easily in small groups. Encourage stakeholders to work together in committees and report findings back to the larger group as a whole.

CONCLUSION

This chapter has described participatory action research as an effective methodology for implementing and evaluating systemic changes in early childhood educator professional development. The approach rests on collaboration among relevant stakeholders who work together to create solutions to real-world problems. Improving the quality of early childhood education entails more than implementing evidence-based programs and practices with fidelity or adhering to an experimental research paradigm. It requires a commitment by individuals and agencies to work together to solve problems in ways that will benefit the community as a whole. This commitment is particularly important when stakeholders want to make broad systemic change. Engaging in participatory action research as a community is rewarding as well as effective. As one participant commented, "It just made me really appreciate the early childhood community even more knowing the dedication and the hard work that everybody is devoting to children." Shared purpose generates its own momentum. When devoted individuals pool their resources and come together for a common good, they can have an enormous impact on the capacity of their community to increase the quality of early childhood education and ultimately to improve the experiences and future possibilities of young children.

REFERENCES

Garet, M.S., Porter, A.C., Desimone, L., Birman, B.F., & Yoon, K.S. (2001). What makes professional development effective? Results from a national sample of teachers. *American Educational Research Journal, 38,* 915–945.

Harms, T., Clifford, R.M., & Cryer, D. (1998). *Early Childhood Environment Rating Scale–Revised.* New York: Teachers College Press.

Harms, T., Cryer, D., & Clifford, R.M. (2003). *Infant Toddler Environment Rating Scale–Revised.* New York: Teachers College Press.

High/Scope Educational Research Foundation. (1992) *Child Observation Record.* Ypsilanti, MI: High/Scope Press.

Kemmis S., & McTaggart, R. (1988). *The action research planner* (3rd ed.). Geelong, Australia: Deakin University.

Putnam, R.D., & Feldstein, L.M. (2003). *Better together: Restoring the American community.* New York: Simon & Schuster.

Reason, P., & Bradbury, H. (2001). *Handbook of action research: Participative inquiry and practice.* Thousand Oaks, CA: Sage.

Reid, D.K., Hresko, W.P., & Hamill, D.D. (2001). *TERA 3 examiner's manual.* Austin, TX: PRO-ED.

Smith, M.W., Brady, J.P., & Anatasopoulos, L. (2008). *Early Language and Literacy Classroom Observation Tool (ELLCO) Pre-K..* Baltimore: Paul H. Brookes Publishing Co.

Straus, D. (2002). *How to make collaboration work: Powerful ways to build consensus, solve problems, and make decisions.* San Francisco: Berrett-Koehler.

Wadsworth, Y. (1998). *What is participatory action research?* Retrieved May 1, 2009, from http://www.scu.edu.au/schools/gcm/ar/ari/p-ywadsworth98.html

III

Where Does Professional Development Occur?

There are many contexts in which professional development occurs, and each of these contexts offers both challenges and opportunities for improving teacher quality. The chapters in this section are representative of some of these contexts, in all of which training is supported through a relationship with higher education institutions. Some of these institutions, such as community colleges, have been at the forefront in forging important relationships with community-based organizations for training purposes. For other institutions, these relationships in the community represent a new vision for higher education, one that focuses on outreach and demonstrates a new flexibility to meet an increasingly diverse population of early educators who wish to continue their education. The three institutions presented in this section serve different clientele, from rural, to mid-sized urban, to large urban locations.

In Chapter 8, Doescher and Beudert report on a project in a relatively rural setting in Oregon where many of the students are often the first members of their families to attend college. Community colleges are a frequent choice by students seeking certifications related to teaching in early childhood settings. However, students often find roadblocks to obtaining higher education in these settings. These authors describe these challenges and report on the ways the Linn-Benton Community College revised its strategies to meet students' needs, with an enormous payback: Students completed their education and received their degrees at higher rates than ever before.

In Chapter 9, Hawkins and colleagues highlight another challenge in professional development: How to adapt the specific training formats (e.g., workshops) in which professional development takes place to meet teachers' needs. Recognizing that these specific formats have different uses at different stages in professional development, the authors recommend a multifaceted approach.

Combinations of several of these formats may be more effective than depending on any single format. This chapter illustrates considerations of how to combine (and, perhaps, not combine) these formats.

Lastly, in Chapter 10, Rubin and colleagues report on a project in southern Texas in which many of the educators and children speak Spanish as their native language. This project included the largest concentration of English language learners of any of the research projects described thus far. Learning from the cultural traditions in the community, the authors describe ways in which the complications of dealing with two languages were resolved, providing important guidance for an increasingly common problem in early childhood centers.

Together, the chapters in this section emphasize the need to take context into consideration when developing training programs. They also demonstrate the important role that higher education institutions may play in early childhood educators' professional development.

8

Professional Development in the Community College Setting

Susan M. Doescher and Jennifer Knapp Beudert

Sheraya has provided family child care for 21 years. She wants new ideas and new information to help in her work. Sheraya completed the short-term training provided by the local resource and referral and is now ready for the next step.

For the past 10 years, Mark has taught in a Head Start program. He needs a degree to keep his job. Mark takes night classes. This is a challenge because offerings are limited, and Mark is discouraged by his slow progress.

Elizabeth graduated from high school last spring. She has 5 brothers and sisters and thinks she might enjoy a job working with children. Elizabeth knows she'll need education beyond high school, but no one in her family has ever attended college. She also worries that she will have to travel some distance from her small rural community.

Many early childhood educators look to community colleges for their professional education (Early & Winton, 2001). Community colleges traditionally offer 2-year degree programs with an emphasis on children's development and practical skills for working in preschool classrooms. These programs extend classroom and on-site experiences, often in a college lab setting, so students will be job-ready upon graduation.

Can this type of traditional degree program effectively educate the early childhood work force, increasingly represented by individuals such as Sheraya, Mark, and Elizabeth? Early care and education has changed since the early 1980s, with trends affecting program composition and quality, thus calling into question the role of community colleges in early childhood professional development. Changes include the following:

- The increased number of young children in a wide variety of nonfamilial child care settings

- The diversity of children in care, including those with special needs, English language learners, and children at risk from poverty

- The diversity in demographics of the early child care work force

To address the school readiness gap, national attention is focusing on preschool teachers and caregivers, a population not previously viewed as professional educators. At least 38 states sponsor initiatives that provide funds for early childhood education, and many of those initiatives require participating programs to employ college-educated early childhood teachers (Barnett, Epstein, Friedman, Boyd, & Hustedt, 2008). Programs such as Good Start, Grow Smart, and Head Start require college degrees for early childhood educators. The Committee on Early Childhood Pedagogy Report (Bowman, Donovan, Burns, & Committee on Early Childhood Pedagogy, 2000) recommended that all children in an early childhood program be assigned a teacher who has at least a bachelor's degree. Federal education policy dedicated to placing highly qualified teachers in classrooms has challenged early childhood communities to develop stronger systems of professional development and to be ready to respond to increased demands for early education (Washington, 2008). If this trend of raising the educational bar continues, however, what are the ramifications for community colleges?

This chapter addresses the benefits and challenges of providing professional development in the community college setting. A wide debate on the value of college-level early childhood programs flourishes. Although requiring college degrees has advanced the professional standing of other caregiving occupations, the field of early childhood remains ambivalent about the desirability of academic credentials (Washington, 2008). This indecisiveness stems from a number of unanswered questions, such as the following:

- Can colleges overcome barriers to recruit participants into degree programs in a field that traditionally prides itself on alternate career paths outside of formal educational requirements?

- Can colleges meet the needs of adult learners from nontraditional backgrounds with extensive work experience and variable academic skill levels?

- Does attainment of a college degree lead to improved classroom quality and teacher outcomes?

Community colleges can have an impact on teacher knowledge and practice. In early studies, college coursework increased teachers' positive attitudes and behaviors with children (Arnett, 1989; Cassidy, Buell, Pugh-Hoese, & Russell, 1995). Since then, the Early Childhood Educator Professional Development (ECEPD) project at the Children's Institute in Rochester, New York (see Chapter 7) and the Early Education Partnership (EEP) program at Linn-Benton Community College in Albany, Oregon (discussed in this chapter) have successfully engaged early education students in college-level professional development. These projects implemented a combination of strategies that included credit-classes and mentoring. The result on student recruitment and retention, knowledge acquisition, and teaching practice was dramatic.

NONTRADITIONAL STUDENTS IN THE EARLY EDUCATION PARTNERSHIP PROGRAM

The EEP program, an ECEPD project conducted in 2005–2008, emerged from a need to engage nontraditional students in early childhood education. Head Start teachers, family and center child care providers, and students wishing to become early childhood educators from two rural counties in Oregon participated in the EEP program. Students were primarily nontraditional learners, sharing many of the same characteristics. For instance, they were single parents, responsible for dependents, and delayed in enrolling in college beyond high school. In addition, they had limited financial resources, worked part- or full-time with children, attended college part-time, had low literacy and basic skill levels, and typically did not view early childhood as a profession. Such nontraditional learners are more likely to leave college before completing their degree because of competing personal, work, and school demands (Whitebook, 2003).

In years prior to the EEP program, enrollment in courses was low because of course inaccessibility and college demands for writing and math. The goal of the EEP program was to develop a rigorous program that would attract and retain students and encourage a greater connection to practice. To accomplish this goal, the EEP program included college classes that led to a certificate or degree and ongoing mentor support. Areas of study included child development, curriculum, working with families, professional issues, and field experience, in addition to the basic education classes such as writing and math. Cumulative coursework incorporated theory, current research, and practice.

Students in the EEP program were paired with life-skills mentors to facilitate successful educational progress. In the past, mentors have effectively supported nontraditional learners as these students pursue their career goals (Weber & Trauten, 2008). In the EEP program, however, mentors helped students succeed in college. Veteran mentors guided, encouraged, and supported students in their professional development. They also engaged them in close working relationships. Life-skills mentors understood college policies and procedures, supportive resources, and problem-solving skills. They displayed excellent practices with children and provided feedback to increase competency in work as well as life skills.

BARRIERS TO COLLEGE EDUCATION

Professional development for early childhood students at the community college level is based on the following assumptions:

- Opportunities to improve knowledge and skills need to be accessible to early childhood educators, which include nontraditional learners, and these students need to receive support in their studies.

- Professional development needs to contain updated research-based content.

- Early childhood educators need to receive support in putting knowledge into practice.

However, significant barriers exist that make the attainment of these goals difficult. These barriers may even discourage colleges from offering programs that include nontraditional learners.

Adult education programs face three types of barriers: situational, institutional, and dispositional (Cross, 1981). These barriers apply directly to the early childhood adult student population and are widely viewed as insurmountable. Many students feel that a degree is not an option due to these roadblocks.

Situational barriers include financial costs of tuition and books, as well as issues such as child care and transportation. Potential students frequently cite financial issues as one of the primary reasons for not pursuing higher education (Washington, 2008). The cost of postsecondary education is not the only concern; more pressing is the fact that most nontraditional students financially support their families and must work during the daytime when classes are offered. Situational barriers are therefore inextricably linked with institutional barriers.

Institutional barriers, including the scheduled times of college classes, make it extremely difficult for working early childhood educators to attend school. College degree programs usually focus on traditional students. Traditional students take a full-time course load, attend classes during the day on the main campus, and participate in several terms of field experience in the college lab setting. Nontraditional students typically are unable to give up jobs to attend daytime classes or to work as unpaid practicum students in college lab schools. Students may live a significant distance from the campus and cannot afford the daily commute. When faculty members at 2-year colleges rated the difficulty of challenges faced in teaching early childhood students, they gave the highest rating to competing work and family responsibilities (Early & Winton, 2001).

Dispositional barriers, which are rooted in attitudes, beliefs, and assumptions, are in many ways the most challenging barriers to overcome. Attitudes toward school and learning, largely influenced by prior experience, low self-esteem, and lack of support from family and friends, may make it impossible for early childhood educators to visualize themselves as successful college students and ultimately as successful professionals (McMurry, Pallotta, & Quinn, 2009; Washington, 2008). Many nontraditional students are the first members of their families to attend college. Friends and family may not support their pursuit of higher education and may discourage their efforts or view school as a self-indulgent luxury. Also, early childhood jobs infrequently offer pay incentives or promotions to reward student efforts.

Returning to college after decades away from school, or after prior negative experiences with school, is very difficult for nontraditional students. Tasks such as filling out registration forms, finding classrooms, setting up e-mail accounts, buying books, or talking with the financial aid office can be extremely daunting. Many nontraditional students are overwhelmed by initial college procedures and give up before even attempting classwork.

Academic issues are also a concern for nontraditional learners. Many early childhood students enter college with low reading, writing, and math skills. Lack of preparedness makes it difficult to be successful in school. Required general education classes can be a big stumbling block to degree achievement. Many colleges will not admit students who cannot demonstrate a certain level of academic proficiency, and those colleges with open enrollment may require remedial work before students can begin taking courses in their field.

Students often postpone taking required classes that they suspect may be beyond their academic skill level. The result is that students attempt these classes in their final term. Many students fail the classes and do not graduate. Students who have almost completely fulfilled the requirements for an early childhood degree will frequently withdraw from the program with only one remaining requirement, such as a math class. Students faced with these academic problems may be reluctant to seek help out of embarrassment, or they may not know where to turn for help. Without help, they are unlikely to succeed on their own.

OVERCOMING BARRIERS

The nontraditional student population does not fit the mold of full-time students who are recent high school graduates in pursuit of a professional career. However, strategies exist that can help bridge the gap between the nontraditional early childhood community and the community college environment in order to help nontraditional students overcome barriers to higher education. Effective strategies that help adult learners succeed in various continuing education programs include mentor support, student cohorts, academic assistance, and flexible scheduling (McMurry et al., 2009; Washington, 2008).

Barriers and solutions for nontraditional students need to be identified before students enroll in early education programs. The Oregon EEP program was designed to overcome financial barriers, for example, by providing comprehensive financial support for all participants, including full tuition, books, and mentoring. Despite skepticism from community agencies that nontraditional educators would enroll in college no matter what supports were available, there was immediate widespread interest in the program. Initial enrollment was 30% higher than expected, and this rate of participation continued for the program's 4-year duration. When financial barriers are completely removed, many early childhood educators leap at the chance to go to school.

Even if financial barriers cannot be entirely removed, any financial resources a college can divert toward nontraditional students makes a difference. College counselors, an instrumental resource, help students secure financial aid for educational expenses, as well as for other living expenses, such as the costs of transportation and child care. Counselors also investigate scholarship programs sponsored by local and state resources and referral offices, community service organizations, and college departments. Many college scholarships go unused, and small amounts of money may make college attendance possible for some nontraditional students.

In order to retain students in an early childhood program and ensure that students succeed, institutional barriers also must be addressed. Surmounting these barriers requires creative and flexible responses from the college. The Oregon EEP program solved these problems by offering evening classes, one-credit modularized classes, online classes, and classes at alternate locations. Through the development of a new system of practicum supervision, students completed field experiences at their own worksites.

Other community colleges also have made some progress in implementing strategies to overcome institutional barriers. As early as 2001, 38.7% of early education programs at 2-year schools offered some form of distance learning (Early & Winton, 2001). With more widely available technological resources, this percentage seems likely to continue to increase. Programs such as the Rochester ECEPD project addressed time and distance barriers by bringing college classes into familiar community settings. However, a comprehensive system that implements multiple strategies is needed to fully overcome these barriers.

College faculty members who are sensitive and supportive of nontraditional students' unique needs can also make a difference in student retention. For example, instructors in the Oregon EEP program were flexible in responding to time and distance barriers, often helping arrange carpools or providing alternate assignments for students who were unable to get to class on a particular week. This enabled students to successfully complete classes instead of dropping out. A program liaison between students and faculty members can help faculty members understand the unique needs of nontraditional students and devise strategies to meet those needs (McMurry et al., 2009). In the EEP program, mentors played the liaison role.

Addressing dispositional or emotional barriers also requires multiple strategies and creative thinking. For instance, mentors can help students succeed in professional development programs by helping students identify professional goals, assisting them with academic concerns, visiting worksites, modeling best practices, and monitoring progress, thus providing a link between work and school (Neuman & Cunningham, 2009). However valuable, this type of support often comes too late for nontraditional students in college degree programs. Traditional mentoring programs assign mentors to students when they begin their course of study, thus overlooking those students who are unable to overcome initial barriers to college access and enrollment on their own. These students need immediate life-skills mentor support to address both institutional and dispositional barriers. They need encouragement as well as basic step-by-step instruction to navigate college bureaucracy in order to persevere with their education despite feelings of self-doubt. Life-skills mentoring was essential in effectively retaining participants in Oklahoma community college early childhood programs (McMurry et al., 2009), for example, and a more intense and individualized program of life-skills mentor support was key to the success of the Oregon EEP program.

Once accepted into the EEP program, participants were connected to mentors who worked with them throughout their course of study. At their initial meeting, mentors helped students enroll in the college, apply for additional financial aid, register for classes, buy books, find classrooms, meet their instructors and advisors, and access college support services. A positive mentor–student relationship was well developed by the time students began courses, and students quickly learned that they could go to their mentors with any questions that arose. Over time, mentor work with students became less focused on life-skills issues and more directed toward on-site practices and the academic program.

Mentors can support nontraditional students with academic needs by connecting them with college resources such as tutoring or developmental studies. Inventive thinking provides solutions for triumph over those especially daunting classes. For example, when it became apparent that the math requirement stopped many students just short of graduation, the EEP program offered smaller sections of the course, encouraged students to take classes in a cohort and study together (thus building a peer support group), assigned a mentor to serve as a course tutor, and encouraged collaboration among course instructors and early childhood faculty members. It is in these circumstances that nontraditional students particularly benefit from instructors who understand ways to successfully complete coursework (Macdonald Fueyo, 1988).

The support that nontraditional students receive from mentors, instructors, and each other can also help fill the emotional void created by lack of support from family and friends. Colleges advance community building among nontraditional students by setting up cohorts of students who take classes together. It is often difficult for nontraditional students to complete class assignments at home due to family responsibilities. The EEP program promoted informal study groups and provided space for student groups to complete homework together after hours and on weekends. Educational and social events sponsored by the college or department (e.g., lectures, workshops, outings) also help students form stronger bonds and provide continuing support for one another.

Another vital element in effective preparation of early childhood professional educators is ongoing mutually responsive interaction among students and faculty (Washington, 2008). This is particularly true in the case of nontraditional students who may not have other beneficial sources of academic, professional, or personal support. Unfortunately many early childhood degree programs have disproportionate numbers of part-time and adjunct faculty members compared with other degree programs. This problem is exacerbated when classes are provided at alternate times and locations. If early childhood courses are taught primarily by contracted faculty members, rather than adjunct instructors hired for a single class, students and faculty members have more opportunities to develop positive relationships. Full-time contracted faculty members are more accessible, have more motivation and opportunities to learn about challenges nontraditional students face, and are better able to meet student needs (Early & Winton, 2001). Recognizing this, EEP program core courses (including nighttime and on-line classes) were taught by the same full-time faculty members who also served as academic advisors for the degree program.

INCREASING CONTENT KNOWLEDGE

A driving force behind the national focus on professional development for early educators is the growing readiness gap between low- and middle-income children in the area of early literacy. An increasing research base supports the hypothesis that improving teacher content knowledge in early literacy will ultimately contribute to improved educational outcomes for children (Neuman & Cunningham, 2009). A common element of successful literacy programs focuses on the core knowledge areas of oral language development, phonological awareness, letter knowledge, print concepts, and general background knowledge necessary for school success in reading (National Reading Panel, 2000; Snow, Burns, Griffin, & Committee on the Prevention of Reading Difficulties in Young Children, 1998). What does this mean for college early childhood degree programs serving nontraditional students?

Few college programs offer classes in early literacy that stress research-based content and instructional intensity and focus. These classes may be difficult for nontraditional students who have low literacy skills themselves and negative memories about reading and language instruction. This student population needs strategies to learn and apply early literacy course content.

In response to these challenges, the Oregon EEP program developed an intensive three-course series of early literacy classes that spanned 9 months. The length and comprehensive nature of this course sequence enabled students to explore how their experiences and emotions might affect their work with children. Many opportunities for students to practice basic literacy skills, such as reading aloud, were also provided. Classes typically included lecture and discussion components, hands-on activities to practice strategies, examination of children's work samples, and video examples of literacy instruction. Assignments linked theory to practice by requiring incorporation of class activities into work with children and ongoing reflection on these experiences. This approach worked: 98% of students successfully completed the three course series and showed substantial gains on the pre/posttest of content knowledge.

CONNECTING COURSE CONTENT TO
TEACHER PRACTICE AND BEHAVIOR CHANGE

To modify teacher behavior, teachers must apply new knowledge in their work with children. Many nontraditional early childhood students already work in the field—some for many years—and need to unlearn long ingrained behaviors before implementing new strategies. Change at this level is particularly difficult. These educators need support and guidance to evaluate and improve their teaching practices. Mentors who have positive relationships with students are in a position to provide support in school and work settings and to help achieve the leap from theory to practice.

Numerous Oregon programs have incorporated relationship-based professional development as an effective strategy for not only increasing content knowledge but also changing teacher behavior (Weber & Trauten, 2008). This type of professional development establishes relationships among more and less skilled members of the early childhood work force (National Child Care Information and Technical Assistance Center, 2008). Studies reveal consistent linkages between relationship-based professional development and positive outcomes for educational practices (Bryant, 2008; Dickinson & Caswell, 2007; Layzer, Layzer, Goodson, & Price, 2007; Pianta, 2006; Ramey, Ramey, Timraz, Grace, & Davis, 2008; Raver et al., 2008). This strategy appears to be an especially successful approach to change teacher behavior when combined with training or education (Weber & Trauten, 2008). Effective characteristics of relationship-based professional development include highly qualified mentors, ongoing training and support of mentors, manageable mentor caseloads, and focused mentor training.

This approach provided the basic foundation for Oregon's EEP program. Initially, nontraditional learners needed life-skills mentoring to enroll and succeed in college. Later in their course of study, they required focused support to apply the content learned in literacy classes to practice when working with children. For these reasons, students received targeted skill-based instruction. Results for EEP students were positive: When measured with the Early Language and Literacy Classroom Observation Tool (ELLCO) Pre-K (Smith, Brady, & Anastasopoulos, 2008), classroom environments, book and writing material usage, and reading and writing activities increased for EEP students at the end of the academic year. These improvements were significantly higher than those of comparison programs.

IMPLICATIONS FOR PROFESSIONALIZING THE EARLY CHILDHOOD WORK FORCE

In other professions, such as nursing, college-level degrees have professionalized the field, increased compensation, and attracted and retained individuals with greater potential for success (Washington, 2008). This can happen in the field of early childhood education as well. Professions, as opposed to jobs, share several common characteristics. These include a code of ethical conduct, performance standards to guide behavior, a research-based body of knowledge, and commitment to ongoing learning and skill development (Barbour & Lash, 2009). Whereas short-term trainings may be effective in improving specific job skills, achievement of a degree provides a broad base of professional education, time to reflect on learning and practice, and opportunities to put information into practice. College degree programs are designed to support early childhood education as a profession rather than a job. An individual who invests the amount of time, energy, and resources necessary to complete a degree program is likely to demonstrate a higher level of professionalism and commitment to the early childhood profession.

Nontraditional students typically do not see themselves as potentially successful professionals. In Oklahoma, faculty referred to early education students as "scholars" and created a formal pinning ceremony. These effective strategies promoted the concept that early childhood teachers *are* professionals both to themselves and the community at large (McMurry et al., 2009). The EEP program dedicated significant resources to individuals working with children. How did participants respond to this investment? The knowledge that professionals devote so much time and money to their education was a transformation experience for many students. They overcame previously insurmountable barriers, achieved academic success, and persevered to attain college degrees or certificates. They increased their content knowledge and changed their teaching practices. They joined early childhood organizations and participated in state and local professional activities. Many reported increased self-esteem, increased sense of professionalism, and pride in their success in the EEP program. We found that 98% of EEP graduates were still working with young children 1 year after completing the program. Nontraditional students can successfully rise to the challenge and complete an early childhood education degree when given the appropriate level of financial, institutional, academic, and personal support.

The quality of early childhood education programs at degree-granting institutions is essential to improving teacher and child outcomes (Burchinal, Hyson, & Zaslow, 2008; Early et al., 2007). Two-year colleges are in a position to play a key role in professionalizing the early childhood work force. Because most early childhood teaching jobs do not require a college degree, many students will start at 2-year colleges (Early & Winton, 2001). Students in these programs are likely to work in a setting serving children prior to kindergarten, whereas the majority of graduates with bachelor's degrees will work in elementary settings.

Two-year institutions typically enroll a population that represents a wide range of economic, ethnic, and racial diversity, and they are uniquely equipped to identify and address the needs and barriers faced by nontraditional students (Early & Winton, 2001; Kee & Mahoney, 1995). If the educational bar for early childhood educators continues to be raised, and if 4-year degrees are increasingly mandated, the issue of barriers for nontraditional students will have to be revisited. A major obstacle is the lack of articulation between 2- and 4-year college degree programs.

In our experience, child care and Head Start directors want EEP graduates to fill vacant teaching positions. The "word in the community" is that EEP teachers are particularly skilled and well-prepared. Graduates are quickly hired, and those already employed are promoted into higher paying or more responsible positions. This immediate response to EEP graduates shows how a comprehensive professional development program can have an impact on a community.

CONCLUSION

Our experiences throughout the 4 years of the EEP program provided a number of critical lessons that might translate well to other community college settings. First, situational, institutional, and dispositional barriers for nontraditional students can be successfully identified and overcome. Colleges that apply unconventional, flexible, and innovative solutions to the unique situations of students can effectively recruit and retain students who might otherwise not be successful in traditional early childhood education degree programs.

Through implementation of such strategies, the EEP program challenged widely held beliefs that nontraditional early childhood students would not enroll in college credit classes, would not persevere to finish a degree program, and would not be academically successful. Our studies showed significant increases in student recruitment and retention over previous years. Student retention was 92% in the EEP program—75% over previous enrollments. Student achievement in courses, compared with similar early childhood students who did not receive such mentoring and financial support, was also notable. More than 64% completed their certificates and degrees on time—35% more than the year prior to the start of the EEP program.

Second, relationship-based supports such as life-skills mentors are essential to the success of nontraditional early childhood education students. Mentors help students navigate the college system, connect to academic resources, and apply knowledge to practice. By providing emotional support and encouragement to participants, mentors also help to build students' self-esteem, confidence, and professional image.

For example, faculty members and mentors observed growth among EEP participants in areas that had not been anticipated—enthusiasm toward books and literacy, sense of self as a professional, willingness to seek out resources and ways to improve practice, interest in ongoing professional education, involvement with fellow colleagues in the community, and commitment to the field of early childhood education. Although the EEP program did not specifically examine the level or pervasiveness of these qualities or the factors that evoked them, participants themselves attributed their growth in these areas to the support and encouragement of their mentors.

In the EEP program, students reported that mentor support was more instrumental to degree completion than the significant financial resources they received. Relationship-based support from individuals at the institutional level, including faculty members, peers, and administrative personnel, added to student success. This type of support does not take a huge financial investment but rather knowledge and commitment by dedicated community members, college administration, and teaching faculty.

Finally, academic course content that is focused and includes time for hands-on learning may be the most effective way to assist early childhood educators make valuable changes in their practices. The same principles that have long been established as best practice to teach young children, specifically hands-on exploration, background knowledge, scaffolded focused instruction, and sufficient time for practice, are those strategies that are successful in teaching nontraditional adult students.

The connection between coursework and practice improved over the course of the EEP program. Increases in quality of the classroom environments and teaching practices of EEP students were greater than comparison settings of teachers who did not participate in the program. EEP participants demonstrated 60% higher scores on the ELLCO Pre-K than teachers in comparison settings. Although not the focus of our studies, the link between teacher behavior change and child outcomes can also result from relationship-based professional development.

Looking to the future, if community colleges take up the challenge of educating the early childhood work force, and degree attainment becomes an expectation rather than an exception, the quality of early childhood educational settings within a community will increase dramatically. Given the choice, early childhood programs will seek out teachers with stronger educational backgrounds, with the hope of ultimately increasing educational outcomes for children.

So what of Sheraya, Mark, and Elizabeth? Sheraya, an experienced family child care provider needs more comprehensive and in-depth professional development, as well as support to change her long-established practices. Mark, a hard-working full-time Head Start teacher, needs online and evening classes in order to make progress toward his degree without taking time off from his job. Elizabeth, unfamiliar with higher education, needs life-skills mentoring and emotional support in order to surmount obstacles to college enrollment. Can community college degree programs meet their needs? If colleges willingly identify the specific challenges facing today's nontraditional learners and creatively apply these proven strategies, then the answer is emphatically "Yes!"

REFERENCES

Arnett, J. (1989). Caregivers in day care centers: Does training matter? *Journal of Applied Developmental Psychology, 10,* 541–552.

Barbour, N., & Lash, M. (2009). The professional development of teachers of young children. In S. Feeney, A. Galper, & C. Seefeldt (Eds.), *Continuing issues in early childhood education* (3rd ed., pp. 158–183). Upper Saddle River, NJ: Pearson Education.

Barnett, W.S., Epstein, D.J., Friedman, A.H., Boyd, J.S., & Hustedt, J.T. (2008). *The state of preschool 2008: State preschool yearbook.* Rutgers, NJ: The National Institute for Early Education Research.

Bowman, B., Donovan, M., & Burns, S., & Committee on Early Childhood Pedagogy. (Eds.). (2000). *Eager to learn: Educating our preschoolers.* Washington, DC: National Academies Press.

Bryant, D. (2008, July 31). *The QUINCE study: Quality interventions for early care and education.* Paper presented at the meeting of the Child Care Policy Research Consortium, Washington, DC.

Burchinal, M., Hyson, M., & Zaslow, M. (2008). Competencies and credentials for early childhood educators: What do we know and what do we need to know? *National Head Start Association Dialog Briefs, 11*(1).

Cassidy, D., Buell, M., Pugh-Hoese, S., & Russell, S. (1995). The effect of education on child care teachers' beliefs and classroom quality: Year one evaluation of the T.E.A.C.H. early childhood associate degree scholarship program. *Early Childhood Research Quarterly, 10,* 171–183.

Cross, K.P. (1981). *Adults as learners: Increasing participation and facilitating learning.* San Francisco: Jossey-Bass.

Dickinson, D.K., & Caswell, L. (2007). Building support for language and early literacy in preschool classrooms through in-service professional development: Effects of the Literacy Environment Enrichment Program (LEEP). *Early Childhood Research Quarterly, 22,* 243–260.

Early, D.M., Maxwell, K.L., Burchinal, M.R., Alva, S., Bender, R.H., Bryant, D., et al. (2007). Teachers' education, classroom quality, and young children's academic skills: Results from seven studies of preschool programs. *Child Development, 78,* 558–580.

Early, D.M., & Winton, P.J. (2001). Preparing the workforce: Early childhood teacher preparation at 2- and 4-year institutions of higher education. *Early Childhood Research Quarterly, 16,* 285–306.

Kee, A.M., & Mahoney, J.R. (1995). *Multicultural strategies for community colleges.* Washington, DC: American Association of Community Colleges.

Layzer, J.L., Layzer, C.J., Goodson, B.D., & Price, C. (2007). *Evaluation of child care subsidy strategies: Findings from project upgrade in Miami-Dade county.* Report prepared for the U.S. Department of Health and Human Services, Administration for Children and Families, Office of Planning, Research and Evaluation, and The Child Care Bureau. Cambridge, MA: Abt Associates.

Macdonald Fueyo, J. (1988). Technical literacy versus critical literacy in adult basic education. *Journal of Education, 170*(1), 107–118.

McMurry, K., Pallotta, S., & Quinn, K. (2009, April 24). *Raising the educational bar for child care professionals in Oklahoma.* Paper presented at the meeting of the National Coalition of Campus Children's Centers, Phoenix, AZ.

National Child Care Information and Technical Assistance Center. (2008, March). *Supporting a skilled and stable workforce: Compensation and retention initiatives.* Retrieved July 13, 2008, from http://nccic.acf.hhs.gov

National Reading Panel. (2000). *Teaching children to read.* Washington, DC: National Institute of Child Health and Development.

Neuman, S.B., & Cunningham, L. (2009). The impact of professional development and coaching on early language and literacy instructional practices. *American Educational Research Journal, 46*(2), 322–353.

Pianta, R.C. (2006). Standardized observation and professional development: A focus on individualized implementation and practices. In M. Zaslow & I. Martinex-Beck (Eds.),

Critical issues in early childhood professional development (pp. 231–254) Baltimore: Paul H. Brookes Publishing Co.

Ramey, S., Ramey, C., Timraz, N., Grace, C., & Davis, L. (2008, July 31). *The "Right from Birth" study: An evidence-informed training model to improve the quality of early child care and education* (PowerPoint slides). Retrieved August 25, 2008, from http://che.georgetown.edu/presentations/

Raver, C.C., Jones, S.M., Li-Grining, C.P., Metzger, M., Champion, K.M., & Sardin, L. (2008). Improving preschool classroom processes: Preliminary findings from a randomized trial implemented in Head Start settings. *Early Childhood Research Quarterly, 23,* 10–26.

Smith, M.W., Brady, J P., & Anastasopoulos, L. (2008). *Early Language and Literacy Classroom Observation Tool (ELLCO) Pre-K.* Baltimore: Paul H. Brookes Publishing Co.

Snow, C., Burns, S., & Griffin, P., and Committee on the Prevention of Reading Difficulties in Young Children. (1998). *Preventing reading difficulties in young children.* Washington, DC: National Academies Press.

Washington, V. (2008). *Role, relevance, reinvention: Higher education in the field of early care and education.* Boston: Wheelock College.

Weber, R.B., & Trauten, M. (2008). *Effective investments in the child care and early education profession.* Corvallis: Oregon State University Family Policy Program, Oregon Childcare Research Partnership.

Whitebook, M. (2003). *Early education quality: Higher teacher qualifications for better learning environments—A review of the literature.* Berkeley, CA: Institute of Industrial Relations, Center for the Study of Child Care Employment.

9

Professional Development in Training Programs

Jacqueline Hawkins, Courtney Crim, Jenifer Thornton, and Amye R. Warren

Among a larger group of teachers, there is a computer specialist, dental hygienist, social worker, and high school teacher sitting in a room waiting for the trainer to arrive. Some are native English speakers, some are not. Their ages and previous professional experiences range widely. You might think this is a community event or a financial planning seminar, but in this case, each of these professionals, and several hundred more like them, are attending a training program in early childhood education. Their career paths have all led them through choice, love of teaching, and love of working with children to their positions as early childhood educators.

What do they have in common? What particular characteristics or skills have brought them to this training? All have a passion for what they do and want to excel. Although they might have come to their positions through different routes, their goals are now the same: They all want additional training to help them do a better job. They all recognize that they will need to acquire skills to better support children's early literacy development. Whether they are in Title I classes, dual language classes, special education classes, or private care settings, each of these participants knows that quality early childhood experiences will make an enormous difference in children's lives and wants to help these children enter school ready to learn. And they know, as research attests, that quality teaching is one of the most influential predictors of their children's ability to be successful.

Training through professional development can provide the opportunity for early educators to become highly qualified teachers if—and this is a big *if*—it is appropriately matched to their needs. Although training programs have no common definition (i.e., one size certainly does not fit all), most occur outside formal education for those already in the field. Unlike degree programs, training programs have no specific admission criteria. Consequently, individuals in training contexts are likely to hail from a variety of backgrounds and previous educational experiences.

This chapter explores the qualities of good training programs. It highlights the needs in the field and provides examples from our training program in Houston, Texas, to demonstrate how training may promote quality practices in early literacy. Finally, it describes several lessons learned in the course of improving teacher quality through training.

FORMATS FOR PROFESSIONAL DEVELOPMENT IN EARLY CHILDHOOD

A number of professional development formats are used to train early childhood educators who are already in the field: workshops, professional development schools, and on-site coaching or mentoring.

Workshops

The most commonly attended form of training in general has been the workshop (Wiley & Yoon, 1995). Typically, a workshop occurs over several hours, or even over an entire day, and it is targeted to a specific focus. For example, workshops on dramatic play may emphasize props, activities, and teaching supports for encouraging quality play behaviors for young children. Although there have been some adaptations to this traditional format, workshop formats have stayed remarkably the same since the early 1990s.

Although workshops are generally thought to be the most cost-effective professional development model, they often are not the most educationally effective model. Critics have condemned "one shot" workshops, arguing that they are minimally effective at best and do not include the key components for effective professional development. Some suggest that they can be superficial, are not always linked to classroom practice in a planned way, and provide no ongoing support or follow-up (Dickinson & Brady, 2006). Others have found that nontraditional early childhood educators may need more time to discuss successes and challenges than can be provided in this format. Given the diversity of need in early childhood education and the variety of educator abilities, workshops have not been particularly sensitive to individual differences in training needs.

Professional Development Schools

Since early 2000s, school districts have been partnering with universities or outside entities to provide professional development experiences for early childhood teachers. These programs have the benefit of training teachers on specific strategies that they will need in their school programs. For example, the Excellence Boys Charter School of Bedford Stuyvesant in New York City developed a collaboration with Hunter College. Teachers receive training on weekends to learn techniques and curriculum strategies that they can use immediately in the classroom. At the same time, the university provides credit hours that may work toward receiving a master's degree over time.

These programs have been successful due to the coherence of their training program. Teachers learn what they will eventually implement in classrooms, and as a result, their focus is very targeted, goal-oriented, and personalized to their working environment.

On-Site Coaching

To date, coaching has become a more common training format, even though there is little research on its effectiveness. Coaching can be experiential, grounded in inquiry and reflection, and collaborative and interactive.

Coaching typically is either directive or collegial (Joyce & Showers, 2002). Directive coaches tell teachers how to adjust instruction; collegial coaches use teacher self-reflection to enhance knowledge and improve instructional practices. The directive approach has been less likely to change the practices of veteran teachers but more likely to appeal to novice teachers (Gersten, Morvant, & Brengelman, 1995). The self-reflection aspects of coaching are considered the more collaborative model in which coaches and teachers focus on instructional concerns and implement changes together (Deussen, Coskie, Robinson, & Autio, 2007). Coaching that involves collaborative team development occurs best in schools with a climate of mutual respect and interdependence, where stakeholders are encouraged to trust each other, share information, and work together to serve students effectively (Reitzug & Burrello, 1995).

Some research suggests that one-to-one coaching is effective in changing teacher practice (Butler, Lauscher, Jarvis-Selinger, & Beckingham, 2004; Dickinson & Caswell, 2007; Joyce & Showers, 1996; Landry, Swank, Smith, Assel, & Gunnewig, 2006). For example, in the Joyce and Showers study, teachers who were coached were more likely to use new strategies appropriately than teachers receiving more traditional professional development. However, other studies have shown no effects of coaching (Gutierrez, Crosland, & Berlin, 2001; Veenman, Denessen, Gerrits, & Kenter, 2001). Although it might seem like the flexibility in coaching models could provide individualization in training, it could also work against improving teacher practices. For example, inexperienced teachers who work with coaches who either do not know the content or have difficulties in delivering information may do more harm than good to improving teacher practice. Variations in teacher experience, training content, delivery format, and the capacity of the coach are some of the areas of study that must be researched to determine the efficacy of specific coaching.

Although there are a number of different formats for training early childhood educators, no one format appears to be superior. Rather, it might be more beneficial to focus on quality components of training, rather than formats, to enhance the professional development and performance of early childhood educators.

QUALITY COMPONENTS OF TRAINING

Many training components described in the research literature appear to be critical components of an effective professional development program. These components range from participating in ongoing training and support to having opportunities to work with colleagues and mentors who are regularly available.

Ongoing Training and Support

Early childhood teachers need ongoing training and support to transform and enhance their early literacy practices in classrooms. Numerous studies (e.g., Boyle, Lamprianou, & Boyle, 2005; Thornton, 2006) have shown that long-term professional development training activities such as ongoing in-class support, modeling of instruction, and constructive feedback are associated with positive changes in teaching practices. Garet and colleagues (2001) suggested that ongoing and "sustained" training is likely to have a greater impact on teachers than brief one-shot trainings. Therefore, professional developers would be wise to establish a long-range plan to improve practices, with review doses of training over time.

Expert Trainers

It has been shown that trainers with specialized expertise (e.g., literacy, math) are more effective than those with generalized knowledge. Boudah, Logan, and Greenwood (2001), for example, reviewed five research projects out of the Office of Special Education Programs and found that effective integration of research and classroom practice was due to the quality of the trainers, whether they came from the classroom, administration, universities, or districts. Expert trainers need to have deep knowledge of early childhood as well as subject matter expertise. It is the depth of their knowledge, and not their degrees, which appears to matter most. Experts with knowledge and experience in the field have been shown to be most effective in gaining the respect of their peers and making significant improvements in practice (Boudah, Logan & Greenwood, 2001).

Ability to Apply Standards and Research into Classroom Strategies

Too often in training participants learn about the *why* (i.e., the rationale for a particular strategy) but not the *how*. For example, it is important to learn why dialogic reading is effective for increasing children's conversation and vocabulary, but in addition to understanding its rationale, early childhood educators will need practice in how to do it. Dialogic reading, for example, involves teachers turning closed-ended questions (e.g., "What is the color of the ball?") into open-ended questions (e.g., "Why do you think the author used this color?"). It is important to demonstrate how research outcomes connect with classroom activities, and this connection incorporates hands-on classroom activities that are tied to research-based effective instructional strategies. Training is unlikely to generalize to the classroom without actual follow-up support in the classroom.

Content Aligned with the Goals and Expectations of the Educational Context

Due in part to the 2002 "Good Start, Grow Smart" White House initiative, states have been required to develop voluntary preschool standards (U.S. Department of Health and Human Services, 2006). Although the quality of these standards varies across states (Neuman & Roskos, 2005), the standards serve as a general guide for determining developmentally appropriate content in working with preschoolers. These standards, available on state web sites, are valuable as a resource for training. They may help teachers frame instructional goals and, at the same time, provide a road map for the skills children will need in order to be successful in kindergarten and beyond. Many states have now begun to develop infant and toddler standards as well. These materials may also help teachers see how the early childhood curriculum serves as a foundation for future learning.

Delivery of Training Content that Meets the Immediate Needs of Children

Teachers will need content that can be easily applied to their classroom settings. Material that is not currently applicable to the needs of the children may not be used and, therefore, may be forgotten. The National Center for Research on Teacher Learning concluded that significant changes in teaching practice are most likely to occur when teachers have ongoing support that is "grounded in classroom practice, so that teachers have both opportunities to try and adapt new practices in their own classrooms and...that enables them to learn concurrently about subject matter" (1991, p. 4). Training that aligns content with effective teaching experiences in the classroom, such as personal examples from the participants and possibly videos, helps to demonstrate instructional and assessment strategies effectively in the classroom while meeting the needs of their students.

Opportunities to Work with Colleagues and Mentors Who Are Regularly Available

Teachers will need ongoing support throughout their teaching careers. Strategies described in this chapter and others emphasize the need for creating a professional community that works to refine its teaching talent through reflective inquiry and discussions with others who teach (Dantonio, 1995). For example, some teachers have formed study groups that meet in informal settings. Others have established interdisciplinary teams, with teachers, social workers, guidance counselors, and parent advocates all working together to establish best practices. These professional communities can help early childhood educators who play a variety of important roles better work together and learn from each other.

All of the components just described guided our training model. Together, they helped us create a design and implementation strategy that proved to be enormously successful for improving language and literacy practices in early childhood settings. The following section briefly describes our project and highlights how we weaved these components together to effectively change and improve practices.

THE C^3 PROJECT

The C^3 Project (2003–2006) was designed to provide professional development to prekindergarten teachers in Houston in the areas of literacy, mathematics, and social skills. It focused on three distinct "Cs"—cognitive, collegial, and collaborative aspects—a model we developed to highlight a team approach to training. The first "C" stood for the cognitive aspects of children's learning. Based on research, we reviewed effective instructional strategies, national and state standards, and research-based practice specifically targeted to early language and literacy. The second "C" stood for the collegial aspects of training. Here, we highlighted the importance of understanding both the culture and the context of early childhood professionals, and the need to be respectful of different perspectives. The third "C" stood for the collaborative aspects of training. In this respect, our goal was to support training teams with different expertise to work together on content, curriculum, and best practices.

Getting started on any project can be a challenge for a training program, but in many respects, our project was able to build on already existing resources. For example, our program was connected with the University of Houston, which already offered a rigorous degree program that met standards from the National Association for the Education of Young Children (NAEYC) and the National Council for the Accreditation of Teacher Education. The program was field-based and, therefore, maintained its relevance to the community and to then-current standards. In addition, we were able to build rapport with schools and districts because of prior relationships and great demand for university support. An Early Childhood Collaborative had begun in 1996 and had grown to include three school districts prior to the C^3 project. With additional funding, we were able to expand to seven school districts—32 campuses and 32 child care centers. The C^3 project involved many steps, including three that are highlighted here: a needs assessment, model lesson design and delivery, and summer prekindergarten academies.

Needs Assessment

Prior to training, our first step was to examine the needs of those who would experience the training. For example, we thought it was essential to understand the teachers' backgrounds, knowledge, skills, and abilities to respond to children with diverse needs, as well as their abilities to perform assessments and monitor children's ongoing progress. Also, it was important to understand their comfort with literacy and mathematics skills to help determine how training might be differentiated to meet their individualized needs.

Our needs assessment indicated that our original plans had to be adjusted. Teachers needed additional support in language and literacy, technology use, and content knowledge. They also needed practice in presenting to a small group of adults, and these opportunities were incorporated into the revised plans. Had we not completed this step, the project would not have been as successful as it turned out for many participants.

Not surprisingly, the training needs assessment showed that most early childhood educators were females who ranged in age from 21 to 69. Almost half were raised in lower to middle income households, and 49% were ethnic minorities. About one third grew up speaking a language other than English, and about half of the group spoke languages in addition to English—Spanish prevailed, but some conversed in Vietnamese, Mandarin Chinese, Urdu, American Sign Language, and Farsi. Houston's educators, like Houston's children, had diverse backgrounds that we believed could be used to enrich training opportunities and the knowledge base of the field.

Much of the information we gathered in the needs assessment was obtained from the teachers at 2-day retreats. The retreats introduced training through our C^3 model. Rather than beginning with the textbooks, training began with educators and presenters engaging directly in activities that could typically be experienced in the classroom. For example, the retreats included centers, music, art activities, language, and literacy opportunities. The teachers made materials to use in their classrooms, took videos of their actions, and discussed work over lunch. Starting with activities that were familiar to the educators, we worked to show them how it might relate to the classroom, building linkages to state standards and research-based outcomes. For example, when working on mathematics standards related to classification and counting, teachers classified the type of shoes they were wearing, graphed the outcome, and then counted how many people in the room wore that type of shoe. To demonstrate how children can graph, we had each teacher add a sticky note to a column on a poster board above a picture of his or her shoe type. The tallest column represented the most popular type of shoe.

One of the unanticipated outcomes of the retreats was the relationship building that occurred among the teachers *and* the presenters. The retreats were a key component of the success of the project and helped build confidence in the participants for change. The rapport that was built at the retreats and the ease with which research and standards were presented gave educators confidence that they were up to the task. The retreats introduced the concept of collaborative teamwork and provided opportunities for educators with different backgrounds and different roles to work together on the same content and skills.

Model Lesson Design and Delivery

Using what we learned from our needs assessment, we developed a set of model lessons. Specifically, we included definitions of terms, model examples, and brief video clips of best practices to help the teachers implement similar lessons in their classrooms. These lessons were developed from the Texas standards for prekindergarten and the national standards from NAEYC. Faculty members and university coaches who were working on advanced degrees in education initially developed four lessons: prekindergarten standards, the environment, developing language, and mathematics. We obtained video footage and information about the curriculum taught from each classroom and embedded it into the lessons. Model lessons included the following:

- A brief review of the current topic and, if applicable, the previous topic that linked standards and research

- A viewing and discussion of clips from each of the classroom videos that were made the previous week that related to the topic

- A research-focused PowerPoint presentation by the university coach

- Suggestions and discussion of classroom practices to implement based on the research presentation

We followed these activities with collaborative discussions to address the challenges to implementation and options for customization of materials for the unique needs of the children in the various classrooms. Sessions were provided in English and/or Spanish. These materials helped teachers implement their activities in their classrooms and provided models of a variety of research-based interventions.

Summer Prekindergarten Academies

Summer academies were designed to supplement and expand the use of the model lesson sessions. The academies provided more intensive training (i.e., Monday to Thursday) and practice opportunities for literacy, mathematics, and social skills instruction. We also included additional teachers who had not attended our original sessions.

The format of each academy followed a typical early childhood classroom day. This strategy was used to help participants have repeated opportunities to experience the type of classroom organization and scheduling that may best benefit children. Faculty, coaches, and participants developed, documented, and delivered the content. The academies included hands-on activity sessions to provide participants with relevant, rigorous trainings anchored in research-based best practice and related to standards. For example, "What's in a Name?" focused on the importance of personalizing instruction for children by using their names. Participants linked their names to their photographs to help link sounds to items, and they used names to practice the phonological and letter–sound correspondence aspects of words.

Each day built on the content of the previous day in a developmental sequence. This ensured that participants experienced the instructional sequences that could be implemented in their own classrooms. Each session focused on objectives aligned with the state guidelines, appropriate use of the classroom materials, teaching strategies, and expected outcomes for children. The participants received materials for their classroom (all of which were used in the training), lessons, PowerPoint presentations, training videos, and books. Participants interacted with materials and each other in both large and small groups, practicing the responses that *children* in their classrooms might give in a particular situation. This interactive format provided immediate feedback, checks for understanding, and opportunities to revise instruction.

Although the content of the academies was important, the format of delivery was essential to their success. Simulations of an early childhood classroom day, pacing instruction, and linking these components over the 4-day time period provided a set of experiential learning opportunities that the participants found novel, relevant, and oftentimes enlightening. Many learned to manage classrooms, sequence their days throughout the year, and begin to explore how to extend activities for the various children in their care. The group activities gave participants opportunities to learn together, discuss challenges, and feel comfortable asking questions to meet their individual classroom needs.

Together, these activities constituted the C^3 approach. We engaged teachers in cognitive, collegial, and collaborative training over a 2-year period, which helped them recognize that they were members of a diverse, talented, and committed professional community of early childhood educators.

The results of our project illustrated significant improvements in the language and literacy environments in the participants' classrooms. Using the Early Language and Literacy Classroom Observation Tool (ELLCO) Pre-K (Brady, Smith, & Anastasopoulos, 2008), we found that teachers improved dramatically in making changes in their literacy environment. For example, teachers designed writing centers, created cozy corner libraries, and increased the amount of functional print throughout the classrooms. Furthermore, using an information survey of linguistic knowledge, developed by Louisa Moats, teachers' knowledge of syllables, morphemes, and phoneme identification were recorded and further improved over time.

LESSONS LEARNED

Our experiences throughout the project highlight several key lessons that are critical for the implication of effective training programs for early childhood educators.

Understand Teachers' Strengths and Needs

Knowing both the strengths and needs of the teachers and the children that they serve is essential to success. Once these facets are known, training can be customized to match individual needs. Our participants, for example, were eager to learn and willing to implement new strategies. However, our needs assessment clearly indicated that they did not have the knowledge, skills, or strategies to implement quality early language and literacy practices. They needed to learn why the strategies were important as well as how to implement them in the classroom. Teachers wanted to be considered professionals in the field. As a result, they were willing to change their teaching and practice when they understood how the new research and practices related to their children's education. We found that they were able to adhere more closely to the prekindergarten standards when they were offered concrete strategies for applying them in practice.

Individualize Learning

Because early childhood teachers vary in their backgrounds, abilities, and formal education, it is important to be aware of these differences and to adjust training to meet varying needs. In our program, some teachers preferred training in Spanish; others, English. Furthermore, different locations and different contexts may require a different emphasis in training. In our case, we kept the prekindergarten standards as our goal, adjusting training in different sites to meet these goals and child outcomes.

Engage Administrators

Administrators can both support and thwart innovation. Therefore, it is important to involve administrators at the very outset of training. Studies have shown that positive changes result when teachers and administrators work together (Dickinson & Caswell, 2007). Isolation does not promote change—educators need to work together, work with their leadership teams, learn from each other, and learn how to critique the work of their peers. Training must include relationship-building opportunities, including visits to other classrooms, observations, and joint projects, if the field is to be assured that change occurs.

The C^3 Project provided a structure for change and was sufficiently flexible to respond to the diverse needs of its early childhood audience. Training was provided in multiple settings, was content focused, and directly applied to what occurred in classrooms. As a result, participants generated their own evidence of best practice—they saw the changes in their classrooms, and these changes were reflected in better child outcomes. Teachers developed knowledge and skills and had more confidence in their teaching at the end of training. Together, this allowed them to connect with the larger school community in the elementary grades and understand the key role they play in early childhood in the bigger picture of student success.

CONCLUSION

So what about the computer specialist, dental hygienist, social worker, and high school teacher? Additional training did help them to do a better job, and they have each acquired skills that help support the literacy, mathematics, and social skills development of young children. The quality of instruction in their classrooms has changed, and these teachers can demonstrate how their efforts have a very positive impact on the future lives of the children in their care.

REFERENCES

Boudah, D.J., Logan, K.R., & Greenwood, C.R. (2001). The research to practice projects: Lessons learned about changing teacher practice. *Teacher Education and Special Education, 24*(4), 290–303.

Boyle, B., Lamprianou, I., & Boyle, T. (2005). A longitudinal study of teacher change: What makes professional development effective? Report of the second year of the study. *School Effectiveness and School Improvement, 16*(1), 1–27.

Butler, D., Lauscher, H., Jarvis-Selinger, S., & Beckingham, B. (2004). *Collaboration and self-regulation in teachers' professional development.* Vancouver: University of British Columbia, Department of Educational and Counseling Psychology and Special Education.

Dantonio, M. (1995). *Collegial coaching: Inquiry into the teaching self.* Bloomington, IN: Phi Delta Kappa.

Deussen, T., Coskie, T., Robinson, L., & Autio, E. (2007). *"Coach" can mean many things: Five categories of literacy coaches in Reading First* (Issues & Answers Report, REL 2007-No. 005). Washington, DC: U.S. Department of Education, Institute of Education Sciences, National Center for Education Evaluation and Regional Assistance. Retrieved September 20, 2008, from http://ies.ed.gov/ncee/edlabs/regions/northwest/pdf/REL_2007005.pdf

Dickinson, D.K., & Brady, J.P. (2006). Toward effective support for language and literacy through professional development. In M. Zaslow & I. Martinez-Beck (Eds.), *Critical issues in early childhood professional development* (pp. 141–170). Baltimore: Paul H. Brookes Publishing Co.

Dickinson, D., & Caswell, L. (2007). Building support for language and early literacy in preschool classrooms through in-service professional development: Effects of the Literacy Environment Enrichment Program (LEEP). *Early Childhood Research Quarterly, 22*(2), 243–260.

Garet, M., Porter, A., Desimone, L., Birman, B., & Yoon, K. (2001). What makes professional development effective? Results from a national sample of teachers. *American Educational Research Journal, 38*(4), 915–945.

Gersten, R., Morvant, M., & Brengelman, S. (1995). Close to the classroom is close to the bone: Coaching as a means to translate research into classroom practice. *Exceptional Children, 62,* 52–66.

Gutierrez, K., Crosland, K., & Berlin, D. (2001, April). *Reconsidering coaching: Assisting teachers' literacy practices in the zone of proximal development.* Paper presented at the annual meeting of the American Educational Research Association, Seattle, WA.

Joyce, B., & Showers, B. (1996). The evolution of peer coaching. *Educational Leadership, 53*(6), 12–16.

Joyce, B., & Showers, B. (2002). *Student achievement through staff development: Fundamentals of school renewal.* White Plains, NY: Longman.

Landry, S.H., Swank, P.R., Smith, K.E., Assel, M.A., & Gunnewig, S.B. (2006). Enhancing early literacy skills for preschool children: Bringing a professional development model to scale. *Journal of Learning Disabilities, 39*(4), 306–324.

National Center for Research on Teacher Learning. (1991). *Findings from the Teacher Education and Learning to Teach Study: Final report.* East Lansing, MI: Author.

Neuman, S.B., & Roskos, K. (2005). The state of state prekindergarten standards. *Early Childhood Research Quarterly, 20*(2), 125–145.

Reitzug, U.C., & Burrello, L.C. (1995). How principals can build self renewing schools. *Educational Leadership, 52*(7), 48–50.

Smith, M., Brady, J.P., & Anastasopoulas, L. (2008). *Early Language and Literacy Classroom Observation Tool (ELLCO) Pre-K.* Baltimore: Paul H. Brookes Publishing Co.

Thornton, J.S. (2006). *The impact of coaching models within an ongoing prekindergarten professional development program on the classroom literacy environment.* Doctoral dissertation, University of Houston. Retrieved July 10, 2009, from http://wwwlib.umi.com/dissertations/fullcit/3243985

U.S. Department of Health and Human Services. (2006, August). *Good Start, Grow Smart: A guide to Good Start, Grow Smart and other federal early learning initiatives.* Available online at http://www.acf.dhhs.gov/programs/ccb/ta/gsgs/fedpubs/GSGSBooklet.pdf.

Veenman, S., Denessen, E., Gerrits, J., & Kenter, J. (2001). Evaluation of a coaching programme for cooperating teachers. *Educational Studies, 27*(3), 317–340.

Wiley, D., & Yoon, B. (1995). Teacher reports of opportunity to learn: Analyses of the 1993 California learning assessment system. *Educational Evaluation and Policy Analysis, 17*(3), 355–370.

10

Professional Development in Culturally Diverse Settings

Renee Rubin, John A. Sutterby, and James V. Hoffman

Little Soul's Child Care Center is located in a small wood frame house on the corner of 4th and Jefferson Streets in South Texas. It is owned and run by Magdalena Vasquez, who started the center 10 years earlier in the garage of her house. Today, she and two assistants care for 22 children, ages 6 months to 4 years old. Magdalena received a certificate in child development many years ago and would like to go back to the local community college for her degree, but she finds it impossible, given the long hours at the center, the college class schedules, and the difficult daily commute. She hopes to find some alternative ways to further her education in the future.

Magdalena and her assistants are typical of many early childhood educators who are working with the nearly 12 million children cared for outside the home. Magdalena is also typical of the many child care providers who are unable to pursue professional development (Dickinson & Brady, 2006). Although she would like to continue her education, inconvenient scheduling and class locations serve as constraints to further training. In fact, one survey indicated that these issues remain the two top challenges to accessing training for many educators in the field (Gable & Halliburton, 2003).

Yet another challenge for professional development, far less detailed in the research however, has been the challenge of meeting the very diverse needs of the early childhood professional audience. Far from being a monolithic group, early childhood educators' interests and needs in professional development vary dramatically. For example, many early childhood educators come to professional development having already taught for many years. Raikes and her colleagues (2006), for example, estimated that 44% have 5 or more years of teaching experience.

Although more seasoned providers and young providers may share similar levels of education and credentialing, they often do not share similar needs or interests when it comes to professional development. More experienced providers may be interested in specific skills or gaps in their knowledge, whereas younger providers may be just learning their craft. Experienced providers may seem to be more interested in professional development in order to gain additional respect from the community and higher pay. Younger providers may be less concerned about the relationship of professional development to increases in salary (Hodgins & Kelleher, 1998).

Early childhood educators may also differ in their education attainment. Some have only high school diplomas; others, master's degrees. In fact, slightly more than half of the teachers working in centers have higher education degrees, whereas less than one third of educators working in home settings have any college degree (Brandon & Martinez-Beck, 2006). Teachers who have at least a bachelor's degree will likely be accustomed to the academic language and theory often presented in college classes and in-service presentations, whereas others might struggle with their own literacy difficulties and the demands of coursework.

Furthermore, early childhood educators often come from the same neighborhoods and cultural backgrounds as the children in their care (Brandon & Martinez-Beck, 2006; Burton et al., 2002). Their connection to the local culture may allow them to better identify with the families and children, but it also means that early childhood educators come from many different backgrounds, unlike elementary school teachers who are still primarily female and from middle-class, non-minority, backgrounds. Consequently, if we are to be successful in improving the early childhood work force, professional development training must address these factors. When new ideas are compatible with existing sociocultural beliefs and norms, they are more likely to be adopted by educators; when they are not perceived as compatible, they are likely to be rejected (Hall & Hord, 2006).

Early childhood educators also work in a variety of settings, including homes, private centers, faith-based centers, state-funded centers, and Head Start centers. Of the 2.3 million paid individuals caring for children ages 0–5 in 2002, about 24% worked in center-based settings, 28% provided family child care, and approximately 48% were paid relatives or nannies working in the child's home (Burton et al., 2002). The policies and family expectations for services may differ across these different settings (Layzer & Goodson, 2006). Teachers who work in schools or larger centers, for example, may have opportunities to interact with other educators during their regular work week. In smaller centers and homes, however, providers may be with children all day and have limited opportunities to discuss ideas with their peers.

The age of children in their care may also influence early childhood educators' interests and needs in professional development. Approximately 29% of educators in the early child care work force care for infants, 49% for toddlers, and 22% for preschoolers (Burton et al., 2002). Not only do the developmental levels of the children vary, but children may also come from different cultural, ethnic, and language backgrounds.

All of these issues must be taken into account if we are to provide successful professional development training for early childhood educators.

THE SOUTH TEXAS EARLY CHILDHOOD PROFESSIONAL DEVELOPMENT PROGRAM

Funded by the State Department of Education, the South Texas Early Childhood Professional Development program was designed to make high-quality professional development accessible to meet the diverse needs of early childhood educators. Our project was located in a primarily Hispanic, low-income, bilingual area along the Texas–Mexico border. More than 70% of the families using child care received subsidies for low-income families, and more than 80% of the third graders in the local school district were considered limited English proficient. Approximately 150 early childhood educators working with children ages 3–5 participated in our project from 2006 through 2008.

To meet the needs of our educators, we provided training in either Spanish or English. Three quarters of our teachers chose to attend English-speaking sessions; the other quarter, Spanish. Training was intense; early childhood educators received twelve 7-hour sessions over a 10-month period. In addition, we provided mentors to help the providers implement these practices in their individual settings. A minimum of 24 hours of mentoring was provided throughout the year.

Given the diversity among our providers, it was important to provide many opportunities for interaction and activity. Professional development sessions included information, hands-on activities, and opportunities for early childhood educators to share ideas with their peers. Topics included oral language development, early literacy and math development, classroom management, children with special needs, classroom environment, and many other topics related to early childhood development and learning. Early childhood educators were provided with curriculum and books (in Spanish and English), as well as manipulatives appropriate for young children. Mentoring was based on the individual needs of the early childhood educators as self-reported and observed by the mentors.

These practices were in marked contrast to previous professional development in the region. At the time our program was implemented, Texas required early childhood educators to have 15 hours of professional development each year to be able to work with young children. Previously, however, professional development was delivered in brief workshops by different people and with little continuity. These types of fragmented workshops with little follow-up have been shown to have little impact on educators or the achievement of the children in their classes (Dickinson & Brady, 2006; Tate, 2004). Therefore, the goal of our project was to provide professional development that would have a long-term impact on the practices of child care educators and help provide a strong foundation for young children.

Surveys were administered to determine the needs of the educators in the area and how best to provide access to high-quality professional development for them. Based on these surveys, professional development was provided in two different locations so that the educators did not have to travel long distances to receive their training. Some educators received professional development in all-day sessions on Saturdays, whereas others preferred meeting more frequently during the week for shorter sessions in the evening. Providers were asked to stay with a particular group for all sessions to encourage ongoing collaboration and support. When necessary, however, they were able to make up sessions at alternate times or locations. The flexibility of time and location provided greater accessibility to professional development.

Furthermore, prior to the implementation of our program, almost all professional development in the region had been presented in English, despite the fact that many early childhood educators spoke Spanish as their first language. In order for them to be able to comprehend and implement the practices discussed during professional development, sessions needed to be offered in their dominant language. By providing them with sessions in Spanish, they were able to ask questions and share information with other educators who also chose to attend Spanish sessions. They participated enthusiastically and had a low absentee rate.

In contrast to the fragmented and sporadic professional development previously provided, **instructional specialists** in the South Texas project provided professional development over a continuous 10-month period. All instructional specialists attended extensive training in early childhood development, early literacy and numeracy skills, children with special needs, English language learners, classroom environment, adult learning, mentoring, and other relevant topics. As much as possible, educators remained with the same instructional specialist and other early childhood educators throughout the 10-month period. In addition, the instructional specialist also mentored the early childhood educators in their own classrooms, ensuring the continuity between coursework and practice and providing greater intensity of treatment. It also created opportunities for feedback, which has been widely supported in the research literature (Barbour & Lash, 2009).

Evidence from successful training programs suggests that professional development is more effective when accompanied with training in the curriculum that teachers use (Fukkink & Lont, 2007). In our case, we adopted a nationally recognized bilingual early childhood curriculum to serve as the foundation for the program. All preschool providers working with children ages 3–5 were given a copy of the curriculum as well as ancillary materials (e.g., big books, manipulatives). To ensure consistency in the presentation of professional development across sites, instructional specialists were required to attend all-day workshops prior to presenting each module. They viewed and asked questions about prepared presentations and engaged in simulations similar to what they would do in training with providers.

Previous research has also indicated that the support of directors or administrators is critical to the implementation of change (Fleming & Love, 2003). In our project, administrators were encouraged to attend professional development along with the early childhood educators. In addition, mentors met regularly with administrators to discuss the professional development program and made recommendations on a regular basis. For example, mentors encouraged administrators to involve the larger school community in parent involvement activities, not just the classrooms of the participating educators.

Becoming a Community of Learners

The early childhood providers in our project were highly diverse in many ways. They differed in level of education, amount of early childhood experience, the settings in which they worked, the ages of children in their care, and their native language. We believed that we needed to be sensitive to these differences in order to have an impact on their practices and in their work with children.

We worked to make connections with their existing knowledge and experience (Wlodkowski, 2008). It was clear from our work that although they might lack formal academic experiences, they had deep and varied **"funds of knowledge"** from years of experience working with young children and their families (Moll & Greenberg, 1990). We encouraged the providers to share their knowledge with other educators during discussions and brainstorming sessions. For example, a number of providers gave examples of ways to incorporate literacy objects in different play centers. Together, they found that these literacy-related activities supported children's language and engagement, creating a shared culture among them. Educators shared songs from their native countries and adaptations of games such as I Spy. They told stories and folk tales that they remembered from their own childhood. In this way, the professional development sessions were designed to build on educators' existing knowledge, support their own culture, and provide rich opportunities for us to show that their ideas were valued and important.

We made efforts throughout the professional development sessions to provide time for feedback; the providers would try a particular strategy, then describe how it was implemented in their centers or homes. For example, the instructional specialists encouraged the providers to have the young children "write" their way, even if it meant scribbling or drawing. Some providers were initially skeptical, even though they were willing to give it a try. Their initial fears, however, were transformed when they saw what 3- and 4-year-olds could do. One teacher, for example, showed samples from her children's journals and detailed their growth in letter knowledge. Even the most reluctant educators seemed to realize its benefits for children. Another way that the educators helped each other was by providing low-cost methods of making materials that were not available to them due to the low socioeconomic level of the region. Examples of these activities included making musical instruments from simple everyday materials and making creative displays of children's work to decorate the room rather than using store-bought materials.

To make connections to providers and their diverse backgrounds, we needed to be aware of the context and local culture in which they lived and worked. In our program, most of the instructional specialists had grown up in the area, and many had worked in child care facilities in the region themselves. Because they also served as mentors, they had opportunities to go into the centers and homes to observe the realities faced by the early childhood educators on a daily basis. For example, we tried to select books and materials that might reflect the local culture. One example was *Friends from the Other Side: Amigos del Otro Lado* (Anzaldúa & Méndez, 1993), which is the story of a girl from the United States who meets and befriends a boy who has immigrated illegally to the United States. She comes to learn about the risks he and his family have taken in order to live in the United States. Because our project was conducted in a border area, this story was one that clearly resonated with both providers and children and helped to build a strong text-to-life connection.

Instructional specialists also used many hands-on experiences and role playing to meet the needs of the early childhood educators. One example was a roleplaying experience to simulate what it is like for a young English language learner. Educators listened to a recording in Thai in which they were asked to come to the front of the room for an extra stipend, but no one came to the front because they did not understand the message. In another activity, the educators were asked to do something in Korean. They listened to the recording several times because many of the educators thought they would improve young children's comprehension by repeating instructions over and over in a language they did not understand. Finally, the instructional specialist acted out what she wanted the educators to do, and the educators understood the message. Because these lessons were based on real-life experiences, the educators better understood the modifications that they needed to make for English language learners in their classrooms.

Our on-site mentoring efforts were also designed to meet the diverse needs of early childhood educators. Providers were encouraged to schedule a mentor visit at the providers' convenience—not the mentors'. Furthermore, goal setting was collaborative and ongoing. The mentors' role was to help meet the providers' objectives by modeling activities with the children, advising them, gathering materials, answering questions, rearranging the environment, and responding to other requests from the educators. In short, the mentoring sessions were as diverse as the educators themselves. For example, after attending professional development, many educators wanted to rearrange their rooms to include more learning areas and more print at the children's eye levels. Since mentors had extensive training and went to many different early childhood facilities, they had knowledge of how the environment affects young children and how other rooms were arranged. On the other hand, early childhood educators had a deep understanding of the children in their classrooms as well as the materials and furniture that were available. By combining their knowledge and experiences, the educators and mentors were able to create more effective classroom environments.

In these ways, our professional development program attempted to address many of the challenges that have traditionally plagued the early childhood field. We provided an intensive program that was flexible, respectful of the local culture, and attuned to the needs of the providers and the parents and children in the community.

The Effects of the South Texas Program

To examine the effects of our culturally sensitive professional development program, we conducted a 2-year evaluation. Specifically, we were interested in whether our program led to measured changes in teacher knowledge, teacher practice, and child outcomes compared with a control group that received no treatment. In the first year, 129 child care facilities were randomly assigned to either the treatment or control groups. We used two measures of classroom environment to measure overall quality improvements: the Early Childhood Environment Rating Scale–Revised Edition (ECERS-R; Harms, Clifford, & Cryer, 1998) for centers and the Family Day Care Rating Scale (FDCRS; Harms & Clifford, 1989) for homes. The literacy environment, in particular, was assessed using the Early Language and Literacy Classroom Observation Tool (ELLCO) Pre-K (Smith, Brady, & Anastasopoulos, 2008). We also developed our own measure of teacher knowledge, the Early Childhood Educator Test of Knowledge, to examine pre- and posttest changes.

Children were given a range of assessments, both prior to professional development and after the program was completed. We used the Peabody Picture Vocabulary Test–Third Edition (**PPVT-III**; Dunn & Dunn, 1997); the Test de Vocabulario en Imagenes Peabody (TVIP; Dunn, Lugo, Padilla, & Dunn, 1986), the Spanish version of the PPVT; the Phonological Awareness Literacy Scale for Prekindergarten (PALS Pre-K; Invernizzi, Sullivan, & Meier, 2001); the Early Literacy Skills Assessment (**ELSA**; HighScope Educational Research Foundation, 2004); and the Test of Early Mathematics Ability–Third Edition (**TEMA-3**; Ginsburg & Baroody, 2003). All data were analyzed to examine the differences among those who had received professional development compared with those who had not.

We found that the knowledge and effective practices of teachers who received professional development improved significantly compared with the control group. Furthermore, an examination of more than 550 children indicated that the children in classes in which teachers had received professional development significantly outscored their counterparts whose teachers did not receive any treatment. In the second year, the 79 control teachers from the first year were provided with the professional development program. A new control group of 55 teachers from a nearby area was incorporated into the study. We used similar pre–post measures as in our first study. Again, the findings from the first year were replicated: Teachers gained knowledge and improved their instructional practices significantly compared with controls, with subsequent enhanced outcomes for children as a result of professional development.

What We Have Learned

Our success in changing the knowledge and practices of early childhood educators and the improvement in learning outcomes for the children in their care demonstrates that intensive, sustained, culturally relevant professional development can improve children's early literacy and mathematical development. As a result, we believe that there are some key take-away messages that might substantially improve the quality of professional development for this highly diverse early childhood population.

The first is that professional development must be adapted to the local culture of child care providers. We worked to learn more about providers' "funds of knowledge," their interests, strengths, and priorities in their work with children. Professional development wasn't a one-size-fits-all approach; rather, we developed strategies that worked differently across settings. As a result, teachers appeared to use these strategies effectively, making them more successful in their work with children. When children receive the kind of instruction they need, they are more likely to be successful in school.

In addition, we learned that programs need to be flexible and tailored to the needs of the early childhood community. We offered providers choices for when and in what location to attend professional development. Participants also had a choice on the language of instruction. These and other options allowed us to maximize the number of participants.

Our professional development program also used multiple strategies to engage participants. We did a bit of lecture on research-based early literacy strategies, but we also provided many hands-on activities that worked to help providers put theoretical knowledge into practice. Bringing both the theoretical and practical ideas together, we helped participants to understand the rationale and the need for changing practices in the classroom.

Finally, we reinforced our professional development workshops with ongoing mentoring, helping providers put these activities into their own classrooms. Mentoring allowed our instructors to meet the individual needs of each participant. It also helped to build strong relationships and reinforce and sustain the research-based practices in classrooms.

CONCLUSION

Addressing the challenges for effective professional development is not simple, but it is necessary if we are to enhance the quality of early education and improve outcomes for children. Programs that provide intensive professional development, offer flexibility, and meet individual needs will be more successful in making changes in the ways young children are nurtured and educated.

REFERENCES

Anzaldúa, G., & Méndez, C. (1993). *Friends from the other side: Amigos del otro lado.* San Francisco: Children's Book Press.

Barbour, N., & Lash, M. (2009). The professional development of teachers of young children. In S. Feeney, A. Galpar, & C. Seefeldt (Eds.), *Continuing issues in early childhood education* (pp. 158–183). Upper Saddle River, NJ: Pearson.

Brandon, R.N., & Martinez-Beck, I. (2006). Estimating the size and characteristics of the United States early care and education workforce. In M. Zaslow & I. Martinez-Beck (Eds.), *Critical issues in early childhood professional development* (pp. 49–76). Baltimore: Paul H. Brookes Publishing Co.

Burton, A., Whitebook, M., Young, M., Bellm, D., Wayne, C., Brandon, R., et al. (2002). *Estimating the size and components of the U.S. child care work force and caregiving population: Key findings from the child care workforce estimate* (preliminary report). Washington, DC: Center for the Child Care Workforce and Human Services Policy Center.

Dickinson, D.K., & Brady, J.P. (2006). Toward effective support for language and literacy through professional development. In M. Zaslow & I. Martinez-Beck (Eds.), *Critical issues in early childhood professional development* (pp. 141–170). Baltimore: Paul H. Brookes Publishing Co.

Dunn, L.M., & Dunn, L.M. (1997). *The Peabody Picture Vocabulary Test, Third Edition* (PPVT-III). Circle Pines, MN: AGS Publishing.

Dunn, L.M., Lugo, D.E., Padilla, E.R., & Dunn, L.M. (1986). *Test de Vocabulario en Imagenes Peabody* (TVIP). Bloomington, MN: Pearson Assessments.

Fleming, J., & Love, M. (2003). A systemic change model for leadership, inclusion, and mentoring (SLIM). *Early Childhood Education Journal, 31*(1), 53–57.

Fukkink, R.G., & Lont, A. (2007). Does training matter? A meta-analysis and review of caregiver training studies. *Early Childhood Research Quarterly, 22*(3), 294–311.

Gable, S. & Halliburton, A. (2003). Barriers to child care providers' professional development. *Child & Youth Care Forum, 32*(3), 175–193.

Ginsberg, H.P., & Baroody, A.J. (2003). *Test of Early Mathematics Ability—Third Edition* (TEMA-3). Austin, TX: PRO-ED.

Hall, G.E., & Hord, S.M. (2006). *Implementing change: Patterns, principles, and potholes.* Boston: Pearson.

Harms, T., & Clifford, R.M. (1989). *Family Day Care Rating Scale.* New York: Teachers College Press.

Harms, T., Clifford, R.M., & Cryer, D. (1998). *Early Childhood Environment Rating Scale–Revised Edition* (ECERS-R). New York: Teachers College Press.

HighScope Educational Research Foundation. (2004). *Early Literacy Skills Assessment* (ELSA). Ypsilanti, MI: Author.

Hodgins, M., & Kelleher, C. (1998). Education of social care workers: The views of course participants. *Studies in the Education of Adults, 30*(2), 208–221.

Invernizzi, M., Sullivan, A., & Meier, J.D. (2001). Phonological Awareness Literacy Screening: Pre-kindergarten. Charlottesville: University of Virginia.

Layzer, J.I., & Goodson, B.D. (2006). *The national study of child care for low-income families.* Washington, DC: U.S. Department of Health and Human Services, Administration for Children and Families.

Moll, L.C., & Greenberg, J.B. (1990). Creating zones of possibilities: Combining social contexts for instruction. In L.C. Moll (Ed.), *Vygotsky and education* (pp. 319–348). Cambridge, United Kingdom: Cambridge University Press.

Raikes, H.H., Torquati, J.C., Hegland, S., Raikes, H.A., Scott, J., Messner, L., et al. (2006). Studying the culture of quality early education and care: A cumulative approach to measuring characteristics of the workforce and relations to quality in four Midwestern states. In M. Zaslow & I. Martinez-Beck (Eds.), *Critical issues in early childhood professional development* (pp. 111–136). Baltimore: Paul H. Brookes Publishing Co.

Smith, M.W., Brady, J.P., & Anastasopoulos, L. (2008). *The Early Language and Literacy Classroom Observation Tool (ELLCO) Pre-K.* Baltimore: Paul H. Brookes Publishing Co.

Tate, M.L. (2004). *"Sit & get" won't grow dendrites: 20 professional learning strategies that engage the adult brain.* Thousand Oaks, CA: Corwin.

Wlodkowski, R.J. (2008). *Enhancing adult motivation to learn: A comprehensive guide for teaching all adults* (3rd ed.). San Francisco: Jossey-Bass.

IV

When to Do It and
How to Know It's Working

Our final section addresses several critical issues in the field of early childhood professional development. First, there is the issue of dosage and density of training. Traditionally, there has been the view that more professional development is better. In Chapter 11, however, Halle and colleagues provide a much more nuanced picture. They argue on the basis of an emerging body of research that we need to better understand the needs of the participants, their background experiences and knowledge, and the particular goals of professional development. All of these issues influence how much and to what extent training is effective.

The last two chapters then begin to address the key question of whether such training is effective. With appropriate measurement tools, we have the capability of determining at what point we may reach a threshold of quality in classrooms. In Chapter 12, Warren and colleagues present a tool they designed and validated with early childhood educators in the field, which measured quality practices and interactions. In Chapter 13, Wright describes an innovative online coaching log that can provide real-time feedback to examine the "active ingredients" of coaching with educators.

Chapter 14 highlights the enormous gains we have made in our understanding of professional development for early childhood educators. We now have amassed a considerable body of research that should aide policy makers in developing quality training programs for a highly diverse field of educators. It is, therefore, incumbent for researchers, practitioners, and policy makers to build on this strong foundation to enhance the quality of teaching practices in early childhood. Our children deserve no less.

11

Beyond How Much

What We Are Learning
About Structuring Effective Early
Childhood Professional Development

Tamara Halle, Martha Zaslow, Kathryn Tout,
Rebecca Starr, Julia Wessel, and Meagan McSwiggan

A common theme running through the literature on best practices in professional development for educators is that professional development must be "intensive and continuous" (Bowman, Donovan, & Burns, 2001). The section on teacher preparation in the National Research Council report *How People Learn* is also clear on this issue: "Teachers need opportunities to be involved in sustained learning, through teaching that models the methods that they are being urged to adopt....[T]ime must be scheduled for teachers to engage in ongoing opportunities to learn" (Donovan, Bransford, & Pellegrino, 1999, p. 27).

This chapter addresses issues of dosage of professional development delivery for the early childhood work force. Because definitions of dosage are not easy to find in the literature of professional development, this chapter begins by providing definitions for important terminology relevant to a discussion of dosage of professional development in order to establish a common language for our approach in this chapter, and perhaps for the field as a whole. The chapter then summarizes key principles of effective professional development delivery related to dosage that are supported by studies in the field.

IMPORTANT TERMINOLOGY

Dosage is a term familiar to us from the field of medicine. Dosage refers to the quantity of an active agent (substance or radiation) taken in or absorbed at any one time, and the term *dose* is the total amount of a toxicant, drug, or other chemical that is administered to, or taken by, an organism (National Institutes of

Health, n.d.). Applying these definitions to the provision of professional development for early childhood educators, we can think of dosage as the amount of professional development (i.e., the intervention that aims to achieve change in the educator's knowledge and/or skill) that is delivered to the recipient. But, the concept of dosage goes beyond answering the question "How much professional development is delivered?" It also involves *timing* (i.e., when the professional development is initiated and also the sequencing of activities within a given program), *duration* (i.e., how long the professional development intervention lasts), *frequency* (i.e., how often the professional development is delivered within the overall time frame), and *intensity* (e.g., how sustained a single instance of the professional development intervention is and how soon the next installation follows, as opposed to the overall length of the intervention).

As an illustration of how these various aspects of dosage may vary in the case of professional development of early childhood educators, we offer the following example: Two professional development programs each deliver 40 hours of professional development to participants, but one program offers its professional development in 1-week long session lasting 8 hours each day, whereas the other provides its professional development program for 4 hours every week for 10 weeks. The overall dose of professional development may be the same, but the duration, frequency, and intensity of the two programs differ.

Two other important concepts, again from the medical field, are *compliance* and *persistence* with the therapeutic regimen (Cramer, Rosenheck, Kirk, Krol, & Krystal, 2003). Medication compliance refers to the degree or extent of an individual's adherence to the recommendations made by a medical provider regarding the timing, dosage, and frequency of a medical treatment. Medication persistence refers to an individual continuing the treatment for the prescribed duration. Both of these concepts are important to take into account when trying to determine the effect of an intervention, be it a medical intervention or an educational intervention such as professional development (Cramer et al., 2003). Regardless of how much medicine an individual is prescribed, the individual may or may not take the medication in the amount and way it was intended (i.e., compliance), or for the full amount of time (i.e., persistence). With regard to professional development programs for early childhood educators, these concepts of compliance and persistence would refer to an early childhood educator not fully participating in all aspects of the professional development offered within a program, or not participating for the intended amount of time. For example, an educator may drop out of a class before completing it, continue in classes or workshops but just not attend them fully (e.g., arriving late, being absent), or intermittently cancel on-site meetings with consultants/mentors. An individual's level of participation in professional development programs is thus relevant to the discussion of dosage, but individual participation also is related to a separate concept of program delivery called *fidelity of implementation*. We will discuss fidelity of implementation in further detail later in the chapter.

Finally, some researchers of early childhood professional development also include in the discussion of dosage the concept of *depth* of intervention (S. Neuman, personal communication, October 2008). Depth can be thought of as the degree to which the content is covered. For instance, does the professional development focus on one concept or multiple concepts? Does the professional development delve deep into a topic or provide a more simplified overview for the beginning practitioner? As we shall see, this concept of depth of content is indeed related to dosage but may not be an aspect of dosage per se. It may, instead, be associated with the level of dosage of professional development necessary to achieve changes in educators' knowledge and/or skill, or changes in the early childhood environment or child outcomes.

INTENSITY AND DURATION OF PROFESSIONAL DEVELOPMENT

Professional development interventions that are delivered in more intensive and extensive ways are associated with better outcomes for educators and children (Zaslow, Tout, Halle, Vick, & Lavelle, 2009). For example, many professional development programs targeting language and literacy development in early childhood settings start off with intensive workshops or kick-off sessions, which tend to last for several full days or weeks. This is followed by shorter follow-up sessions and/or classroom observations at regular intervals over the course of several weeks or months (e.g., Adger, Hoyle, & Dickinson, 2004; Justice, Pence, & Wiggins, 2008; Landry, 2002; Landry, Assel, Gunnewig, & Swank, 2008; McCutchen et al., 2002; McGill-Franzen, Allington, Yokoi, & Brooks, 1999; O'Connor, Fulmer, Harty, & Bell, 2005; Podhajski & Nathan, 2005). Professional development programs targeting children's social skills also show greater positive effects for educators and/or children when they are longer and more intensive (Domitrovich, Cortes, & Greenberg, 2007; Rhodes & Hennessy, 2000). Furthermore, the literature suggests that to change and sustain the quality of environments, on-site consultation may not be effective at low levels of intensity, even when combined with training (Campbell & Milbourne, 2005; Fiene, 2002) but may be more successful at higher levels of intensity (longer and more frequent on-site visits over a longer period of time; Palsha & Wesley, 1998).

Even though much research indicates that longer, more intense periods of professional development lead to positive outcomes, shorter, less intense programs are also found to be effective in certain circumstances. Even brief doses of professional development (e.g., 10 hours in one case, 30 minutes in another) are associated with positive child outcomes (Neuman, 1999; Whitehurst et al., 1999). Examples include professional development interventions targeting language and literacy, mathematics, and social-emotional domains (Zaslow et al., 2009).

With regard to professional development targeting language and literacy in the early childhood setting, a series of studies by Whitehurst and colleagues involved a one-time, 30-minute training in dialogic reading, a specific interactive book reading technique, which resulted in mostly favorable child outcomes among preschoolers at posttest, although there were some mixed results, and effects did not last through first and second grade (Whitehurst, Arnold, et al., 1994; Whitehurst, Epstein, et al., 1994; Whitehurst et al., 1999). Similarly, Wasik and Bond (2001) employed a 4-week professional development training (not necessarily implemented in consecutive weeks) on interactive book reading. The training resulted in significant effects on both educator practice, such as using relevant vocabulary words during book reading, and children's vocabulary and expressive language development.

Similar findings are seen for professional development programs targeting the teaching of early mathematics. One study reported effects of professional development on teacher knowledge and attitudes regarding mathematics (Arnold, Fisher, Doctoroff, & Dobbs, 2002). This successful professional development intervention was of very brief duration: a 2-hour workshop with brief weekly follow-up visits. Teachers in the intervention group reported significant increases in their positive attitudes towards and sense of competence in the teaching of mathematics from pre- to posttest, and teachers in the intervention group had higher scores on these attitudinal measures at posttest than teachers in the nonintervention group.

There are also examples of successful professional development interventions of minimal dosage targeted at supporting social-emotional development. For example, a single workshop on child temperament resulted in change in provider knowledge but not in provider attitudes of acceptance of the range of child behaviors (Franyo & Hyson, 1999). In fact, Franyo and Hyson found sustained changes in knowledge about child temperament 4 weeks after the workshop providing training on this topic. In addition, the experimental evaluation of the *Ready to Learn* curriculum (Brigman, Lane, Switzer, Lane, & Lawrence, 1999), for which training involved two full-day workshops with three half-day follow-up workshops, resulted in better scores on observed attending behavior and teacher report of child social behavior.

Taken together, all of these studies' findings suggest that intensive and extensive administration of professional development tends to be associated with positive outcomes for both educators and children. However, even small dosages of professional development can be associated with positive outcomes for educators and children.

How can these seemingly contradictory findings be reconciled? We think that one explanation hinges on keeping the goals and scope of the intervention in mind. Professional development targeted on a *discrete set* of skills (e.g., dialogic reading) may only require short-term and brief professional development activities. But professional development that has a *broad focus* (e.g., programs that aim to affect change across a wide range of language and literacy skills, from phonological awareness to letter recognition to emergent writing) may require more extensive professional development activities, perhaps spread over time. In particular, it has been noted that time constraints limit the number and depth of discussions on discrete topics that can be covered within professional development sessions (Dickinson & Brady, 2006).

Professional development that aims to teach early childhood educators *new* skills may require models that are more intensive and/or longer in duration. However, it is also possible that even a small dose of professional development focused on a new skill will be beneficial compared with no exposure at all. For example, in a study regarding early mathematics, Arnold and colleagues (2002) found that meaningful input in teacher practices, even in a low dose, resulted in a marked improvement to prior educator knowledge. This may be particularly true if educators have very limited background or do not feel a great sense of competence in mathematics. These conclusions are very much in keeping with the perspective presented by Joyce and Showers (2002) based on their work in providing training and structuring peer coaching for teachers of K–12 classrooms. They conclude that trainers need to be able to gauge both the complexity of what teachers are being instructed to implement and the newness of the content in terms of previous knowledge and practice of the teachers. "Trainers need to be able to gauge the difficulty level to help plan the intensity and duration of training and select the components they will use accordingly" (Joyce & Showers, 2002, p. 2).

An intriguing question is whether keeping the goals and scope of professional development the same but varying the frequency of the professional development will help isolate the importance of dosage for achieving outcomes. A rigorously evaluated professional development program for low-income communities aimed to examine just this question (Tout, Halle, Zaslow, & Starr, 2009). An evaluation of a program focused on multiple content areas in early childhood education, including language and literacy, social and emotional development, and the use of early childhood assessment, systematically varied receiving weekly visits from a mentor lasting up to 3 hours for 28 weeks (i.e., 84 hours of on-site work) with monthly visits of up to 3 hours for 7 months (i.e., 21 hours of on-site work) and monthly telephone calls for 7 months (the duration of the telephone calls was not clearly stated). The evaluation of this program found that participants receiving monthly on-site sessions had more favorable outcomes in terms of educator knowledge/skill and child outcomes compared with participants who received either weekly visits or monthly phone calls. We can conclude from these findings that more is not necessarily always better in terms of provision of on-site early childhood professional development. It is possible that monthly visits allow the early childhood educator to consolidate better what he or she has learned in the professional development sessions; this is an empirical question worth further exploration.

Nevertheless, there are still major questions in terms of isolating the elements of dosage that really matter. Specifically, this study that compared different dosages, although well-designed, still introduced confounds between *frequency* and *overall dosage* of professional development. The early childhood educators who received weekly visits from on-site mentors/coaches received not only more total hours of professional development (i.e., a higher overall dosage) but also more frequent installments (i.e., a higher frequency of professional development) than those who received monthly on-site visits. In addition, the comparison of monthly on-site visits with monthly phone calls does not permit us to conclude that on-site professional development is superior to more remote contact via the telephone because this study did not fully contrast *duration* and *mode* of professional development delivery. That is, we do not know that the duration of the monthly telephone calls matched the duration of the monthly on-site visits. A more systematic examination of the mode of professional development delivery (i.e., face-to-face versus over the telephone or Internet) contrasted with duration and frequency is needed.

In addition to the usual dosage questions of duration and frequency, it is important to ask whether there is an *optimal amount* of professional development that is needed in order to observe changes in educator practice and/or child outcomes, or whether providing professional development above this "watershed" amount provides substantially more change in outcomes. A further possibility is that one needs to have a minimum level of existing classroom quality in place in order for professional development to be effective (Burchinal, Kainz, & Cai, in press; Burchinal, Vandergrift, Pianta, & Mashburn, 2008). Not a lot is known yet about thresholds, but this may become an important issue, especially when scaling up professional development efforts and considering cost–benefit analyses of such efforts.

TIMING OF PROFESSIONAL DEVELOPMENT DELIVERY

Professional development is more effective when it is ongoing or renewed periodically (Burchinal, Cryer, Clifford, & Howes, 2002; Norris, 2001). Ongoing participation in professional development throughout an educator's career has been linked to positive interactions between the educator and children (Norris, 2001). In addition, Raikes and colleagues (2006) found that *more intensive training*, involving sequenced rather than stand-alone workshops, may be more closely linked with observed quality.

There is also a component of timing that has to do with the pacing of professional development within the time frame provided to deliver it. For example, when someone is on site to provide coaching or mentoring to an early childhood educator, how much of his or her on-site time should be spent on observing, on modeling, or on reflecting? This is still an open, empirical question worth further exploration.

Yet another factor of timing of professional development is the sequencing of professional development strategies within a single program. Two strategies are typically used in early childhood professional development: 1) coursework or training sessions that tend to address the knowledge-focused components of the program that are typically delivered in group settings and 2) activities to address the practice-focused components that are typically delivered on an individual basis, often on site. The sequencing or timing of knowledge-focused and practice-focused components should be taken into consideration when structuring a professional development program. For example, what is the timing of a training session in relation to on-site coaching? Do these two strategies occur during the same time frame, or do they follow one another temporally within a professional development program? Is the coaching interspersed with the training during a single time frame? During the on-site work, which activity should be initiated first: observing, modeling, or discussion/reflection? These are all questions related to the timing and sequencing of the professional development that are important to consider when determining what makes an effective program for early childhood educators.

Although in many instances the training or coursework precedes the on-site practice-based component of professional development, in some instances these are interspersed. In a review of 18 professional development interventions, a great deal of consistency was found in the total amount of classroom instruction offered across programs, even though there was still variability in duration and frequency of professional development delivered across the programs (Tout et al., 2009). Case in point: Two different programs offered a total of 45 hours of coursework worth three credits, but in one program the class met twice a week for 3 hours per class for 7.5 weeks, and in the other program the class met once a week for 3 hours for 15 weeks.

In contrast, the dosage for training sessions varied more widely across eight selected programs. (These eight programs were selected for in-depth study based on rigor of evaluation design and evidence of effects on educator and/or child outcomes associated with the intervention.) For example, one program that addressed language and literacy as well as mathematics and socialization provided several full-day training sessions (either as single days, 2-day trainings, or 4-day trainings), as well as two 90-minute sessions per month for a semester. Another language and literacy professional development program offered twelve 7-hour sessions over 10 months for a total of 84 hours of training. Yet another program offered 3 hours of training per month over an 18-month period for a total of 54 hours of training. Another program that provided professional development for implementing a commercially available, comprehensive early childhood curriculum offered fourteen 2-hour training sessions once a week for a total of 28 hours of training.

Many of the programs combined coursework or training sessions with on-site professional development support (with some incorporating the knowledge-based component into their on-site work). The dosage of the on-site work varied considerably within and across programs. Specifically, the *periodicity* of the visits varied across programs; some on-site staff visited participants at their sites once a month, some twice a month, some once a week, some for 5 days straight. In addition, *the amount of time of any given on-site session* varied; most programs were designed to provide visits of 1–2 hours in duration, although some programs had on-site staff work with participants for 1 half day or 1 full day at a time. In practice, however, on-site staff often provided more or less on-site work based on their judgment of the need of individual participants within the program (Tout et al., 2009).

Individualized professional development delivery often means that individual participants receive different content and/or different overall amounts of professional development than other participants in the same program. It also makes it difficult to determine the optimal dosage of professional development needed to affect change in educator knowledge/practice and child outcomes. It is important to examine the dosage of each mode of professional development, as well as the overall dosage when offered in combination, in order to understand the associations with outcomes of such approaches.

COMPLIANCE, PERSISTENCE, AND ENGAGEMENT IN PROFESSIONAL DEVELOPMENT

In addition to frequency, duration, intensity, and timing, the concepts of educator compliance and persistence in professional development initiatives are important to consider. It is not guaranteed that any given participant in a program will receive the full dosage due to absence and/or noncompliance. Therefore, programs should take compliance and persistence into account when planning dosage of the professional development. Two early childhood professional development programs have reported monitoring participant attendance/absence from the training/coursework by use of an attendance log and/or a sign-in sheet (Tout et al., 2009). Another program required participants to take 11 of the 12 training sessions (77 out of 84 total hours). Yet another program incentivized attendance by offering a certificate to those participants who did not miss more than two sessions per 9-month block of time over an 18-month intervention. This certificate awarded clock hours that could count toward a higher degree in child development. Programs should be encouraged to report on such efforts to address compliance and persistence in professional development interventions in order to more fully understand the effectiveness and the actual dosage that individual participants receive in their programs.

Compliance and persistence can lead to positive outcomes in educator knowledge and practice. For example, Norris (2001) found that educators who attended child care–related training sessions and workshops throughout their careers were consistently rated higher on measures of quality than intermittent attendees or nonparticipants.

Despite what the program is designed to deliver, individual participants may receive varying amounts of professional development, based on how faithfully they attend classes or training sessions (discussed in terms of compliance and persistence), or whether on-site professional development is delivered in the frequency and amount it was intended. This latter concept is called *fidelity of implementation*. Fidelity of implementation relates to the degree to which the intervention was carried out as planned, and also whether the early childhood professionals who receive the intervention then implement the new practices as intended. Fidelity may be related to dosage in that further professional development may be needed if it is determined that an approach is not being implemented with fidelity; less or no follow-up may be needed if a practice has been quickly and fully adopted.

Pence and colleagues (2008) tracked fidelity of preschool teachers' adherence to a language-focused curriculum over time, and reported that treatment teachers' fidelity to the intervention transitioned from high scores in the fall to low scores in the winter and then to a rebound in high scores in the spring (matching those in the fall). These findings suggest that it may be important to assess treatment fidelity at multiple time points in order to get a complete understanding of teachers' adherence to an intervention. These findings also suggest that "booster" dosages of professional development may be needed if fidelity is waning.

CONSIDERING MODERATORS

Clearly, there are many different aspects of dosage to consider in an early childhood professional development program. However, the same dosage may affect individual early childhood settings differently because of preexisting factors for the educators and/or the setting. These factors are called *moderators* because they can moderate the strength of a professional development program's effect on outcomes.

One moderator is the educator's willingness or readiness to change. When an educator does not approach a professional development experience with the willingness to change attitudes or practices based on what they will learn, the likelihood of positive effects of the intervention on attitudes or practices diminishes (Fixsen, Naoom, Blase, Friedman, & Wallace, 2005). The key for sustaining educator practice outcomes appears to be engaging educators in the intervention process and encouraging them to "own" the changes they are making. Some professional development programs are beginning to measure readiness to change as a baseline indicator for success for their initiative; they are also using stage-of-change measures to monitor change in attitudes throughout a professional development initiative, in addition to measuring change in educator knowledge and skills (Children's Institute, 2008).

Another moderator to dosage is the match between the characteristics and personality of the person delivering the professional development and the educator receiving the professional development. These characteristics include having a positive attitude, being able to relate to individuals from diverse backgrounds, and having good oral and written communication skills. In addition, a sense of trust and mutual respect is crucial for a positive relationship between the professional development provider and the educator (Tout et al., 2009). Downer and colleagues (2009) examined the characteristics of teachers that were associated with responsiveness to an online professional development program for early childhood educators and found that the effectiveness of individual coaches varied but that research has not identified the characteristics that underlie the variations in effectiveness of different professional development.

There is evidence that coaches vary in their effectiveness, at least when providing online professional development (Downer et al., 2009). However, we have little evidence of the characteristics that are important for this variation in effectiveness. Tout and colleagues (2009) interviewed directors of 18 professional development programs and identified the following attributes as possible bases for variation in effectiveness of professional development staff:

- A college degree in early childhood education or development

- Experience working with young children and adult learners

- Expertise in the target area of the professional development program

A final potential moderator to dosage of professional development is the environment of the educator. Evidence has shown that there are benefits to engaging the environment as a whole in the professional development, including a group or cohort of teachers in the program, as well as getting the support or involvement of the director or principal in the education setting (Dickinson & Brady, 2006). This can create a learning community for those involved in the program in which educators can share resources and practices and also has the potential to create more sustainable changes in the setting. A lack of support from the director, principal, or administration in an early childhood education setting has been shown to lead to decreased interest in the professional development by the educators. This can lead to rejection of the new practices being learned or difficulty in implementing new practices amongst the existing practices in the education setting (Ginsburg et al., 2006). Thus, involving the administration of the early childhood setting where the professional development program will take place can be beneficial when planning a professional development program.

SUMMARY OF EMERGING PRINCIPLES OF EFFECTIVE PROFESSIONAL DEVELOPMENT DELIVERY

This chapter has discussed many important aspects of dosage of professional development. When making decisions about a professional development program, it is important to consider all of these aspects and how they work together. Some emerging principles of effective professional development delivery include the following:

- Professional development interventions that are delivered in more intensive and extensive ways are associated with better outcomes for educators and children; however, success can be found in shorter, less intense programs as well.

- The appropriateness of the intensity/duration of the professional development intervention depends on the goals of the professional development.

- Professional development targeted on a discrete set of skills may only require short-term and brief professional development activities.

- Professional development that has a broad focus or that covers more complex content may require the provision of more background on children's development and, therefore, more extensive professional development activities, perhaps spread out over time.

- Professional development that is geared toward teaching early childhood educators new skills may require professional development models of more intensity and/or longer duration.

- Sustainability of practices acquired through professional development may require periodic infusions of additional professional development opportunities and on-site support.

- Characteristics of the educators receiving the professional development (including the educators' readiness to change attitudes or practices), as well as the characteristics and previous training of those delivering the professional development, and the potential match between the two, need to be taken into account in order to determine the appropriate delivery of professional development.

- A supportive educational environment is beneficial for the educators involved in a professional development program. Support from other educators, directors, and principals can lead to better outcomes in the classroom.

CONCLUSION

Dosage is an integral part of any early childhood professional development initiative. Aspects mentioned in this chapter, such as intensity, duration, timing, compliance, and persistence, should be considered when planning a program. In addition, educators' readiness to change, the match between the on-site professional development staff and the early childhood educator, and the amount of support from others in the early childhood setting can influence the level of effectiveness of a professional development program, no matter what the dosage. Considering dosage is important not only for improvements in educator knowledge and practice but also for ensuring sustained levels of quality of the early childhood setting and subsequent child outcomes.

REFERENCES

Adger, C.T., Hoyle, S.M., & Dickinson, D.K. (2004). Locating learning in in-service education for preschool teachers. *American Educational Research Journal, 41*(4), 867–900.

Arnold, D.H., Fisher, P.H., Doctoroff, G.L., & Dobbs, J. (2002). Accelerating math development in Head Start classrooms. *Journal of Educational Psychology, 94,* 762–770.

Bowman, B.T., Donovan, M.S., & Burns, M.S. (Eds.). (2001) *Eager to learn: Educating our preschoolers.* Washington DC: National Academies Press, National Research Council, Committee on Behavioral and Social Sciences and Education, Committee on Early Childhood Pedagogy.

Brigman, G., Lane, D., Switzer, D., Lane, D., & Lawrence, R. (1999). Teaching children school success skills. *Journal of Educational Research, 92*(6), 323–330.

Burchinal, M., Cryer, D., Clifford, R.M., & Howes, C. (2002). Caregiver training and classroom quality in child care centers. *Applied Developmental Science, 6*(1), 2–11.

Burchinal, M., Kainz, K., & Cai, Y. (in press). How well are our measures of quality predicting to child outcomes: A meta-analysis and coordinated analyses of data from large scale studies of early childhood settings. In M. Zaslow, I. Martinez-Beck, K. Tout, & T. Halle (Eds.), *Measuring quality in early childhood settings.* Baltimore: Paul H. Brookes Publishing Co.

Burchinal, M., Vandergrift, N., Pianta, R., & Mashburn, A. (2008). *Threshold analysis of association between child care quality and child outcomes for low-income children in prekindergarten programs.* Paper presented at the annual meeting of the National Association for the Education of Young Children, Dallas, TX.

Campbell, P.H., & Milbourne, S.A. (2005). Improving the quality of infant-toddler care through professional development. *Topics in Early Childhood Special Education, 25*(1), 3–14.

Children's Institute. (2008). *Educator survey: State of Change Scale.* New York: Author.

Cramer, J., Rosenheck, R., Kirk, G., Krol, W., & Krystal, J., for the VA Naltrexone Study Group 425 (2003). Medication compliance feedback and monitoring in a clinical trial: Predictors and outcomes. *Value Health, 6,* 566–573.

Dickinson, D.K., & Brady, J.P. (2006). Toward effective support for language and literacy through professional development. In M. Zaslow & I. Martinez-Beck (Eds.), *Critical issues in early childhood professional development* (pp. 141–170). Baltimore: Paul H. Brookes Publishing Co.

Domitrovich, C.E., Cortes, R.C., & Greenberg, M.T. (2007). Improving young children's social and emotional competence: A randomized trial of the preschool "PATHS" curriculum. *Journal of Primary Prevention, 28,* 67–91.

Donovan, M.D., Bransford, J.D., & Pellegrino, J.W. (Eds.). (1999). *How people learn: Bridging research and practice.* Washington, DC: National Academies Press.

Downer, J.T., Locasale-Crouch, J., Hamre, B., & Pianta, R. (2009). Teacher characteristics associated with responsiveness and exposure to consultation and online professional development resources. *Early Education and Development, 20*(3), 431–455.

Fiene, R. (2002). Improving child care quality through an infant caregiver mentoring project. *Child & Youth Care Forum, 31*(2), 79–87.

Fixsen, D.L., Naoom, S.F., Blase, K.A., Friedman, R.M., & Wallace, F. (2005). *Implementation research: A synthesis of the literature.* Tampa: University of South Florida, Louis de la Parte Florida Mental Health Institute, The National Implementation Research Network.

Franyo, G.A., & Hyson, M.C. (1999). Temperament training for early childhood caregivers: A study of the effectiveness of training. *Child & Youth Care Forum, 28*(5), 329–349.

Ginsburg, H.P., Kaplan, R.G., Cannon, J., Cordero, M.I., Eisenband, J.G., Galanter, M., et al. (2006). Helping early childhood educators to teach mathematics. In M. Zaslow &

I. Martinez-Beck (Eds.), *Critical issues in early childhood professional development* (pp. 171–202). Baltimore: Paul H. Brookes Publishing Co.

Joyce, B., & Showers, B. (2002). *Student achievement through staff development* (3rd ed.). Alexandria, VA: Association for Supervision and Curriculum Development.

Justice, L., Pence, K., & Wiggins, A. (2008). Language-Focused Curriculum: University of Virginia (Virginia site). In Preschool Curriculum Evaluation Research Consortium, *Effects of preschool curriculum programs on school readiness: Report from the Preschool Curriculum Evaluation Research Initiative* (pp. 109–115). Washington, DC: U.S. Department of Education, National Center for Research on Education, Institute for Education Sciences.

Landry, S.H. (2002). *Supporting cognitive development in early childhood.* Paper presented at A Summit on Early Childhood Cognitive Development: Ready to Read, Ready to Learn, Little Rock, AR.

Landry, S., Assel, M., Gunnewig, S., & Swank, P. (2008). Doors to Discovery and Let's Begin with the Letter People: University of Texas Health Science Center at Houston (Texas site). In Preschool Curriculum Evaluation Research Consortium, *Effects of preschool curriculum programs on school readiness: Report from the Preschool Curriculum Evaluation Research Initiative* (pp. 86–98). Washington, DC: U.S. Department of Education.

McCutchen, D., Abbott, R.D., Green, L.B., Beretvas, S.N., Cox, S., Potter, N.S., et al. (2002). Beginning literacy: Links among teacher knowledge, practice, and student learning. *Journal of Learning Disabilities, 35*(1), 69–86.

McGill-Franzen, A., Allington, R.L., Yokoi, L., & Brooks, G. (1999). Putting books in the classroom seems necessary but not sufficient. *Journal of Educational Research, 93*(2), 67–75.

National Institutes of Health, National Institute of Environmental Health Sciences. (n.d.). *Glossary.* Retrieved July 21, 2009, from http://science.education.nih.gov/supplements/nih2/chemicals/other/glossary/glossary1.htm

Neuman, S. (1999). Books make a difference: A study of access to literacy. *Reading Research Quarterly, 34*(3), 286–310.

Norris, D.J. (2001). Quality of care offered by providers with differential patterns of workshop participation. *Child & Youth Care Forum, 30*(2), 111–121.

O'Connor, R.E., Fulmer, D., Harty, K.R., & Bell, K.M. (2005). Layers of reading intervention in kindergarten through third grade: Changes in teaching and student outcomes. *Journal of Learning Disabilities, 38*(5), 440–455.

Palsha, S.A., & Wesley, P.W. (1998). Improving quality in early childhood environments through on-site consultation. *Topics in Early Childhood Special Education, 18*(4), 243–253.

Pence, K.L., Justice, L.M., & Wiggins, A.K. (2008). Preschool teachers' fidelity in implementing a comprehensive language-rich curriculum. *Language, Speech, & Hearing Services in Schools, 39,* 329–341.

Podhajski, B., & Nathan, J. (2005). Promoting early literacy through professional development for childcare providers. *Early Education and Development, 16*(1), 23–41.

Raikes, H.H., Torquati, J.C., Hegland, S., Raikes, H.A., Scott, J., Messner, L., et al. (2006). Studying the culture of quality early education and care: A cumulative approach to measuring characteristics of the workforce and relations to quality in four Midwestern states. In M. Zaslow & I. Martinez-Beck (Eds.), *Critical issues in early childhood professional development* (pp. 111–136). Baltimore: Paul H. Brookes Publishing Co.

Rhodes, S., & Hennessy, E. (2000). The effects of specialized training on caregivers and children in early-years settings: An evaluation of the foundation course in playgroup practice. *Early Childhood Research Quarterly, 15*(4), 559–576.

Tout, K., Halle, T., Zaslow, M., & Starr, R. (2009). *Evaluation of the Early Childhood Educator Professional Development Program: Final report.* Washington, DC: Unpublished report submitted to the U.S. Department of Education.

Wasik, B.A., & Bond, M.A. (2001). Beyond the pages of a book: Interactive book reading and language development in preschool classrooms. *Journal of Educational Psychology, 93*(2), 243–250.

Whitehurst, G.J., Arnold, D.S., Epstein, J.N., Angell, A.L., Smith, M., & Fischel, J.E. (1994). A picture book reading intervention in day care and home for children from low-income families. *Developmental Psychology, 30,* 679–689

Whitehurst, G.J., Epstein, J.N., Angell, A.L., Payne, A.C., Crone, D.A., & Fischel, J.E. (1994). Outcomes of an emergent literacy intervention in Head Start. *Journal of Educational Psychology, 86,* 542–555.

Whitehurst, G.J., Zevenberegen, A.A., Crone, D.A., Shultz, M.D., Velting, O.N., & Fischel, J.E. (1999). Outcomes of an emergent literacy intervention from Head Start through second grade. *Journal of Educational Psychology, 91*(2), 261–272.

Zaslow, M., Tout, K., Halle, T., Vick, J., & Lavelle, B. (2009). *Towards the identification of features of effective professional development for early childhood educators: A review of the literature.* Washington, DC: Unpublished report submitted to the U.S. Department of Education.

12

Measuring Early Childhood Educators' Instructional Practices and Interactions

Amye R. Warren, Jenny M. Holcombe,
Sarah Jo Sandefur, Anne B. Gamble, and Heather K. Hicks

One of the most difficult challenges faced by those implementing Early Childhood Educator Professional Development (ECEPD) programs concerns how best to measure the program's effectiveness. Clearly, the ultimate goal of any ECEPD program is better outcomes for young children. But measuring children's outcomes will only take us so far. If children do not make substantial progress, we need to know how and why professional development failed. If children's outcomes *are* improved, what made the professional development successful? It is critically important to examine each step in the professional development process, including teachers' knowledge, practice, and classroom environments and how these factors contribute to children's outcomes (e.g., Guskey, 2000).

Many professional development evaluations have been limited to documenting early childhood educators' satisfaction with the training they have received. Other evaluations have taken the next step, reporting changes in relevant content knowledge. But improvements in content knowledge are insufficient for predicting whether teachers will apply their knowledge in practice (e.g., Davidson & Moore, 2007; Ramey & Ramey, 2006). For example, Neuman and Cunningham (2009) found that completing a college course on early literacy enhanced teachers' knowledge but did not improve their practices. In their meta-analysis, Fukkink and Lont (2007) concluded that training had substantially larger effects on early childhood educators' attitudes and knowledge than on their skills.

Other evaluations of professional development have therefore begun to focus greater attention to actual teacher practices, but most have used fairly global measures of classroom quality and teacher interactions rather than examining specific teacher practices. By global measures, we refer to broad areas of teacher interactions, such as a single item rating the richness of the language environment or the extent to which the teacher encourages children to talk to teachers and to one another. A measure of specific instructional practices, however, might include separate items regarding the use of open-ended questions, the use of recasts, and whether appropriate wait time is provided for responses.

Such fine-grained analyses of practices are necessary for the development of effective early childhood professional development approaches. Detailed analyses can allow us to determine the practices that teachers are effectively implementing even before training so that additional training can be "tailored to fill in the gaps and to increase skills in needed areas" (Ramey & Ramey, 2006, p. 364). Detailed analyses can also distinguish the practices more effectively implemented after training from those that proved more resistant to improvement. Moreover, there may be different patterns of implementation across subgroups of early childhood educators, such as prior formal education levels, settings, or beliefs. If so, we may find that different types of educators require different amounts or forms of professional development to implement different types of practices (Ramey & Ramey, 2008).

Two studies illustrate the value of such detailed analyses of instructional practices. First, Landry and colleagues (2006) reported that teachers showed comparatively less growth in the area of phonological awareness during the first year of their professional development project and benefited from an additional year of professional development in the areas of phonological awareness and vocabulary. In addition, children showed significant growth in phonological awareness, but they made greater gains when their teachers had more prior formal education.

Second, in an earlier ECEPD project, Schwanenflugel and colleagues (2005) provided professional development to 37 public school pre-K classrooms in Georgia. Some of the teachers received training in supporting phonological awareness, others were trained in vocabulary enhancement strategies, still others received both types of training, and the remainder received no training. Vocabulary enhancement training included both implicit and explicit practices—meaning that some practices were more indirect (e.g., talking more with children and reading books interactively), whereas others directly focused on introducing new vocabulary words (e.g., didactic-interactive book reading with a focus on selected vocabulary words, activities designed to teach new vocabulary words). Training involved 3 days of professional development before school started, followed by biweekly classroom visits over a 15-week period. The program had very little effect on expressive vocabulary but significant effects on receptive vocabulary. Children improved more when they had teachers who used more of the practices on which they were trained (both implicit and explicit, but especially the explicit).

Schwanenflugel and colleagues (2005) found that teachers were initially resistant to some strategies and tended to drop those they deemed to be time consuming or demanding when the intervention period was over (i.e., the second half of the school year). For example, teachers had reservations about finding the time for small-group reading and one-to-one conversations. Most eventually translated the interactive book reading techniques into large-group times. Many teachers abandoned the practices of selecting theme- or book-based target vocabulary words to focus on each week and developing activities to extend the vocabulary learning.

We begin this chapter by briefly discussing some of the instruments designed to measure instructional interactions of early childhood educators and documenting the need for new measures. Other comprehensive reviews are available (see Davidson & Moore, 2007; National Research Council, 2008; Wiggins, Marshall, & Friel, 2007), and we refer readers to those for more detailed discussions. We then discuss the formative assessment tools we developed for use in two ECEPD projects: the Strategy Checklists. The Strategy Checklists were used by coaches to assess the extent to which early childhood educators used specific instructional strategies to support children's language, literacy, mathematical, and social development. We present our rationale, an overview of the development process, preliminary data regarding psychometric properties, and summaries of the results we obtained when using the Strategy Checklists in our two large-scale professional development efforts. Finally, we present an Abbreviated Strategy Checklist that can be used for coaches, teachers, and administrators for formative assessments in their own professional development programs.

AVAILABLE MEASURES OF EARLY CHILDHOOD INSTRUCTIONAL INTERACTIONS

With the increasing emphasis on early childhood education in general and early literacy in particular, the availability of tools to measure early childhood program quality is expanding rapidly. We focus our discussion on three available measures of language and/or literacy instructional interactions: The Early Language and Literacy Classroom Observation Tool (ELLCO) Pre-K (Smith, Brady, & Anastasopoulos, 2008), the Classroom Assessment Scoring System™ (**CLASS**™; Pianta, La Paro, & Hamre, 2008), and the Observation Measure of Language and Literacy Instruction (**OMLIT**; Abt Associates, 2006).

The original ELLCO (Smith, Dickinson, Sangeorge, & Anatasopoulos, 2002), was designed for pre-K to third-grade classrooms. Developed for a professional development program in Head Start classrooms (see Dickinson & Caswell, 2007), the ELLCO was widely used as a professional development outcome measure (e.g., in Early Reading First grants). It could be administered in a fairly short period of time (less than 2 hours) by administrators and teachers with relatively little training.

The current ELLCO targets preschool and pre-K classrooms. The ELLCO Pre-K contains 19 items divided into five sections. The first two sections deal with classroom organization, management, materials, and curriculum but not specific language and literacy practices. The language environment section has four items, including one new item that assesses instructional strategies for promoting phonological awareness. The final two sections include five items relating to books and book reading and three items relating to print and early writing.

The CLASS was explicitly designed as a formative assessment measure of teaching quality in preschool through third-grade classrooms. It has been used in statewide evaluations of pre-K programs in 11 states. The CLASS measures emotional support, classroom organization, and instructional support. The instructional support subscales include concept development, quality of feedback, and language modeling. The concept development and quality of feedback scales cover general instructional practices across academic areas, such as making connections to the real world and providing scaffolding. The language modeling subscale contains five items assessing specific language facilitating practices such as asking open-ended questions and using advanced language. Observations with CLASS allow program administrators to provide detailed, individualized feedback that is used to develop professional development plans (Hamre, LoCasale-Crouch, & Pianta, 2008).

The OMLIT also examines language and literacy instruction in preschool and pre-K classrooms. It is more comprehensive and detailed than either the ELLCO or the CLASS, consisting of five different instruments:

1. The Classroom Literacy Opportunities Checklist (54 items about materials available)

2. The Snapshot of Classroom Activities (literacy activities, literacy materials included in other activities, number of children and adults present during activities)

3. The Read Aloud Profile (assessing use of dialogic/interactive reading practices)

4. The Classroom Literacy Instruction Profile (a time-sampling measure of literacy events/strategies used/quality)

5. The Quality of Instruction in Language and Literacy (11 items assessing the frequency and quality of instruction and support for language and literacy development)

THE NEED FOR NEW FORMATIVE ASSESSMENTS OF INSTRUCTIONAL INTERACTIONS

In its 2008 review of measures of quality in early childhood environments, the National Research Council provided this summary:

> Most existing measures assess the social environment well and the learning environment at a general level, but only a few adequately assess practices related to cognition or academic skills domains. Development of observation measures is just beginning to catch up with the increased political emphasis on academic preparation. Early measures included only a few very general items related to practices designed to promote language and cognitive development. (2008, p. 156)

In fact, out of 22 assessments discussed in the National Research Council review, only 8 were rated as having "substantial representation" of language and literacy. The original ELLCO had only a few, fairly broad instructional items—a single item covered all language facilitation practices, and there were no items concerning the promotion of phonological awareness. The ELLCO Pre-K has one additional item on phonological awareness and an expanded language facilitation section (increased from one item to four). Even so, the items remain fairly global. Although it is more detailed than the ELLCO Pre-K, the CLASS has only nine items on classroom practices and does not include items concerning specific literacy and numeracy practices (National Research Council, 2008). The CLASS was designed to be conducted by highly trained external observers and requires significantly more time to administer than the ELLCO. Finally, the OMLIT is the most comprehensive and specific measure presented herein; yet, it was designed as a research tool and may be too difficult and time consuming for program administrators or coaches to administer and use as a formative assessment.

Very few available measures assess early childhood educators' practices outside of the typical preschool or pre-K classroom setting. In the National Research Council (2008) review, only eight measures were appropriate for infants and toddlers; most of those were designed for use in home settings with parents or family caregivers, and few addressed early language and literacy instruction. The Child/Home Early Language and Literacy Observation (**CHELLO**; Neuman, Dwyer, & Koh, 2007) was designed to fill the gap for home-based settings. However, more professional development programs are beginning to include teachers of infants and toddlers in center-based care, although they typically focus on areas other than literacy (e.g., social-emotional development, joint attention; Cain, Rudd, & Saxon, 2007; Campbell & Milbourne, 2005). There is a growing need for adequate definition and measurement of practices that support language and literacy development in our youngest learners (e.g., see Snow, 2006). The authors of the CLASS are also developing a version for infant and toddler settings (Child Trends, 2007).

USING THE STRATEGY CHECKLISTS
IN EARLY SUCCESS AND PROJECT REEL

With this backdrop, we turn now to a discussion of the Strategy Checklists, measures of instructional practices that we developed for use in two ECEPD projects: Early SUCCESS (Strategies for Urban Child Care Education Support and Services) and later Project REEL (Resources for Early Educator Learning). (See Chapter 5 for more information.)

Early SUCCESS

Early SUCCESS provided 80 hours of research-based professional development to 137 early childhood educators in the Chattanooga, Tennessee, area. Early

SUCCESS participants worked in 5 family settings, 16 group settings, 49 centers, and 1 public school pre-K classroom, with children from birth through age 5. They came from a wide range of educational backgrounds: 22% had completed only high school or a GED and only 16% had completed a bachelor's degree or higher.

The year-long professional development program included 32 hours of training workshops (weekly 2-hour sessions for 16 weeks), a workshop manual to accompany each session, 16 hours of observations of master teachers at early childhood model sites, 26 hours of individualized coaching in the participants' classrooms/settings (family child care does not have classrooms), 4 hours of guided viewing of videotapes showing best practices in teaching young children, and a 2-hour "Celebration of Learning" to showcase the teachers' growth. The content provided the research background and specific strategies to support children's development of oral language, literacy (phonological awareness, alphabet knowledge, concepts of books and print, emergent writing, and interest in print/motivation to engage in print-related activities), and social skills.

We evaluated the effectiveness of our professional development program in many ways (e.g., pre–post tests of content knowledge, teacher self-ratings of practice, independent 2-hour observations of practice, checklists of the literacy materials in the settings). Partway through the first year of training, however, we discovered that we needed an additional measure to determine how well teachers were implementing the specific strategies presented via the workshops, coaching sessions, and observations at model sites. This measure needed to apply across age groups and settings yet be adapted for specific age groups; therefore, we developed the Strategy Checklists.

The Strategy Checklists for Early SUCCESS

The Strategy Checklists were developed for use by early literacy coaches and teachers. Coaches first observed teachers' instructional practices on several occasions. After determining teachers' strengths and weaknesses, coaches provided specific feedback to teachers and assisted them in developing professional development goals and plans for achieving them.

Using our training manual, we developed a comprehensive list of the strategies presented during training. Strategies were divided into those appropriate for younger children (infants and toddlers) and those appropriate for older children (preschool and pre-K). They were further divided into strategies promoting language and literacy development and those fostering social development. Thus, there were four versions of the Strategy Checklist: Younger Language and Literacy (115 items), Younger Social Skills (18 items), Older Language and Literacy (152 items), and Older Social Skills (18 items). There was some overlap for strategies that applied across the entire age range, but examples were adapted for the appropriate age group. Examples of items are available in Appendix 12.1.

After working and observing for several hours in the teachers' settings, coaches were asked to reflect on their observations and complete the checklists, marking "present" for each strategy observed and "absent" for each strategy that had not been observed; strategies that did not apply (e.g., for a setting with infants, posting classroom rules would be inappropriate) were also indicated. Checklist scores were calculated as the sums of the strategies present divided by the total number of recommended strategies applicable for the age group/setting.

The Strategy Checklists were not developed until partway through the first year of training, and the early literacy coaches needed to spend several hours in each teacher's setting before the checklists could be completed. Therefore, the first ratings (Time 1) did not reflect a pure pretraining baseline but performance after some training had occurred (social skills was the first training topic, followed by oral language development). Posttraining (Time 2) ratings were conducted following the conclusion of the formal workshops, approximately 4 months after the first ratings were obtained, and a subgroup of the second cohort's teachers were assessed again 4–6 months later (Time 3). Internal reliability was excellent for both versions of the checklist (*alpha* = .968 for the Younger version and .967 for the Older version at Time 1).

At Time 1, teachers of younger children were using only one tenth of the language and literacy strategies and one fourth of the social skills strategies, whereas teachers of older children initially used approximately one third of the language and literacy strategies and more than half of the social skills strategies (see Table 12.1). Analyses indicated that improvement between Times 1 and 2 was significant (p = .000) for teachers of younger and older children and for strategies promoting language and literacy as well as those promoting social skills. Repeated measures analyses of the second cohort's scores at all three times revealed statistically significant improvement (p = .000) for all four checklists (see Table 12.1).

Table 12.1. Strategy checklists percentage scores by time

Version	Time 1	Time 2	Time 3
Younger—Language and Literacy			
Overall	11.79	32.17	
Cohort 2	8.27	31.24	42.24
Younger—Social Skills			
Overall	20.70	51.20	
Cohort 2	11.76	51.68	59.66
Older—Language and Literacy			
Overall	31.38	50.57	
Cohort 2	24.67	45.78	60.97
Older—Social Skills			
Overall	58.27	76.87	
Cohort 2	45.37	62.35	79.01

Improvement was greater for the social skills dimension between Times 1 and 2 but approximately equal for social skills and literacy and language between Times 2 and 3. For teachers of younger children, there was more improvement in the area of social skills strategies than for language and literacy strategies. Importantly, further improvements were made after the formal training period ended (between Times 2 and 3), especially for those who worked with older children.

In addition, we examined teacher performance and improvement (Time 1 to Time 2) as a function of prior formal education level. Teachers were grouped into three levels: those with a high school education or GED; those with some college experience or a child development associate (CDA) credential; and those who had completed an associate's, bachelor's, or master's degree. There were significant differences by education level for combined scores on the Older Language and Literacy and Older Social Skills checklists. The teachers with the most education at the beginning of the training performed significantly better at Time 1; they used approximately 46% of the recommended strategies, compared with 33% for the teachers with less education. However, all three groups of teachers improved significantly and equally, increasing their use of strategies between Times 1 and 2 (to 65% for teachers with the most prior education and to around 50% for the other two groups); there was no time by education interaction.

The pattern was similar for the combined Younger Language and Literacy and Younger Social Skills subscales, although the differences were not statistically significant. Teachers with a college degree (associate's or bachelor's) and those with some college averaged using about 20% of the recommended strategies at Time 1, whereas those with high school educations used about 15%. At Time 2, all groups had improved; the group with the highest education level used 49% of the strategies, followed by those with some college education (43%) and those with a high school diploma (38%).

Perhaps more importantly, the Strategy Checklists allowed us to examine which specific strategies were most and least likely to be implemented by the teachers. Using these data, we fine-tuned our professional development workshops and coaching efforts in our next project, Project REEL, giving greater emphasis to areas of lower implementation.

Project REEL

Project REEL expanded on and differed from Early SUCCESS in several key ways. First, we extended our service area to the entire state of Tennessee by working with the Child Care Resource and Referral Network (CCR&R). Tennessee's CCR&R already provided professional development workshops and technical assistance (on-site targeted technical assistance is very similar to what we did in coaching sessions); we aligned our workshops and coaching to their standards such that early childhood educators would earn credit toward their annual professional development requirements. The CCR&R provides training and support using *The*

Creative Curriculum (Dodge & Colker, 1991; Dodge, Colker, & Heroman, 2002; Dodge, Rudick, & Berke, 2006). Therefore, we used *The Creative Curriculum* as our foundation, providing the curriculum manuals and related assessments to all participating sites. Second, we added a focus on numeracy (early mathematics). Third, we used a train-the-trainer model, with each trainer (Project REEL specialist) being responsible for delivering workshops and coaching to approximately 20 early childhood educators in their local CCR&R region. Fourth, we expanded the overall professional development hours from 80 to 120; the emphasis on coaching was almost tripled (from 26 to 74 hours), whereas the number of workshops was slightly reduced (from 32 to 28 hours). Finally, our two cohorts of early childhood educators were assigned to receive their professional development at different times; participants in the second cohort began their training approximately 6 months after participants in the first cohort.

All early childhood educators were assessed using multiple measures appropriate for their settings. The Creative Curriculum for Preschool Implementation Checklist (Heroman & Jones, 2003) was used for center-based classrooms serving 3- to 5-year-olds, and new versions of the checklist were developed for the infant–toddler classrooms and family settings. The ELLCO (Smith et al., 2002) was used for preschool classrooms.

Revisions to the Strategy Checklists for Project REEL

As we wrote our expanded and updated training manual for Project REEL, we revised our Strategy Checklists accordingly, adding a numeracy subscale and new items for the other subscales. We also divided the items into subscales representing each component (social skills, oral language, phonological awareness, print awareness, book concepts, alphabetic principle, comprehension, emergent writing) to allow the coaches/trainers to easily determine areas of strength and weakness and to adjust their coaching efforts accordingly. We could clearly link the subscales to the skills identified by the National Early Literacy Panel (2008) as important predictors of later literacy.

We then carefully examined each item and determined which were applicable across the entire age range and which were specific to infants and toddlers versus older children. The common items were listed first in each subscale, followed by items unique for that age group. Ultimately, the version for older children included 249 items, and the version for younger children included 144 items. We also developed a "Multi-age" version for use in group and family child care programs with children from birth through age 5; it contained all common items as well as the items specific to younger and older children. Examples of items are available in the Abbreviated Strategy Checklist in Appendix 12.1.

Finally, we expanded the checklist score from two responses (strategy present/absent) to three responses: not using strategy (absent), using strategy but needs improvement (present), and using strategy well. The literacy coaches in

Early SUCCESS had suggested making this distinction, and it allowed us to better track improvement over the 3 years of Project REEL. The idea was that early childhood educators would move from using few strategies during the early training period to using more strategies (although perhaps not adeptly), eventually progressing to using many strategies well.

Analyses of the psychometric properties of our revised Strategy Checklists yielded promising results. Internal reliability was high for each subscale (*alphas* ranging from .88 to .985 on the Younger version, from .921 to .993 for the Older version, and from .924 to .983 on the Multi-age version). Criterion-related validity data came from examining concurrent correlations between the Strategy Checklists and other measures of teacher and classroom quality. For the Older version (combined), correlations with the ELLCO Classroom Observation Scale ($r = .74$) and the Literacy Environment Checklist ($r =. 55$) were significant ($p < .01$); surprisingly, the correlation with the ELLCO Literacy Activities Rating Scale was not significant ($r = .228$). In addition, the Older version of the Strategy Checklists correlated significantly ($r = .75$, $p < .01$) with the Creative Curriculum for Preschool Implementation Checklist. The Younger version (combined) of the Strategy Checklists also correlated significantly ($r = .620, p < .01$) with the Creative Curriculum Implementation Checklist for Infants and Toddlers. The correlation between the Multi-age version and the Creative Curriculum Family Child Care Implementation Checklist was not significant ($r = .349, p = .203$).

Examining scores on a present/absent basis, as in Early SUCCESS, we found that teachers in Project REEL began their training with fairly high scores (more than 60% of the strategies were being used on both the Younger and Older versions; the Multi-age version averaged 56%). Teachers also improved significantly after training, to 70%–80% for all versions. However, there was evidence of some decline 1 year after training had been completed, especially for the teachers of younger children.

The pattern was somewhat different when examined with our expanded scale(not using/using/using well). Teachers' initial scores increased substantially when more credit was given for using strategies well; moreover, there was less evidence of decline. Although further analyses are necessary, it appears that teachers used more new strategies (quantity) and used more strategies well (quality) over the course of the project. In addition, the declines seen one year after training ended appear to be attributable primarily to dropping some previously used strategies altogether (quantity) rather than declines in the quality of strategies being used. Similar to the findings of Schwanenflugel and colleagues (2005), without the support of our on-site coaches, teachers may have consciously dropped strategies that they believed to be especially difficult, time-consuming, or ineffective, or those for which they did not receive administrative or parent support.

Analyses of the Strategy Checklists by subscale revealed important information about the type of strategies that teachers were most or least likely to use initially and after training. For teachers of older children, the top two areas of performance at all assessment periods were Social-Emotional and Comprehension. Teachers were already implementing more than 80% of the Social-Emotional strategies and 70% of the Comprehension and Oral Language strategies at the first assessment. Modest improvements were seen in these three areas. Emergent Writing and Alphabet Knowledge scores, however, were consistently at the bottom. Emergent Writing scores showed improvements after training (from approximately 55% to 65%), but Alphabet Knowledge scores hovered around 50%–55% at all measurement periods.

The subscale analysis for the Younger versions of the Strategy Checklists revealed different patterns of strategy use by the two cohorts of teachers. The first year training cohort initially exhibited high rates of use of strategies supporting Social-Emotional, Oral Language, and Comprehension development, whereas the second cohort began highest in using Numeracy, Comprehension, and Emergent Writing strategies. Both groups scored lower initially in Alphabet Knowledge strategies. Moreover, the first cohort improved on most subscales and maintained their improvements, whereas the second cohort actually showed significant declines in their use of Alphabet Knowledge and Print Awareness strategies.

Finally, the subscale analysis for the Multi-age version showed more frequent use of Social-Emotional, Comprehension, and Oral Language strategies; less frequent use of Numeracy and Emergent Writing strategies; and least frequent use of strategies supporting an understanding of the alphabet. Although Emergent Writing, Numeracy, and Alphabet Knowledge were consistently among the lowest subscale scores, substantial improvements in all three (15%–20%) were made after training. For Numeracy and Emergent Writing, the gains were maintained 1 year later, but there was some decline in use of Alphabet Knowledge strategies for the first cohort of teachers by the end of the project.

Lessons Learned

After using the Strategy Checklists in both the Early SUCCESS and Project REEL professional development projects, we have found that the Strategy Checklists apply equally well in home, infant-toddler, preschool, and pre-K settings. Coaches used the Strategy Checklists to pinpoint areas in which teachers needed more assistance, and teachers used the checklists to select goals for their individual development plans. The Strategy Checklists became the teachers' and coaches' quick reference guide to our 243-page training manual.

We also used the Strategy Checklists to determine the effectiveness of our professional development efforts. We saw in both projects that teachers in all settings improved in their overall use of strategies and maintained their improvements over time. Examining the scores at the subscale level allowed us to see that teachers were generally doing better with using Social-Emotional, Oral Language, and Comprehension strategies, but they needed help with implementing

Alphabet Knowledge, Print Awareness, and Emergent Writing strategies. Even after training, teachers had particular difficulty applying the Alphabet Knowledge strategies they had been taught; we will use that information to refine our professional development activities in the future.

As the Strategy Checklists included every strategy presented in our professional development manual, they were lengthy and not easily applied to other early childhood education settings or professional development programs. Therefore, we developed an Abbreviated Strategy Checklist comprising the most important and universally applicable strategies from each area (see Appendix 12.1).

Although most of the items on the Abbreviated Strategy Checklist were present on the original checklists, we revised a few of the original items and added a very small number of new items. We have examined the internal reliability of the Abbreviated Strategy Checklist by reanalyzing the subset of items retained from the original checklists for each subscale. Even with the reduced number of items, internal reliability remains high (from .738 for Emergent Writing, to .931 for Social-Emotional; all alphas were greater than .8 except Emergent Writing). We will be conducting further analyses using the Abbreviated Strategy Checklist and will use the results to develop scoring guidelines.

CONCLUSION

Because so few measures of early childhood educator instructional interactions exist, and because most of these measures became available within the last decade, many professional development programs have put substantial time and effort into developing their own instruments. Each measure necessarily reflects unique aspects of the programs they were designed to assess, resulting in difficulty comparing findings across professional development efforts. Recognizing this limitation, the ECEPD program began requiring use of a common metric, the ELLCO (Smith et al., 2002), in 2005. But the ELLCO is a fairly global instrument, primarily useful for describing overall classroom quality rather than measuring implementation of practices taught in professional development programs or assisting teachers and administrators in developing improvement plans. Moreover, although the ELLCO Pre-K (Smith et al., 2008) has been developed for use with preschool and pre-K programs and the CHELLO (Neuman et al., 2007) applies in home/family child care settings, there is no equivalent instrument for use in center-based infant and toddler classrooms. Thus, there is a continued need for measures with greater specificity to inform professional development efforts for all early childhood education settings.

The Strategy Checklists were designed to meet that need. The Abbreviated Strategy Checklist (see Appendix 12.1) represents a balance between precision and practicality. It is sufficiently detailed to allow administrators, coaches, and teachers to reliably determine areas of strength and weakness from which to develop individualized improvement plans, yet it can be administered and thus provide feedback relatively quickly and easily. We plan to continue developing and refining this tool, and we hope that others engaged in formative assessments of professional development will find it useful.

REFERENCES

Abt Associates. (2006). *Observation training manual: OMLIT early childhood.* Cambridge, MA: Author.

Cain, D.W., Rudd, L.C., & Saxon, T.F. (2007). Effects of professional development training on joint attention engagement in low-quality child care centers. *Early Child Development and Care, 177*(2), 159–185.

Campbell, P.H., & Milbourne, S.A. (2005). Improving the quality of infant-toddler care through professional development. *Topics in Early Childhood Special Education, 25*(1), 3–14.

Child Trends. (2007). *Quality in early child care and education: A compendium of measures.* Washington, DC: Author.

Davidson, M.R., & Moore, P.F. (2007). Assessing professionals' knowledge and skills. In K. Pence (Ed.), *Assessment in emergent literacy* (pp. 54–71). San Diego: Plural Publishing.

Dickinson, D.K., & Caswell, L. (2007). Building support for language and early literacy in preschool classrooms through in-service professional development: Effects of the Literacy Environment Enrichment Program (LEEP). *Early Childhood Research Quarterly, 22,* 243–260.

Dodge, D.T., & Colker, L.J. (1991). *The Creative Curriculum for Family Child Care.* Washington, DC: Teaching Strategies.

Dodge, D.T., Colker, L.J., & Heroman, C. (2002). *The Creative Curriculum for Preschool* (4th ed.). Washington, DC: Teaching Strategies.

Dodge, D.T., Rudick, S., & Berke, K. (2006). *The Creative Curriculum for Infants, Toddlers, and Twos* (2nd ed.). Washington, DC: Teaching Strategies.

Fukkink, R.G., & Lont, A. (2007). Does training matter? A meta-analysis and review of caregiver training studies. *Early Childhood Research Quarterly, 22,* 294–311.

Guskey, T.R. (2000). *Evaluating professional development.* Thousand Oaks, CA: Corwin.

Hamre, B.K., LoCasale-Crouch, J., & Pianta, R.C. (2008). Formative assessment of classrooms: Using classroom observations to improve implementation quality. In L.M. Justice & C. Vukelich (Eds.), *Achieving excellence in preschool literacy instruction* (pp. 102–119). New York: Guilford.

Heroman, C., & Jones, C. (2003). *The Creative Curriculum for Preschool Implementation Checklist.* Washington, DC: Teaching Strategies.

Landry, S.H., Swank, P.R., Smith, K.E., Assel, M.A., & Gunnewig, S.B. (2006). Enhancing early literacy skills for preschool children: Bringing a professional development model to scale. *Journal of Learning Disabilities, 39*(4), 306–324.

National Early Literacy Panel. (2008). *Developing early literacy: Report of the National Early Literacy Panel.* Jessup, MD: National Institute for Early Literacy.

National Research Council. (2008). Measuring quality in early childhood environments. In C.E. Snow & S.B. Van Hemel (Eds.), *Early childhood assessment: Why, what, and how* (pp. 145–177). Washington, DC: National Academies Press.

Neuman, S.B., & Cunningham, L. (2009). The impact of professional development and coaching on early language and literacy instructional practices. *American Educational Research Journal, 46*(2), 322–353.

Neuman, S.B., Dwyer, J., & Koh, S. (2007). *Child/Home Early Language and Literacy Observation (CHELLO)*. Baltimore: Paul H. Brookes Publishing Co.

Pianta, R.C., La Paro, K.M., & Hamre, B.K. (2008). *Classroom Assessment Scoring System (CLASS)*. Baltimore: Paul H. Brookes Publishing Co.

Ramey, S.L., & Ramey, C.T. (2006). Creating and sustaining a high-quality workforce in child care, early intervention, and school readiness programs. In M. Zaslow & I. Martinez-Beck (Eds.), *Critical issues in early childhood professional development* (pp. 355–368). Baltimore: Paul H. Brookes Publishing Co.

Ramey, S.L., & Ramey, C.T. (2008). Establishing a science of professional development for early education programs. In L.M. Justice & C. Vukelich (Eds.), *Achieving excellence in preschool literacy instruction* (pp. 41–63). New York: Guilford.

Sandefur, S.J., Warren, A.R., Hicks, H.K., & Gamble, A. (2006). *The Strategy Checklists.* Unpublished instrument, Project REEL, University of Tennessee at Chattanooga.

Schwanenflugel, P.J., Hamilton, C.E., Bradley, B.A., Ruston, H.P., Neuharth-Pritchett, S., & Restrepo, M.A. (2005). Classroom practices for vocabulary enhancement in prekindergarten: Lessons from PAVEd for Success. In E.H. Hiebert & M.L. Kamil (Eds.), *Teaching and learning vocabulary* (pp. 155–177). Mahwah, NJ: Lawrence Erlbaum Associates.

Smith, M.W., Brady, J.P., & Anastasopoulos, L. (2008). *Early Language and Literacy Classroom Observation Tool (ELLCO) Pre-K.* Baltimore: Paul H. Brookes Publishing Co.

Smith, M.W., Dickinson, D.K., Sangeorge, A., & Anatasopoulos, L. (2002). *Early Language and Literacy Classroom Observation Tool (ELLCO)*. Baltimore: Paul H. Brookes Publishing Co.

Snow, C.E. (2006). What counts as literacy in early childhood? In D. Phillips & K. McCartney (Eds.), *Blackwell handbook of early childhood development* (pp. 274–294). Malden, MA: Blackwell Publishing.

Wiggins, A.K., Marshall, K.A., & Friel, S.A. (2007). Assessing classroom language and literacy richness. In K. Pence (Ed.), *Assessment in emergent literacy* (pp. 3–51). San Diego: Plural Publishing.

Abbreviated Strategy Checklist

Social-Emotional

For all children, the teacher:

- Develops reasonable and fair limits and states them effectively (Tells children what to do, e.g., "use soft touches," rather than what not to do).
- Teaches helpful or appropriate behavior (e.g., how to ask for something, listen without interrupting, join a group, put things away).
- Ignores inappropriate behavior (only when it is appropriate to do so; dangerous or hurtful behavior cannot be ignored, crying in infants cannot be ignored).
- Uses positive guidance (strategies that teach appropriate behavior rather than punishment or time-out for inappropriate behavior).
- Changes the context/situation if problems develop (changes the physical setting, increases/decreases options available to the child).
- Redirects children's behavior to more appropriate activities.
- Recognizes signs of stress, anxiety, or strong emotions; prevents overstimulation and assists children in calming down.
- Uses affirmations with all children (verbally praises appropriate behaviors and points out what children do well).
- Provides words for feelings (through children's books, by labeling the child's feelings, e.g., "It looks like you are frustrated") .
- Uses "teachable moments" to prevent behavioral escalation (intervenes with suggestions for appropriate behaviors before a situation becomes a discipline encounter).
- Responds quickly and consistently to children's needs (e.g., promptly responds to an infant's cry).
- Models appropriate social-emotional behaviors (e.g., "I think we'll do something quiet for a little while now. I need to calm down.").

For toddlers and older children, the teacher:

- Develops a set of no more than 3–5 rules and posts them, reviewing them every day.

Oral Language

For all children, the teacher:

- Expands and elaborates upon whatever children say/vocalize.
- Asks open-ended questions.
- Uses routine and transition times as language-enrichment opportunities (diaper changing, lunch, lining up, cleaning up).
- Gives children time to talk to each other; encourages conversation.
- Talks to each child one-on-one every day.
- Restates "child dialect" (e.g., Child says, "I runned." Teacher responds, "Oh, you ran.").
- Uses a rich vocabulary; reads books with new or "rare" words; explains what those words mean.
- Uses "event casts," talking about what teacher/children is/are doing, what they are going to do, what they have done.
- Is a good listener, participates in respectful communication, does not interrupt, allows sufficient "wait time" for children to say what they want to say.

Appendix 12.1. Abbreviated Strategy Checklist. (From Sandefur, S.J., Warren, A.R., Hicks, H.K., & Gamble, A. [2006]. *The Strategy Checklists.* Unpublished instrument, Project REEL, University of Tennessee at Chattanooga.) (*Note:* The full versions of the Strategy Checklists along with instructions for administration and use are available from the authors. Contact Amye Warren at Amye-Warren@utc.edu or Psychology Department #2803, University of Tennessee at Chattanooga, 615 McCallie Avenue, Chattanooga, TN, 37403.)

For infants and toddlers, the teacher:
- Speaks in an easily understandable way (uses child-directed speech slightly above the child's level).
- Talks about whatever babies and toddlers are looking at or currently doing (joint attention).

For preschoolers/pre-K, the teacher:
- Uses dialogic/interactive reading strategies with open-ended questions (competence, abstract, and reflection) about books.
- Selects and explicitly teaches new vocabulary words with age-appropriate activities.
- Encourages narratives (asks children to tell personal narratives, imaginative stories, and to retell stories they have read).

Phonological Awareness

For all children, the teacher:
- Calls attention to rhyming words in books, songs, chants, fingerplays, and poems.
- Encourages and praises children's curiosity and experimentation with language sounds.
- Integrates a sound focus throughout the day (calls attention to beginning sounds and rhyming words when reading books, chart paper texts, children's names, recipes, signs, labels, etc.)

For infants and toddlers, the teacher:
- Reproduces sounds when reading books ("What sound do cows make? Mooooooo.")
- Calls their attention to sounds in the environment (cars, airplanes, bells, music, Mother's voice, peers' voices, etc.).

For preschoolers/pre-K, the teacher:
- Counts out syllables in children's names and other familiar words.
- Focuses on beginning sounds of children's names and other words important to the child.
- Calls children's attention to words that have the same rhyme pattern.
- Calls children's attention to compound words, both adding the two parts together and separating the two parts.

Concepts About Books

For all children, the teacher:
- Reads aloud with enthusiasm, drama, inflection, and fluency.
- Integrates books in multiple places around the setting (cribs, crawling areas, block play, dramatic play areas, library center, etc.).
- Reads high-quality books that are developmentally appropriate for individual/small groups.
- Labels, explains, ask questions, and describes objects and characters in a book.
- Encourages children to "read" (tell the story through pictures) to peers and to stuffed animals/toys.

For infants/toddlers, the teacher:
- Uses board books and other sturdy formats so that children may freely explore.
- Encourages "book babble" and responds as if children are reading in a conventional way.

For preschoolers/pre-K, the teacher:
- Uses book related language when reading aloud to children: cover, title, author, illustrator, page, top, bottom, word, sentence, letter, front, back, beginning, end, etc.
- Encourages storytelling by children and enriches/expands what the children say.

Print Awareness/Alphabet Knowledge

For all children, the teacher:

- Encourages play with age-appropriate alphabet manipulatives, magnetic letters, sorts, blocks, games, stamps, stencils, etc.
- Shows and discusses print that appears on items in the immediate environment (on cereal boxes, toys, clothes, labels, baby food jars, etc.).
- Reads an ABC book aloud at least daily and points out items that begin with the target letter.
- Writes their names when they are watching.

For preschoolers/pre-K, the teacher:

- Takes dictation (shared writing experiences) from children on paper for subsequent shared reading opportunities.
- Places and uses the children's names on labels in several places in the setting.
- Creates and calls attention to displays of environmental print to which both teachers and children have contributed familiar items.
- Uses write alouds and shared writing to show the formation of letters.
- Places and demonstrates the use of print materials in multiple area/centers of the setting.

Comprehension

For all children, the teacher:

- Introduces new vocabulary words and explains places in a book that are likely to be confusing for a child.
- Uses repeated dialogic/shared reading experiences with varied questioning strategies.
- Labels, explains, and describes images in books and connects them to children's experiences.
- Reads aloud to individuals and small groups from fiction, information, and poetry books.

For infants/toddlers, the teacher:

- Encourages the child to point and/or say an object's or character's name in a book illustration.
- Encourages the child to say a familiar word in the book by pausing and helping the child "fill in the blank."

For preschoolers/pre-K, the teacher:

- Supports children in creating retellings of stories through oral language, toys, puppets, felt boards, dramatic play, etc.
- Encourages children's connections to the book before, during, and after teacher read alouds.
- Talks about setting, characters, problems, and solutions during and after the reading.

Emergent Writing

For all children, the teacher:

- Provides daily opportunities to explore drawing and writing; tapes paper down on the floor or table for child's convenience.
- Sits with both younger and older children when they're scribbling and praises children's writing efforts, from dots/line by infants to letter forms by preschoolers.
- "Thinks aloud" while modeling writing of her/his own labels, notes, lists, etc.

For preschoolers/pre-K, the teacher:

- Supports understanding of multiple reasons to write multiple times every day: signs, recipes, menus, messages, greeting cards, etc.
- Models the conventions of writing: begin at the left and move to the right; begin at the top and work toward the bottom of the page; begin sentences with a capital letter, places spaces in between words, etc.

- Demonstrates through writing aloud, shared writing, and guided writing that letters represent the sounds in words.
- Provides rich materials for writing, demonstrates their use, and offers writing opportunities in all centers (block play, home living center, post office, etc.).
- Encourages attempts at name writing and other meaningful genres of writing.

Numeracy

For all children, the teacher:

- Models mathematical language in her/his own speech (half, shortest, before, first, second, higher, under, etc.).
- Provides multiple types, sizes, shapes, and colors of blocks, cups, containers, molds, spoons, and toys.
- Shares songs, chants, fingerplays, and poems to support focus on numbers and patterns.
- Shows numerals and shapes on items in the everyday environment.
- Integrates early mathematical books in multiple places around the setting.
- Reads counting/shape/size and other math-concept books (simple concept board books for younger children).
- Models counting of age-appropriate sets of items.

For preschoolers/pre-K, the teacher:

- Provides opportunities to sort objects by size, shape, and color.
- Provides opportunities to create simple patterns and talk about the patterns they create.

13

Online Logs

A Tool to Monitor Fidelity of Implementation in Large-Scale Interventions

Tanya S. Wright

As early childhood interventions are scaled up, it is essential for researchers, practitioners, and policy makers to ensure accountability in the field. The push for educational researchers to test interventions in field-based settings has brought the issue of fidelity of implementation into focus. *Fidelity of implementation* is defined as, "the extent to which a program is implemented as intended and operating up to the standards established for it" (Rossi, Lipsey, & Freeman, 2004, p. 57). In order to attribute program outcomes to the intervention, it must first be established that the intervention is actually carried out as planned (O'Donnell, 2008). Fidelity of implementation is critical for researchers testing the effectiveness of new interventions (Institute of Education Sciences, 2009), as well as for practitioners who are working to institute research-based interventions in educational settings (see also National Implementation Research Network web site, http://www.fpg.unc.edu/~nirn/).

Two key constructs make up fidelity of implementation: fidelity to program structure and fidelity to program process (Mowbray, Holter, Teague, & Bybee, 2003; O'Donnell, 2008). Fidelity to program structure includes both adherence and duration. Was the program delivered as designed? Did participants receive the appropriate number of sessions? Did the sessions last the correct amount of time? Were sessions delivered according to the schedule that was planned (Mowbray et al., 2003; O'Donnell, 2008)? Fidelity to program process focuses on the quality of program delivery. Did the implementer deliver the program using the techniques and processes that were planned? Can the program be clearly distinguished from other interventions or comparison conditions?

In a small-scale study that occurs in one or two nearby locations, these questions can be answered with relative ease by sending trained individuals to observe the program on a regular basis. However, as intervention studies become larger in scale, the following question arises: How can we ensure fidelity of implementation using feasible and cost-efficient methods?

This chapter discusses the Project Great Start Professional Development Initiative study as an example to demonstrate considerations that arise when trying to ensure fidelity of implementation in a large-scale professional development intervention for early childhood teachers and child care providers. The chapter describes the development and use of an online coaching log tool that was piloted during this study. This tool enabled us to examine fidelity to both structural and quality features of a professional development coaching intervention during a large-scale, field-based study.

Funded through the Early Childhood Educator Professional Development Grant (USDOE), the Project Great Start study (Susan Neuman, Principal Investigator) focused on coaching as a nontraditional method for providing professional development in language and literacy to early childhood teachers and child care providers in comparison to the more traditional model of college coursework. One-to-one, on-site coaching has been suggested as a method for providing longer-term, context-specific professional development to teachers and has been effective in large-scale studies as one component of a multifaceted professional development initiative. For example, Neuman and Cunningham (2009) found that college coursework combined with 32 weeks of coaching was more effective than college coursework alone in improving early childhood providers' teaching practice. They also found that college coursework alone led to no measurable improvements in teachers' early literacy practice compared with a control group who received no professional development at all.

This intriguing finding led to the second part of the Project Great Start study, which sought to isolate coaching as the potential mechanism for improving teacher practice. To disentangle the effects of coaching from other components of professional development interventions, this study included a coaching-only professional development treatment. Early childhood providers ($N = 148$) who worked at centers in low-socioeconomic communities were randomly assigned to receive 1) 10 weeks of language and literacy coaching in their classroom ($n = 58$), 2) a 10-week language and literacy college course ($n = 58$), or 3) business as usual (control group; $n = 32$). By including the coaching-only group, this study sought to examine the independent effect of coaching on the language and literacy practice of early childhood teachers. (See Neuman & Wright, in press, for more details on the study.)

DESIGNING A FIDELITY TOOL
FOR LARGE-SCALE INTERVENTIONS

To answer the research question in the Project Great Start study, it was imperative to ensure that there was fidelity to the coaching professional development treatment. We needed a scalable and cost-efficient method for monitoring coaching sessions at 58 sites across the state of Michigan. We needed to be certain that coaching sessions were occurring as planned and on the prescribed schedule of one session per week for 10 weeks.

In addition, for the purposes of measuring and improving the quality of coaching, we needed to elicit detailed information about each coaching session. What was the exact duration of the session? What content did the coach address with the teacher? How did the coach impart new ideas and information to the teacher?

To accomplish all of these goals, we developed an online self-report log that coaches completed after each coaching session. The logs were structured response surveys that were completed on a repeated basis over time.

Rationale for Tool Development

Before developing a new tool for monitoring fidelity of implementation, we began by considering the benefits and disadvantages of methods that we had already been using. During the first year of the Project Great Start study, we used observers to gather data on the quality of coaching (Neuman & Cunningham, 2009). These observers visited coaching sessions at random and provided descriptive information using qualitative notetaking. The observations provided rich data about the quality and content of a few coaching sessions that we were able to analyze after the study was complete, but these notes did not allow for real-time monitoring of all coaching sessions. Also, these data provided only random fidelity checks because it would not have been efficient or cost effective to send observers to every session.

In addition, during the first year of the study, we held focus groups with the coaches after coaching was complete. Again, these data helped us to learn more about coaching after the study was complete.

Finally, we asked coaches to fill out open-ended paper and pencil logs in which they provided notes describing their goals for each coaching session and whether or not they accomplished these goals. Again, these documents were not thoroughly analyzed until months after the study was complete. This technique did not meet the need to gather more immediate fidelity of implementation data.

For the second year of the study, we sought a scalable and cost-efficient means of gathering fidelity data on coaching that would also allow for close to real-time monitoring of all coaching sessions. We designed the online coaching log to meet these needs. Coaches completed the online log within 48 hours of each coaching session, and we had access to this data immediately after it was submitted electronically. Our goal was to pilot a real-time tool to monitor both structure and process components of fidelity of implementation during a large-scale intervention project.

From Research Method to Fidelity Tool

The most well-documented use of logs for research purposes was during a large-scale study of school reform initiatives (Rowan, Camburn, & Correnti, 2004). In this study, logs were used to examine how elementary school teachers implemented new curricula in their classrooms. The teachers completed daily logs to document the instruction that they provided for target children in their classrooms (Rowan et al., 2004; Rowan & Correnti, 2009). In piloting the use of instructional logs for this study, researchers found that when teachers and expert observers completed the log on the same day, they had almost the same interrater reliability as a pair of expert observers who also completed the log (Camburn & Barnes, 2004). This indicated that teachers could document their own instruction as reliably as expert observers. In addition, the authors argued that in a large-scale study of this type, logs were far more cost-effective than paying observers to spend time in classrooms on a daily basis (Rowan et al., 2004).

Logs were also found to be more accurate than one-time, post-intervention surveys (Rowan & Correnti, 2009). In one-time surveys, teachers have difficulty accurately accounting for how much time they spend on one practice or another (Mayer, 1999). Logs allowed teachers to record practice on a daily basis, thereby improving accuracy in teachers' self-reporting.

We adapted this log methodology to create a tool for monitoring fidelity of implementation during the coaching professional development treatment in the Project Great Start study. Logs were selected for their clear benefits over one-time surveys as far as accuracy of information. In addition, this methodology was appealing because of its cost-efficiency when compared with using trained observers in a study of this scale.

In creating the coaching log, we conceived of the coach as providing one-to-one instruction to the early childhood teacher. Therefore, in the Project Great Start study, the coach completed a log to detail the professional development that she provided for the early childhood teacher, in contrast to the previously described use of logs in which a classroom teacher completed the log to describe the instruction he or she provided to a child.

Also, rather than having the coaches complete logs on a daily basis, as in the previous studies, coaches completed logs after each coaching session. This was appropriate because coaches met with providers for 10 coaching sessions over the course of 10 weeks.

Another substantial difference between the coaching log and teacher logs used in previous studies was that coaches completed the log online. Putting the log online rather than using a pencil and paper version met the pressing need to collect real-time information about coaching sessions. This allowed day-to-day monitoring of a professional development program that was occurring in 58 sites throughout the state.

The Online Coaching Log

To design the online coaching log, we modeled the format after published examples of logs (e.g., Rowan et al., 2004), changing the structure as necessary to move to an online format. Items on the log were written specifically for this study to measure both structural and process fidelity to the coaching intervention.

Which coaching techniques did you use during today's session (Check all that apply):

☐ Setting goals and objectives with teacher

☐ Engaging teacher in professional self-reflection

☐ Providing teacher with professional resources

☐ Explaining new ideas or concepts to teacher

☐ Helping the teacher change the physical environment

☐ Co-planning lessons

☐ Co-teaching

☐ Modeling instructional strategies

☐ Observing teacher's interactions with children

☐ Providing feedback about observed teaching practices

Figure 13.1. Sample items to monitor fidelity to coaching methodology.

The online log had items to monitor fidelity to program structure, including the date and duration of sessions and the coaching techniques used by the coach during the session (Figure 13.1), as well as the coach's key goal for the session. Responses to these items provided information on fidelity to structures that were key to professional development, including the timing of coaching as well as the coach's fidelity to the coaching model that he or she was trained to use.

To measure coaching quality, we needed to ensure that coaches were working on content that reflected program language and literacy goals for providers. We aligned items on the coaching log with key language and literacy practices that are measured by the Early Language and Literacy Classroom Observation Tool (ELLCO; Smith, Dickinson, Sangeorge, & Anastasopoulas, 2002) and the Child/Home Early Language and Literacy Observation (CHELLO; Neuman, Dwyer, & Koh, 2007). We knew that we would use these observational measures to evaluate teachers' language and literacy practice, so it was important to ensure that coaches provided professional development that moved teachers toward improvement on the research-based content included in these measures. For example, both of the observation measures examine whether there is an area in the classroom set aside just for reading books. In turn, on the log we asked coaches to tell us whether creating or improving a dedicated book area was a focus of the session, was touched on briefly during the session, or was not addressed during the coaching session.

Items on the log also reflected recommended early childhood language and literacy practices from the book *Nurturing Knowledge* (Neuman, Roskos, Wright, & Lenhart, 2007). All coaches were provided with this book during their training to guide their work with providers. The log also asked coaches to check practices that they addressed during each session within the following key areas: 1) general classroom environment, 2) assessment, 3) book area, 4) book/print availability, 5) writing materials, 6) environmental print, 7) shared book reading (see Figure 13.2 for a sample item on shared book reading), 8) play, 9) phonological awareness, 10) developmental writing, 11) teacher–child interactions, and 12) oral language and vocabulary development. There were 65 items on the log, and it took approximately 15 minutes to complete.

The log was placed online, allowing real-time access to data from our base at the University of Michigan. We could monitor sessions that were occurring throughout the state of Michigan.

Coaches were trained on the use of the online log as part of a day-long Coaching Training Institute that was provided by researchers from the University of Michigan. In addition to the regular training on the diagnostic/prescriptive coaching model (Neuman & Cunningham, 2009) and a review of key language and literacy content, the coaches were introduced to the definitions of all terms used in the log and were taught how to complete the questionnaire. Coaches were also provided with the contact information for a staff member on the project who could help with technical difficulties and follow-up questions in using the online coaching log.

Completing the log was considered part of the coach's job responsibilities, and as such, coaches were compensated for completing logs after each coaching session. Coaches were expected to complete one session per week with each provider.

A staff member monitored log completion and contacted the coaching supervisors at each site if logs were not completed in a timely manner. Coaching supervisors determined why logs were missing (e.g., Did the coach forget to complete the log? Did the provider reschedule the session?) and reported back to project staff members once the issue was resolved. This tracking process ensured fidelity to the professional development intervention, which called for one coaching session per week.

In addition to tracking that sessions were occurring as planned, the web site that we used allowed us to download the data at any time. It also created summary data in the form of bar graphs for each item across all logs that were completed to that point. At regular times during the 10-week coaching intervention, coaching supervisors were given this data so that they could provide feedback to their coaches on whether content areas were being adequately addressed.

Coaches were informed that the logs would not be used to evaluate their individual coaching; rather, log data was used to better understand the overall quality of the intervention across all coaches. The log measured fidelity of implementation across this large-scale intervention. It was the role of the coaching supervisor to meet weekly with all coaches in his or her area and to assist in solving problems at the individual coach level.

Findings from Online Log Data

In total, we collected 505 coaching logs over the course of the Project Great Start study. Overall findings from the online log data were that providers who received 10 weeks of coaching made improvements to the reading and writing physical environment (measured on the Environmental Checklists of the ELLCO) compared

PROJECT GREAT START COACHING LOG

Part III: Teacher-Coach Session Elaboration

Focus of session = main area addressed during the session

Touched on briefly = area addressed but not the main focus of the session

Not discussed = this area was not covered at all during the session

Today we worked on or discussed...

SHARED BOOK READING

	Focus of Session	Touched on Briefly	Not Discussed
Planning regular times for reading aloud to children	○	○	○
Using discussion and questioning during shared book reading	○	○	○
Methods for reading to children in a variety of groupings (one-on-one, small groups, whole group)	○	○	○
Coordinating book reading with ongoing projects and learning experiences	○	○	○
Reading books from a variety of genres (i.e., storybooks, alphabet books, informational books, rhyming books)	○	○	○
Using shared book reading to introduce children to new vocabulary	○	○	○
Using shared book reading to introduce children to new information	○	○	○
Demonstrating concepts of print (print is read from left to right, front cover, back cover, etc)	○		○
Other (please specify)			

Figure 13.2. Sample items to measure fidelity to language and literacy content goals: shared book reading.

with providers who took a college course or were in the control group. Teachers who received coaching maintained improvements to the language and literacy environment 4 months after coaching was completed, at the end of the school year. However, teachers who took the language and literacy college course made no improvements compared with the control group. No teachers in the study made progress on the Teaching Strategies section of the ELLCO, indicating that neither the 10-week college course nor 10 weeks of coaching helped teachers to improve in their language and literacy instructional strategies (Neuman & Wright, in press). Data from the logs allow us to say with confidence that coaches demonstrated strong fidelity of implementation to the key components of the study. Most providers received all 10 coaching sessions with 87% of expected logs submitted, providing data on the timing and duration of coaching. A few coaches had technical difficulties in submitting a log or needed to reschedule sessions, but fast resolution when logs were not submitted on time allowed us to be confident that across all participants, the coaching professional development was delivered as planned.

As for coaching quality, coaches completed a write-in section documenting the goal that the coach and provider worked on for each week, indicating that coaches were following the diagnostic/prescriptive coaching model in which they examined provider needs and worked with the provider to provide professional development to meet those needs. Coaches used a range of techniques to address provider needs, using all methods on which they were trained.

Another important process component of literacy coaching was to better understand the language and literacy content that coaches were addressing during their sessions. This is particularly interesting in light of study findings that coaching led to improvements in the language and literacy physical environment but not in teacher's instructional strategies. Data from the logs provide insight into why teachers who received 10 weeks of coaching improved the language and literacy physical environment at their sites but did not improve in their instructional strategies.

For example, for writing, we created two theoretical clusters of log items. The Writing Environment included 1) creating or improving a dedicated writing area, 2) ensuring that there was a variety of paper available for children, and 3) ensuring that there was a variety of writing/drawing tools available to children. Writing Instructional Strategies included 1) helping children practice writing their own names, 2) writing stories with children, and 3) encouraging children's early invented spelling. We tallied items for all coaches and calculated a mean number of sessions devoted to each content cluster. Conducting a t-test, we found significant differences between these two factors, with individual coaches addressing the writing environment in more sessions than writing instruction ($t = 1.98$, $p = .05$).

On average, creating a writing area, ensuring a variety of paper was available to children, and ensuring a variety of drawing tools were available to children were each addressed by coaches in at least two sessions. However, the only writing instructional strategy that was addressed in at least two sessions was children's

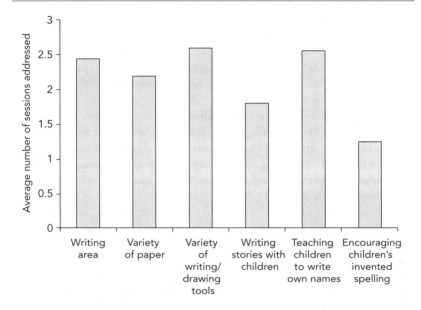

Figure 13.3. Writing content covered by coaches.

name writing (see Figure 13.3). It seems that for writing, coaches spent more time improving the environment than focusing on developmentally appropriate writing instruction. In turn, teachers made improvements in environmental supports for writing but not in writing instructional techniques. Because Project Great Start was a research study in which we were testing the effectiveness of the coaching intervention, we could not retrain coaches on writing instruction during the study. However, if online logs were used during an implementation study, this data could be used for improving the quality of implementation in real time as the intervention is carried out in the field.

A similar analysis was repeated for reading. Here, we clustered items associated with the reading environment that included 1) creating or improving a dedicated book area, 2) ensuring that there are an appropriate number of books in the space, and 3) making a variety of books available to children. Reading instructional strategies included 1) creating daily times for reading aloud to children, 2) coordinating shared book reading with ongoing themes or projects, and 3) using discussion and questioning during shared book reading. A t-test revealed marginal differences ($t = 1.86$, $p < .06$). Coaches spent more time on the environmental characteristics in centers than on the teaching strategies associated with literacy improvements.

The time spent on improving reading instruction was obviously not as effective as work on the reading environment. Providers who received coaching did not improve on the instructional strategies sections of the ELLCO. In light of previous finding that providers who received a college course and 32 weeks of coaching made improvements to instruction as well as the environment (Neuman & Cunningham, 2009), we wondered whether coaches in the Project Great Start study simply did not have enough time to effectively work with teachers on improving their instruction.

The logs provided us with initial answers to this research question because coaches completed a log after each of the 10 sessions. As such, we were able to use the logs to look at changes in coaching across time. The possibility to examine changes in coaching over the duration of the 10-week intervention is an analytical strategy that would not be possible with either posthoc surveys or random observational fidelity checks.

When we used the logs to examine the content that coaches addressed over time, we found that coaches were more likely to address the literacy environment in an earlier session, whereas instruction was addressed across all sessions. For example, Figure 13.4. presents a graph that looks across coaches to demonstrate when "creating or improving a dedicated book area" was addressed as compared with "strategies for improving shared reading." This suggested that coaches were able to address weaknesses in the literacy environment early on in their work and with relative efficiency, but they needed longer-term work to improve instruction.

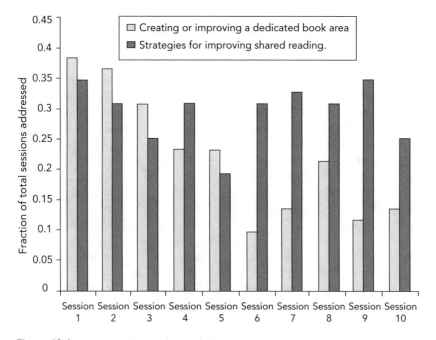

Figure 13.4.   Content addressed over time—books.

As coaching in the area of shared reading instructional strategies did not taper off, even in the last session, it seems that at the end of their professional development, providers may still have needed continued coaching in this area. We can use log data to surmise that 10 coaching sessions did not provide enough time to inculcate improvement in this key area of early childhood literacy instruction. Future studies should examine the appropriate dosage of coaching to improve both the literacy environment as well as literacy instructional strategies.

CONCLUSION

After piloting the online coaching log during the Project Great Start study, we found that online logs have strong potential as a method for tracking fidelity of implementation during large-scale, field-based interventions. Online logs have many strong points when compared with other methods for monitoring fidelity.

For one, online logs can be designed to measure constructs that make up fidelity of implementation, including both structural and process components of the program being evaluated. The structural aspects of the program include timing, frequency, and total dosage of the intervention. Process components differ by intervention but should always include the quality with which the intervention was delivered. In the Project Great Start study, we measured quality by asking coaches to log information on the methods they used during their sessions as well as the language and literacy content that they addressed each week. A strong point of the online log is that it can be flexibly adapted to reflect fidelity of implementation of various programs. In a different intervention, the online logs could be designed so that the program implementer, for example, could complete them to document implementation of key features and processes of that particular program.

Online logs also provide real-time data to monitor fidelity of implementation. Real-time data allows researchers or practitioners to plan for improvement when fidelity is sub-par. In the Project Great Start study, if logs were not completed as scheduled, this information was funneled back to the coaching supervisor, who could look into and resolve the problem. Real-time data also has the potential for similar feedback loops related to quality. If log data indicates that implementers are not addressing key areas of the intervention, they can be given additional training or support to ensure that the program is delivered with the intended quality. Using online logs to make changes mid-intervention was not possible in the Project Great Start study because, as researchers, we were examining the effectiveness of a particular intervention. However, using online log data to make improvements during the intervention would be particularly useful to practitioners as they implement and monitor a new program in the field.

In addition, online logs are far more cost-efficient than collecting observational data. Although coaches were compensated for the time they spent logging, we did not need to train observers or pay for their time and transportation to attend coaching sessions around the state. It would have been an unthinkable investment of money and manpower to send observers to attend 580 coaching sessions over a 10-week period, yet this would have been the only other way to capture the level of detail that we gained from coaching logs. Sending observers on a few fidelity visits or asking coaches to fill out a single survey after coaching was completed would not have yielded the quantity or quality of data that we were able to capture through the use of online logs.

Because online logs were completed after every coaching session, we were able to examine the intervention as a whole with many data points, but even more useful is that we could track changes in implementation over time. Examining an intervention by only asking what happened on average during the intervention provides a static and unrealistic view of a program as it plays out in the field. Perhaps an intervention is delivered with low quality when implementers are first learning the program, quality improves as implementers become more comfortable, but then fidelity tapers off as the program continues. The only way to monitor change over time, and to remedy problems that occur, is to collect regular fidelity data throughout the intervention. Online logs provide this capacity to researchers and practitioners. In the Project Great Start study, monitoring the language and literacy content delivered over time allowed us to learn that changes to the language and literacy environment were addressed by coaches with relative efficiency early in the coaching professional development. Work on language and literacy instruction required more ongoing attention by coaches, and likely needed more than 10 weeks of coaching.

Online log data also can be used to determine areas of improvement for the intervention. In the case of our study, we used log data to determine that coaches likely need more upfront training on addressing issues of language and literacy instruction with early childhood providers. We also learned that the coaching intervention likely requires more than 10 weeks to be effective for improving both the language and literacy environment as well as language and literacy instruction. Future research must address the appropriate dosage for coaching as a professional development intervention.

After completing the pilot study of online coaching logs, we found several critical features that should be noted when using such a tool. During training, in addition to reviewing items on the log, a glossary should be provided explaining each item to improve item reliability across coaches. Also, a reliability check comparing coaches' use of the log with log use by trained observers would provide confirmation that coaches are interpreting items as intended. Items can be reworked if necessary to improve the accuracy of the information that coaches are providing.

Another area of consideration when using the logs is to plan for a feedback loop between those analyzing the log and practitioners implementing the intervention. In the Project Great Start study, supervisors received information about missed logs as well as summary log data on areas that were or were not being addressed by coaches. In future studies, we would plan for supervisors to make even better use of this information, making this feedback loop part of the program being studied. For example, if log data indicates that coaches, as a group, are not using modeling to demonstrate instructional techniques, supervisors could provide ongoing training to coaches on this technique during weekly supervision meetings.

As we consider using logs in this way, it is important to note that log data does not replace the need to have supervisors who work with coaches. Log data cannot be used to evaluate the work of individual coaches. If this data were used at the individual level, and individual coaches were critiqued based on their logs, it would encourage coaches to provide desirable information on the logs rather than valid accounts of their work. Coaches in our study were informed that log data would be used to examine the program and not to evaluate individuals. However, log data provides invaluable, real-time feedback on how the intervention as a whole is being implemented. This information is not simply data to be analyzed after the intervention is complete, but rather it has strong potential to be used at the group level to strengthen the quality of an intervention while it is being delivered.

Online logs are an effective tool to monitor fidelity of implementation in the field. They allow day-to-day progress monitoring, which enables researchers and practitioners to ensure that interventions are delivered as planned. The online log methodology enhances the ability to scale up interventions with confidence in the quality of program delivery while also providing the real-time information required to make adjustments to the intervention when necessary.

REFERENCES

Camburn, E., & Barnes, C.A. (2004). Assessing the validity of a language arts instruction log through triangulation. *The Elementary School Journal, 105,* 49–73.

Institute of Education Sciences. (2009). *Request for applications: Education research grants* (CFDA Number: 84.305A). Retrieved http://ics.cd.gov/funding/pdf/2010_84305A.pdf.

Mayer, D. (1999). Measuring instructional practice: Can policymakers trust survey data? *Educational Evaluation and Policy Analysis, 21,* 29–45.

Mowbray, C., Holter, M.C, Teague, G.B. & Bybee, D. (2003). Fidelity criteria: Development, measurement, and validation. *American Journal of Evaluation, 24,* 315–340.

Neuman, S.B., & Cunningham, L. (2009). The impact of professional development and coaching on early language and literacy instructional practices. *American Educational Research Journal, 46*(2), 532–566.

Neuman, S.B., Dwyer, J., & Koh, S. (2007). *Child/Home Early Language and Literacy Observation (CHELLO).* Baltimore: Paul H. Brookes Publishing Co.

Neuman, S.B., Roskos, K., Wright, T.S., & Lenhart, L. (2007). *Nurturing knowledge: Building a foundation for school success by linking early literacy to math, science, art and social studies.* New York: Scholastic.

Neuman, S.B., & Wright, T.S. (in press). Coaching in early language and literacy: Effects on teacher practice and child outcomes. *The Elementary School Journal.*

O'Donnell, C.L. (2008). Defining, conceptualizing, and measuring fidelity of implementation and its relationship to outcomes in K–12 curriculum intervention research. *Review of Educational Research, 78,* 33–84.

Rossi, P.H., Lipsey, M.W., & Freeman, H.E. (2004). *Evaluation: A systematic approach* (7th ed.). Thousand Oaks, CA: Sage.

Rowan, B., Camburn, E., & Correnti, R. (2004). Using teacher logs to measure the enacted curriculum: A study of literacy teaching in third-grade classrooms. *The Elementary School Journal, 105,* 75–101.

Rowan, B., & Correnti, R. (2009). Studying reading instruction with teacher logs: Lessons from the Study of Instructional Improvement. *Educational Researcher, 28,* 120–131.

Smith, M., Dickinson, D., Sangeorge, A., & Anastasopoulas, L. (2002). *Early Language and Literacy Classroom Observation.* Baltimore: Paul H. Brookes Publishing Co.

14

The Research We Have; The Research We Need

Susan B. Neuman

Emphasis on the need for evidence-based professional development programs has grown from both the research and policy perspectives with the passage of the No Child Left Behind Act of 2001 (PL 107-110) and the Good Start Grow Smart initiatives. As the demands for greater accountability of children's academic performance have intensified, so too have the demands for quality teachers in the early childhood years (Neuman, 2009). Today, early childhood educators are being asked to have deeper knowledge of child development; to provide richer education experiences for children, including those who are especially vulnerable; to engage children of varying abilities, backgrounds, and languages; and to do so with greater accountability than ever before. Together, these needs have placed professional development at the forefront of policy initiatives for improving the overall quality of early childhood experiences and children's academic outcomes (Zaslow & Martinez-Beck, 2006).

Since the late 1990s, knowledge has burgeoned about the key foundational skills children need to enter kindergarten ready to learn academic skills (National Reading Panel, 2000; Snow, Burns, & Griffin, 1998). However, knowledge about how best to prepare teachers to convey these skills is still emerging (Snow, Griffin, & Burns, 2005). Given the enormous attention to professional development, and early education in general, this conclusion highlights what we have learned and suggests further research directions. It also addresses the research from a policy perspective and focuses on the ways in which these principles can be applied to practice.

WHAT WE NOW KNOW

Professional development in early childhood has taken many guises. Professional development can refer to training, continuing education, and workshops, and it can involve many forms, such as classroom training, coaching, and mentoring. Despite its many types and forms, the purpose of professional development is to increase the knowledge base, skill set, and dispositions of teachers already in the field of early childhood, with the understanding that higher quality teaching can improve child outcomes.

The early childhood work force is neither a young nor a well-educated work force. According to one report, the largest age cohort of teachers in the early childhood field is in their late 50s (Herzenberg, Price, & Bradley, 2005). Current population survey data show that teachers in center-based early childhood education are older and have much less education than they once did in the past; further, education levels of those in home-based care have fared even worse. Considering early childhood educators' nontraditional status, therefore, it is not appropriate to apply what we have learned from professional development with K–12 teachers, who have college degrees, credentials, and subject matter expertise.

Drawing from the research described in this book, as well as from extensive reviews of the literature, it is now possible to derive some basic conclusions about what enhances our goals of quality teaching and improved child performance (Bowman, Donovan, & Burns, 2000; Strickland, Snow, Griffin, & Burns, 2002).

Certification and Qualification Are Not Synonymous

With the publication of the consensus report *Eager to Learn* (Bowman et al.) in 2000, policy makers turned to emphasizing education as a strategy for improving quality teaching. One of the policy recommendations in this publication was to encourage early childhood educators to obtain bachelor's degrees and additional specialization. The view was that higher levels of formal education and specialization in early childhood could lead to higher quality interactions with children and overall program improvements.

However, one comprehensive review has shown that having teachers who hold a degree or certification does not predict a quality program (Zaslow & Martinez-Beck, 2006). For example, studies by Early and colleagues have reported little relationship between teachers' level of education and overall classroom quality or child outcomes (Early et al., 2006; Early et al., 2007). In fact, it is unclear what levels of education are required for early childhood teachers and whether there might be a threshold of knowledge that is necessary to improve practice.

Although certification and formal education may not serve as an adequate predictor of observed quality, it still may be an important goal. For example, increased education might improve salaries and concomitantly draw more people and increase the talent pool to the profession (Phillips, Mekos, Scarr, McCartney, & Abbott-Shim, 2000). Nevertheless, the recognition of the weak link between formal education and quality should provide a cautionary note to policy makers: We cannot assume that we will reach our goal of quality teaching through certification or degree programs.

Structured Coursework May Not Lead to Better Practice

As of this writing, 44% of all states offer the Teacher Education and Compensation Helps (**T.E.A.C.H.**) scholarship program, a unique scholarship opportunity that ties increased compensation to the attainment of a prescribed number of credit hours (T.E.A.C.H. Early Wages and Childcare Project, 2008). It is designed to not only improve the competencies of individual teachers but to have an impact on child care programs by addressing staff retention. Recognizing the diverse educational backgrounds of the early childhood work force, it provides a structure for a comprehensive sequence of early childhood professional development opportunities through coursework in community settings and local colleges.

T.E.A.C.H. is a signature program. It gives scholarships, materials, and stipends to teachers who wish to take advantage of professional development. It creates a demand for coursework that builds the capacity of educational institutions in local communities. Nevertheless, several studies have called into question the effectiveness of such coursework on improvements in teacher quality (Koh & Neuman, 2009; Neuman & Cunningham, 2009; Neuman & Wright, in press).

Examining the effects of professional development coursework, my colleagues and I conducted a large-scale study comparing groups that received coursework, coursework plus coaching, or neither coursework nor coaching (comparison group) (Neuman & Cunningham, 2009). In this case, coursework was intensive; teachers participated in 45 hours of coursework plus outside assignments for the course. Still, we found negligible effects for changes in teacher knowledge and practice compared with teachers who had no professional development training. We then conducted a follow-up study with a slightly more educated work force (Neuman & Wright, in press). This time, we compared professional development coursework to coaching and a comparison group. Evidence from this study, as well, showed minimal growth resulting from coursework alone in teacher knowledge and very limited application to language and literacy practices.

To the contrary, however, Dickinson and Caswell (2007), in a small-scale study, reported significant gains in practice resulting from the Literacy Environment Enrichment Program (LEEP), a professional development course. Differences in these findings might be related to the fact that our larger scale intervention was targeted to individual teachers, often isolated in settings, as opposed to Dickinson and Caswell's study in which teachers and supervisors engaged in the professional development together. Furthermore, it may relate to the power relationships between supervisors and teachers and the potential authority that could enable supervisors to mandate changes in teacher classrooms.

Clearly, more research is needed, and once again, we must be careful to not overstate conclusions based on a small body of studies. At the same time, if our goal is targeted to changes in teacher practices, in particular, it suggests that coursework must be augmented with other activities.

Specialized Training Can Improve Teacher Competencies

In contrast to formal education programs, specialized training does appear to improve the competencies of early childhood teachers—under certain conditions (Fukkink & Lont, 2007). All training programs, however, are not equal. In fact, one meta-analysis (Fukkink & Lont) found some can do more harm than good. For example, programs that have no structure or curriculum have limited success. Those with a variety of formats delivered to a wide variety of learners are not particularly effective.

Rather, training programs that are targeted to specific learning outcomes can be effective. Whitehurst and colleagues (1994), for example, demonstrated that engaging early childhood providers in 30 minutes of specialized training in storybook reading could have a significant impact on children's receptive and expressive language and phonological awareness. Similarly, Neuman (1999) found sustainable benefits on teaching practices and child outcomes in a study of 500 child care centers as a result of 10 workshops targeting read-aloud skills. These programs demonstrate that when clear goals are established with opportunities for teachers to practice and review, targeted skills can be refined and improved, leading to improved child performance.

Scaffolding Skills in Context Helps to Improve Practice

To develop strategies and practices, emerging evidence suggests that teachers need ongoing, supportive experiences in field-based settings (Neuman & Cunningham, 2009). In the past, these experiences have typically included practicum activities in laboratory schools that allowed teachers to practice skills in context. In the last several years, a different type of scaffolding has been shown to be effective: coaching and consultation that relates directly to a teacher's individual practice.

Although coaching has long been used in athletic training programs and leadership programs (Nettles, 1993), its application to reading and early childhood teaching is relatively new. Nevertheless, as detailed throughout the chapters in this book, there are promising indications that coaching can lead to improvements in teacher practices. For example, in our studies we found that 8 months of weekly coaching was directly tied to high-quality language and literacy practices in center- and home-based care (Neuman & Cunningham, 2009).

In a subsequent study, we examined some of the critical features that seem to be linked to improved practices (Koh & Neuman, 2009). We found the following features important in a coaching model:

- *On-site:* Successful coaches meet teachers in the teachers' own practice settings to help them learn through modeling and demonstrating practices (Poglinco & Bach, 2004).

- *Balanced and sustained:* Coaches involve teachers in ongoing continuing education rather than just a temporary infusion or a rapid-fire string of professional development activities (Darling-Hammond & McLaughlin, 1999; Guiney, 2001; Speck, 2002).

- *Facilitative of reflection:* Effective coaches observe, listen, and support instructional practices that improve child outcomes; they don't dictate the "right" answer (Guiney, 2001; Harwell-Kee, 1999).

- *Highly interactive:* Coaches establish rapport, build trust, and engender mutual respect among practitioners and interact extensively to benefit children's outcomes (Herll & O'Drobinak, 2004).

- *Corrective feedback:* Coaches provide descriptive, not evaluative or judgmental, feedback based on observable events in settings to enable practitioners to engage in collaborative problem-solving for improving practice (Gallacher, 1997; Schreiber, 1990).

- *Prioritizes:* Coaches assist teachers in identifying priorities and developing action plans for improving children's language and literacy practices (Herll & O'Drobinak, 2004).

Successful programs appear to engage teachers in reflection and goal setting; they help to identify desired outcomes and strategies to achieve these outcomes, they collaboratively develop an action plan for the implementation of new practices, and they evaluate their results. This continuous process of evaluation and review appears to be related to successful interventions.

Web-Based Programs with Additional Support Can Be Effective

Innovations using web-based designs have shown that we can improve teacher quality using cost-effective means (Pianta, Mashburn, Downer, Hamre, & Justice, 2008; Powell, Diamond, & Burchinal, 2009). These approaches demonstrate that the Internet may be an especially effective partner in professional development. However, it cannot do the work alone. Teachers will need ongoing support and feedback in conjunction with these programs to provide successful professional development programs that enhance teacher practices.

Pianta and colleagues (2008), for example, developed a web-based system of professional development, MyTeachingPartner, that included video exemplars and a series of modules on best practices. They compared the effects of the program for teachers who had ongoing consultation and feedback with teachers who only used the web-based program. The results indicated positive effects for teachers who engaged in feedback with a consultant. The positive effects were particularly evident for teachers who worked in classrooms with a higher proportion of at-risk children.

Focusing specifically on language and literacy, Powell and colleagues (2009) compared two professional development approaches: one that involved on-site coaching and one that involved remote coaching for more than 100 teachers. Teachers who received remote coaching relied on feedback from teacher-submitted videotapes of teaching practice (15 minutes in length) plus links to case-based hypermedia resources of nearly 100 exemplars of evidence-based practices. Both interventions showed positive effects on teaching practices and on children's literacy skills that were moderately to strongly predictive of later conventional literacy outcomes (National Early Literacy Panel, 2008). These results suggest that technologically mediated (remote) delivery of professional development can be a promising alternative to in-person (on-site) classroom visits.

Professional developers in early childhood have often been wary of remote online education. There is the belief that teachers need hands-on materials and relational programs to improve practices. However, these studies demonstrate that technology can help to deliver instruction effectively. It cannot substitute for processes of observed practice and individualized feedback, but it can help scale up professional development in ways that may provide greater access to training than ever before.

Mentorship May Overcome Many of the Barriers to Professional Development

Early childhood educators may face even more barriers to professional development than traditional teachers. Costs, schedules, and strategies for accessing professional development, detailed in several chapters in this book, are among the many barriers that may be viewed by the early childhood educator as insurmountable at times.

Mentorship can help. Traditionally used in teacher induction programs, a mentor is a highly respected professional who supports and assists both novice and experienced teachers in their professional growth (Ingersoll & Kralik, 2004). Although sometimes the terms *mentoring* and *coaching* are used simultaneously, there are some subtle differences. A mentor is a leader who helps guide the teacher in the profession. He or she offers support, assistance, and orientation to professional development programs. Coaches, however, may mentor teachers, but their chief role is to help teachers implement new teaching strategies effectively. They are on the ground, working collaboratively with teachers in their setting, whereas the mentor may be more involved in overseeing the entire program of professional development for the educator.

Mentoring usually lasts for 1 year for teachers in elementary and secondary education. Yet in early childhood education, mentorship has taken on a somewhat different role and may continue for several years. For example, in Michigan, mentors in the T.E.A.C.H. program help to design professional development programs for teachers, provide information on scholarship opportunities, assist in enrolling teachers in coursework at community colleges, and work to ensure that the teachers' program articulates well to a 4-year institution. At each stage, they work to support teachers and their professional opportunities through conferences, organizations, and graduate courses. Similarly, as reported in Chapter 8, college mentors have been vital in helping students plan and carry out their professional program.

Although there is anecdotal information indicating the benefits of mentoring, especially for nontraditional students, there are no definitive studies to date on its efficacy for early childhood educators. However, studies that have examined teacher quality in K–12 schools have shown that mentoring increases the retention rate of teachers (Gallacher, 1997; Ingersoll & Kralik, 2004). Still, researchers are trying to understand the mechanisms for why these programs are effective. For example, questions arise regarding the intensity, duration, and selection of mentors, as well as the relation of mentoring to child outcomes and achievement.

Researchers do know, however, that retention in teaching is related to stability of programs. In addition, keeping teachers involved in professional development throughout their careers appears to improve their sense of professionalism and the quality of their program. Mentorship can cut down on many of the barriers that are unique to the early childhood educator and should be considered as an essential component of a professional development program.

Curriculum Aligned with Training Enhances the Intensity of Professional Development

Studies suggest that training and curricular improvements often go hand in hand. For example, the Preschool Curriculum Evaluation Research grant program, funded out of the Institute for Education Sciences, was designed to align training with curriculum programs (Preschool Curriculum Evaluation Consortium, 2008). The underlying logic model was that quality training plus curriculum supports could lead to greater intensity of treatment to preschoolers and, consequently, improved child outcomes. Although these studies were designed to examine the efficacy of various curricula, the projects illuminated both the importance and the process of professional development. These reports suggest that teacher training and ongoing support help to improve the implementation of curricula and that such training and support is often associated with improvements in teacher behavioral and instructional practice as well as enhanced child outcomes (Caswell, 2008).

The Head Start REDI program, for example, was designed to make the integration of research-based practices easier by providing teachers with a manualized enrichment curriculum and specific instructional strategy training arranged to support a scope and sequence of social-emotional and language and literacy skills (Bierman et al., 2008). Their findings indicated that the combination of training practices and research-based instructional strategies improved children's cognitive and social-emotional school readiness.

More broadly, the Bierman study and several others (e.g., Lonigan, Farver, Clancy-Menchetti, & Phillips, 2005) have suggested that a curriculum may provide teachers with more intentional guidance for teaching. Together, professional development and a curriculum may help teachers understand both "what" to teach and "why" to use certain teaching methods, in a way that is better coordinated with child outcomes. Given the limited number of hours in a day, this dual focus integrated in an intervention model may effectively and simultaneously promote gains in teacher knowledge, teacher practice, and child outcomes.

Professional Development Programs Need to Address Teachers' Beliefs and Dispositions to Be Effective

Research suggests that teachers' positive perceptions of professional development, specifically its potential effectiveness and appropriateness for the needs of their children, are important precursors of effective program implementation (Domitrovich, Gest, Gill, Jones, & DeRousie, 2009). Teachers are more likely to participate in a professional development program if it is congruent with their beliefs and fits well with their personal teaching style. In contrast, teachers who do not see the value of fostering particular skills may be more likely to ignore or modify their instructional practices. Furthermore, when professional development is perceived as being easy to understand, with jargon-free language, it is implemented more effectively.

In our studies (Neuman & Wright, in press), teachers often chaffed at the theoretical nature of their professional development training. They wanted to learn what to do, rather than just why to do it. Difficult names and new terms were often seen as barriers to learning. Teachers wanted information that was more centrally tied to practice. They wanted to be challenged, but at the same time, they wanted to feel successful in making a positive impact in their classroom or home-based care settings.

Professional Development Programs Must Be Held Accountable

The goal of any professional development program, regardless of its form or process, must be to improve teacher quality as a means to improve child outcomes—nothing less will do. Therefore, every program needs to put in place a method to hold itself accountable.

Accountability, of course, can take many forms. It also can take place during many phases of the program. For example, Hawkins and colleagues (see Chapter 9) began their program with a needs assessment to determine teachers' prior knowledge, strengths, and weaknesses. Similarly, my colleague and I (Neuman & Dwyer, 2006) developed a Teacher Knowledge Assessment to measure prior knowledge of language and literacy before professional development. We then used a different form to assess the effects of professional development coursework on changes in teacher knowledge of language and literacy development.

Similarly, throughout this book, researchers have developed accountability strategies for purposes of progress monitoring. Warren and colleagues (see Chapter 12), for example, developed strategy checklists to determine whether teachers were engaged in research-based activities as a result of the professional development training. These checklists provided a transparent means for teachers to examine their ongoing practices. It also provided a method for trainers to determine whether they were successful in conveying these strategies and allowed them to adjust their strategies to better meet teachers' needs.

Peterson and Valk (see Chapter 3) adapted the Transtheoretical Model to understand teacher belief systems and to better tailor services to participants' stage of change (precontemplation, contemplation, preparation, action, maintenance). This instrument provided feedback to trainers on teachers' ability to change; this, in turn, could help trainers to better frame their professional development. The goal was to use this information in order to enhance the acceptability of research-based practices in order to have a positive impact on children's achievement.

In our studies, we approach accountability at every stage and in multiple directions. For example, as Wright describes in Chapter 13, even in large-scale intervention, it is possible to hold coaches accountable for their activities. Our coaching logs permitted real-time accountability of coaches' activities and follow-up recommendations. At the same time, however, coaches also held teachers accountable. In their weekly visits, coaches reviewed previous recommendations with teachers to determine the degree to which they had implemented changes. Teachers anecdotally reported that they often felt on call to make the changes discussed the previous week. As one teachers articulated, "If you have a one-to-one relationships with someone, you don't want to disappoint them. So whether or not you like it, you do the work." In addition, the weekly goal setting appeared to help teachers focus on particular practices. By establishing priorities, the changes that were recommended could be more attainable.

Accountability provides a critical road map (Neuman, 2009): It helps us to understand where teachers are; it assesses along the way the effects of professional development programs; and it allows for mid-course corrections in programs, when necessary, so they can be more effective. It also ensures that we maintain our focus. Although the effects of professional development may be indirect, affecting quality practices in classrooms, ultimately our road map must lead to enhancing child outcomes. Accountability allows us to see whether or to what extent we have achieved our goal.

These principles, articulated throughout the chapters in this book, highlight the fact that there is a growing body of research-based knowledge that policy makers and practitioners may use to improve program quality. We now have an abundance of evidence to suggest that high-quality professional development can lead to improved practices in multiple care settings, which can improve children's outcomes. Furthermore, these projects have illuminated the processes and forms that are most directly related to outcomes. Together, this research has demonstrated that when teachers devote a high level of dedication and energy to professional development, greater benefits in quality practices and overall children's achievement are likely to occur.

Still, further research is needed to evaluate the relative contributions of professional development in early childhood. Specifically, we need more empirical evidence to determine what works, for whom, within which contexts, and at what cost. If we are to establish a scientific base for early childhood professional development, there are vital questions that must be addressed to enhance evidence-based exemplars for best practice.

THE RESEARCH WE NEED

Research in early childhood professional development must go beyond basic questions of teacher characteristics, credentials, experience, and their associations with practice (Sheridan, Edwards, Marvin, & Knoche, 2009). Rather, if we are to establish professional development as a scientific endeavor, we need to address the following questions of critical relevance to both policy makers and practitioners who are designing programs to serve teachers in the current era of service expansion and accountability.

What Combination of Strategies Yield the Greatest Impact?

Different components of training are known to support different types of outcomes (Joyce & Showers, 2002). Nevertheless, most projects use multiple professional development opportunities (e.g., workshops, coaching, individual group reflections) as integral parts of a single training package. Although the bundling of strategies might be useful as a professional development package, it has thwarted our efforts to understand what particular strategy might be most powerful for what purpose.

We need studies to disentangle some of these strategies. Comparisons of the effects of individual training strategies could lead to a better understanding of how each component works. This information could then lead to a better understanding of how different components of training might work together to benefit the needs of their audience.

What Are the Best Measurement Tools?

Most professional development programs have relied on environmental measures to examine changes in teacher practice. These measures typically look at the structural features of the environment (e.g., number of books) and their availability, the schedule, and other physical environmental features that have been shown to be adequate in predicting quality practices. The Environmental Language and Literacy Classroom Observation Tool (ELLCO) Pre-K (Smith, Brady, &

Anastasopoulos, 2008) and the Early Childhood Environmental Rating Scale, Revised Edition (ECERS-R; Harms, Clifford, & Cryer, 2004) are examples of the most common measures used to examine the quality of the language and literacy environment and overall quality of environment, respectively.

Neither of these measures, however, is sensitive to the critical processes of teaching or qualitative changes in instructional practices that are most predictive of child outcomes. These changes include teacher–child interactions, increases in the quality of language and reasoning abilities, and the activities that support higher quality thinking. Recognizing the importance of these factors, we need additional measures that can detect the more subtle changes in the features of quality instruction that may become more pronounced over time.

What Are the Threshold Levels of Implementation, Fidelity, and Dosage?

Chapters throughout this book have highlighted the importance of quality implementation and fidelity for achieving positive outcomes. These studies have demonstrated that dosage (i.e., the intensity of treatment) matters and that treatments that are diluted often fail to achieve results.

Nevertheless, as Halle and colleagues (see Chapter 11) correctly point out, not all participants necessarily need the same dosage of professional development at the same time. Yet, to date, most professional development programs provide a similar dosage of treatment to all participants, regardless of their backgrounds and previous expertise.

To better calibrate the needs of participants, Hawkins and colleagues (Chapter 9) have argued for better needs assessments. Such measures could help us identify the most critical elements of an effective program and could also provide a better sense of how much professional development activity is needed to achieve desired results. Along with other measurements, this information could potentially represent significant cost savings and help to differentiate instruction to better meet teachers' needs.

What Are the Functional and Effective Behaviors Used by Trainers, Coaches, and Mentors?

Many chapters throughout this book have highlighted the importance of the relational factors among trainers, coaches, mentors, and teachers. Participants in professional development programs who feel respected and supported by trainers appear more likely to implement quality practices. Research on coaching has suggested that these relational components, as well as competency, objectivity, adaptability, and a well-developed knowledge base, are important characteristics of an effective coach (Sheridan et al., 2009). Most of the information, however, is anecdotal and has not been systematically justified beyond teacher reports.

Research is needed to determine more specifically the characteristics of effective coaches. Furthermore, we need to know what activities or strategies effective coaches use that appear to result in the positive changes. In addition, dosage remains an issue. Given that coaching tends to be an individual one-to-one approach to professional development and, therefore, likely to be more costly than other techniques, we need to better understand how much time and effort may be necessary to reach the goal of improving practice.

What Workplace Characteristics Influence Professional Development?

Most research to date has focused on the individual teacher—his or her knowledge development, changes in practice, and subsequent achievement changes in classrooms. Nevertheless, rarely have workplace characteristics and their potential influences on change been examined in the literature on professional development.

In our studies (Neuman & Cunningham, 2009; Neuman & Wright, in press), for example, we found that classroom aides who wished to become prospective teachers often did not have the authority to make changes in the environment. Although in some cases aides and assistant teachers would jointly participate in professional development, acting as a team, in other cases, there was more of a hierarchy of decision making that would sometimes thwart efforts to make change. In addition, many schools had very limited budgets and could not even supply the very basic materials such as books for programs.

Clearly, research is needed to examine the institutional constraints and supports that enable teachers to take advantage of what they have learned through professional development. For example, Dickinson and Caswell (2007) found that administrator support and participation in professional development was key to ensuring that research-based methods were used in practice. In addition, some schools have particularly benefited by establishing *communities of practice,* or working groups that continue to study and examine their own practices as a strategy for supporting individuals and strategies internal to the organization responsible for practice.

The benefits of professional development may be mediated by workplace characteristics. Further research is needed to explore how characteristics such as administrative organization, program auspices, and other institutional factors may moderate or potentially intensify the effects of professional development.

How Sustainable Is Professional Development?

The sustainability of professional development is a topic of great interest among policy makers and practitioners. To date, however, research has generally followed the trajectory of improvements in practice by looking at gains immediately following professional development. Rarely have researchers measured change over time. Nevertheless, the maintenance of skills beyond immediate training and initial supports is critical to enhancing quality in early childhood.

If these changes are sustained, professional development could be a highly efficient mechanism to improve children's achievement. After all, changes in practice may influence one year and one classroom but may extend to subsequent years and classrooms. However, if professional development only provides immediate gains without longer term sustainability, then it may not be a cost-efficient strategy to improve children's achievement.

Therefore, we need studies that examine the affect of professional development over time. Such studies could provide vital information on the real costs of professional development. Studying the cost-benefit ratio of professional development, particularly in the field of early childhood in which turnover has been high, is essential to determine its overall capacity to improve the quality of early childhood programs.

Can Professional Development Attract New Teachers to the Field?

Most studies have focused on the professional development needs of teachers who are currently in the field (Zaslow & Martinez-Beck, 2006). Research has not addressed questions related to new entrants to the world of early childhood. However, a program of professional development could potentially help recruit a new work force, one that sees early childhood education as a vital profession that involves continuous learning and continuous challenge. We need studies to investigate how or if professional development has the capacity to attract and retain teachers, potentially addressing the career pipeline for those who enter and want to stay in the early childhood field.

The early childhood field attracts many but keeps few; turnover in the teaching profession is problematic generally, but for early childhood it has been devastating. It often robbed the field of a knowledge base that could be used to build a more solid foundation of research and practice. Studies are needed to determine if professional development in any way can stem this tide.

WHERE WE NOW STAND

The field of early childhood education is on the radar of policy makers and practitioners. It is enjoying more prestige and recognition as a vital part of children's early education than ever before. Today, there is a proliferation of strategies and efforts to help teachers develop quality early childhood practices. Professional development is available in many different forms and uses many different training models.

We have made significant progress in the past few years identifying some of the mechanisms that can improve teacher quality. We now know that professional development can produce benefits in teacher behavior. We know that teachers who receive significant dosages of training can improve their classroom instructional practices. We also know that teacher quality can have an impact on child outcomes, ranging from academic achievement to social-emotional development.

But we still have much to learn. Research is needed to determine the most efficient and effective means for promoting changes in teachers' knowledge skills and dispositions. We need to better understand how to alter hard-to-change practices. We also need to understand institutional supports and how they help or thwart innovative practices. Exploring these and other factors in future research can help elucidate the potential effects of professional development efforts with greater precision to better ensure evidence-based practice.

REFERENCES

Bierman, K., Domitrovich, C., Nix, R., Gest, S., Welsh, J., Greenberg, M., et al. (2008). Promoting academic and social-emotional school readiness: The Head Start REDI program. *Child Development, 79,* 1802–1817.

Bowman, B., Donovan, S., & Burns, M.S. (2000). *Eager to learn: Educating our preschoolers.* Washington DC: National Academies Press.

Caswell, L. (2008). *Promoting children's early language and literacy development in the contexts of early intervention and care: A review of the importance of federally-funded research initiatives on young children's school readiness.* Washington, DC: Health and Human Services.

Darling-Hammond, L., & McLaughlin, M. (1999). Investing in teaching as a learning profession. In L. Darling-Hammond & G. Sykes (Eds.), *Teaching and the learning profession* (pp. 120–145). San Francisco: Jossey Bass.

Dickinson, D., & Caswell, L. (2007). Building support for language and early literacy in preschool classrooms through in-service professional development: Effects of the Literacy Environment Enrichment Program (LEEP). *Early Childhood Research Quarterly, 22,* 243–260.

Domitrovich, C., Gest, S., Gill, S., Jones, D., & DeRousie, R. (2009). Individual factors associated with professional development training outcomes of the Head Start REDI program. *Early Education and Development, 20,* 402–430.

Early, D., Bryant, D., Pianta, R., Clifford, R., Burchinal, M., Ritchie, S., et al. (2006). Are teachers' education, major and credentials related to classroom quality and children's academic gains in pre-kindergarten? *Early Childhood Research Quarterly, 21,* 174–195.

Early, D., Maxwell, K., Burchinal, M., Alva, S., Bender, R., Bryant, D., et al. (2007). Teachers' education, classroom quality, and young children's academic skills: Results from seven studies of preschool programs. *Child Development, 78,* 558–580.

Fukkink, R., & Lont, A. (2007). Does training matter? A meta-analysis and review of caregiver training studies. *Early Childhood Research Quarterly, 22,* 294–311.

Gallacher, K. (1997). Supervision, mentoring and coaching. In W.P.J. McCollum & C. Catlett (Eds.), *Reforming personnel in early intervention* (pp. 191–214). Baltimore: Paul H. Brookes Publishing Co.

Guiney, E. (2001). Coaching isn't just for athletes: The role of teacher leaders. *Phi Delta Kappan, 82,* 740–743.

Harms, T., Clifford, R., & Cryer, D. (2004). *Early Childhood Environment Rating Scale–Revised Edition (ECERS-R)*. New York: Teachers College Press.

Harwell-Kee, K. (1999). Coaching. *Journal of Staff Development, 20*(3), 28–29.

Herll, S., & O'Drobinak, B. (2004). Role of a coach: Dream keeper, supporter, friend. *Journal of Staff Development, 25*(2), 42–46.

Herzenberg, S., Price, M., & Bradley, D. (2005). *Losing ground in early childhood education*. Washington, DC: Economic Policy Institute.

Ingersoll, R., & Kralik, J. (2004). *The impact of mentoring on teacher retention: What the research says*. Denver, CO: Education Commission of the States.

Joyce, B., & Showers, B. (2002). *Student achievement through staff development* (3rd ed.). Alexandra, VA: Association for Supervision and Curriculum Development.

Koh, S., & Neuman, S.B. (2009). The impact of professional development on family child care: A practice-based approach. *Early Education and Development, 20*(3), 537–562.

Lonigan, C., Farver, J., Clancy-Menchetti, J., & Phillips, B. (2005). *Promoting the development of preschool children's emergent literacy skills: A randomized evaluation of a literacy-focused curriculum and two professional development models*. Atlanta, GA.: Society for Research on Child Development.

National Early Literacy Panel. (2008). *Developing early literacy*. Washington, DC: National Institute for Literacy.

National Reading Panel. (2000). *Teaching children to read*. Washington, DC: National Institute of Child Health and Development.

Nettles, S.M. (1993). Coaching in community settings. *Equity and Choice, 9*, 35–37.

Neuman, S.B. (1999). Books make a difference: A study of access to literacy. *Reading Research Quarterly, 34*, 286–312.

Neuman, S.B. (2009). *Changing the odds for children at risk: Seven essential principles of educational programs that break the cycle of poverty*. Westport, CT: Praeger.

Neuman, S.B., & Cunningham, L. (2009). The impact of professional development and coaching on early language and literacy instructional practices. *American Educational Research Journal, 46*(2), 532–566.

Neuman, S.B., & Dwyer, J. (2006). *The teacher knowledge assessment of language and literacy*. Ann Arbor: University of Michigan.

Neuman, S.B., & Wright, T. (in press). Promoting language and literacy development for early childhood educators: A mixed-methods study of coursework and coaching. *Elementary School Journal*.

No Child Left Behind Act of 2001, PL 107-110, 115 Stat. 1425, 20 U.S.C. §§ 6301 *et seq.*

Phillips, D., Mekos, D., Scarr, S., McCartney, K., & Abbott-Shim, M. (2000). Within and beyond the classroom door: Assessing quality in child care centers. *Early Childhood Research Quarterly, 15*, 281–303.

Pianta, R., Mashburn, A., Downer, J., Hamre, B., & Justice, L. (2008). Effects of web-mediated professional development resources on teacher-child interactions in prekindergarten classrooms. *Early Childhood Research Quarterly, 23*, 431–451.

Poglinco, S., & Bach, S. (2004). The heart of the matter: Coaching as a vehicle for professional development. *Phi Delta Kappan, 85*(5), 398–402.

Powell, D., Diamond, K., & Burchinal, M. (2009). *Effects of a professional development intervention on teaching processes and child language and literacy outcomes*. Paper presented at the Society for Research on Child Development, Denver, CO.

Preschool Curriculum Evaluation Consortium. (2008). *Effects of preschool curriculum programs on school readiness.* Washington, DC: U.S. Department of Education, Institute of Education Sciences.

Schreiber, B. (1990). Colleague to colleague: Peer coaching for effective in-house training. *Education Libraries, 15*(1–2), 30–35.

Sheridan, S., Edwards, C., Marvin, C., & Knoche, L. (2009). Professional development in early childhood programs: Process issues and research needs. *Early Education and Development, 20*(3), 377–401.

Smith, M.W., Brady, J.P., & Anastasopoulos, L. (2008). *Early Language and Literacy Classroom Observation Tool (ELLCO) Pre-K.* Baltimore: Paul H. Brookes Publishing Co.

Smith, M.W., Brady, J.P., & Clark-Chiarelli, N. (2008). *Early Language and Literacy Classroom Observation Tool (ELLCO) K–3, Research Edition.* Baltimore: Paul H. Brookes Publishing Co.

Snow, C., Burns, M.S., & Griffin, P. (1998). *Preventing reading difficulties in young children.* Washington, DC: National Academies Press.

Snow, C., Griffin, P., & Burns, S. (Eds.). (2005). *Knowledge to support the teaching of reading.* San Francisco: John Wiley.

Speck, M. (2002). Balanced and year-round professional development: Time and learning. *Catalyst for Change, 32,* 17–19.

Strickland, D., Snow, C., Griffin, P., & Burns, M.S. (2002). *Preparing our teachers: Opportunities for better reading instruction.* Washington, DC: John Henry Press.

T.E.A.C.H. Early Wages and Child Care Project. (2008). *Annual report.* Chapel Hill, NC: Child Care Services Association.

Whitehurst, G., Arnold, D., Epstein, J., Angell, A., Smith, M., & Fischel, J. (1994). A picture book reading intervention in day care and home for children from low-income families. *Developmental Psychology, 30,* 679–689.

Zaslow, M., & Martinez-Beck, I. (Eds.). (2006). *Critical issues in early childhood professional development.* Baltimore: Paul H. Brookes Publishing Co.

Glossary

alphabetic principle Knowledge of the alphabetic principle is awareness that written words are composed of letters that are intentionally and conventionally related to phonemic segments of the words of oral language.

at-risk A characteristic of the child's home, family, or community that is associated with low achievement. The three risk factors that are most frequently reported are poverty, mother's education, and mother's native language (if other than English).

CDA Child development associate credential indicating that an individual has successfully completed several early childhood courses and an assessment process. It identifies the individual as a qualified trained child care provider able to meet the specific needs of children, as well as work with parents or other adults to nurture children in various aspects of child development.

CHELLO The Child/Home Early Language and Literacy Observation (Neuman, Dwyer, & Koh, 2007) is an observational tool designed to examine the quality of an early language/literacy environment in home-based child care settings.

CLASS™ The Classroom Assessment Scoring System™ (Pianta, La Paro, & Hamre, 2008) is a formative assessment measure of teaching quality in preschool through third-grade classrooms. It measures emotional support, classroom organization, and instructional support.

coach/coaching Coaches provide technical support to develop specific job-related skills. A coach, for example, often uses observation, data collection, reflective questioning, and nonjudgmental feedback to help teachers develop specific strategies for improving quality instruction and set goals for children's achievement.

comprehension Understanding of the meaning of text and stories.

Child Observation Record (COR) COR (HighScope, 2000) is an observational assessment tool for preschool children (ages 2.5–6 years), designed to measure the progress of children in early childhood programs by looking at 32 dimensions of learning.

developmentally appropriate practice A framework of guidelines and principles for best practice in the education and care of young children (ages birth through 8 years), which is based on how young children develop and learn.

dialect   A regional or social variety of a language distinguished by pronunciation, grammar, or vocabulary, especially a variety of speech differing from Standard American English.

dialogic reading   An interactive and shared picture book reading practice used to promote the language and literacy skills of young children.

Early Reading First   Federal grant targeted to improving instruction in the preschool years. It provides funding to local education agencies as well as to public and private organizations serving children from low-income families and is designed to help prepare children for success in learning to read.

ECERS   The Early Childhood Environmental Rating Scale (Harms, Clifford, & Cryer, 2005) is an assessment tool used to examine the quality of the early childhood environments or group programs for young children (ages 2.5–5 years) using a 43-item scale.

ELLCO   The Early Language and Literacy Classroom Observation Tool Pre-K (Smith, Brady, & Anastasopoulos, 2008) and K–3, Research Edition (Smith, Brady, & Clark-Chiarelli, 2008), is designed to measure the quality of the language and literacy environment for pre-K to third-grade classrooms. It includes a classroom observation to gather information about five subscales (classroom structure, curriculum, the language environment, books and book reading opportunities, and print and early writing supports) and a teacher interview.

ELSA   The Early Literacy Skills Assessment (HighScope, 2004) is used to measure progress in four key areas: comprehension, phonological awareness, alphabetic principle, and concepts of print. The assessment is in the form of a children's storybook.

emergent literacy   A range of activities and behaviors related to written language—including pretend reading, play, invented spelling, 'driting (drawing and writing)—that changes over time and culminates in conventional literacy skills in middle childhood.

expressive language   Accuracy and fluency in producing language.

FDCRS   The Family Day Care Rating Scale (Harms, Cryer, & Clifford, 2007) assesses the quality of family day care with a 32-item scale covering six categories.

fidelity of implementation   The extent to which a program is implemented as intended and operated up to the standards established for it.

funds of knowledge   Family background knowledge and experiences that may contribute to working with young children and their families.

Good Start, Grow Smart   An initiative introduced by the Bush Administration in 2002 to enhance the development of preschool early learning standards and professional development to support quality instruction.

Head Start A federally funded early childhood program that provides comprehensive services and support to young low-income children and their families in the areas of education, nutrition, health, and parental involvement.

instructional specialists Instructional specialists have similar roles as coaches in early childhood settings. They work individually with early childhood educators in their own setting to enhance the continuity between training and practice.

intervention A supplementary program designed to address an identified or anticipated problem. Often described as a "treatment," an intervention may propose a different professional development model in contrast to "business-as-usual."

ITERS-R The Infant/Toddler Environment Rating Scale–Revised (Harms, Cryer, & Clifford, 2003) is an assessment instrument designed to examine the quality of programs for very young children (ages birth through 2½ years).

literacy Reading, writing, and the creative and analytical skills involved in decoding and understanding texts.

mentor/mentoring A mentor is both a tutor and a guide who strives to integrate and extend the teaching techniques of her or his protégé. The mentor often facilitates learning opportunities for someone new to the field or returning for additional learning. In many cases, mentors will guide their colleagues throughout their educational or professional development program.

nontraditional learners Students who tend to be older with limited previous education.

OMLIT The Observation Measure of Language and Literacy Instruction (Goodson, Layer, Smith, & Rimdzius, 2006) is designed to measure the quality of the environment and instruction and consists of five instruments: the Classroom Literacy Opportunities Checklist, the Snapshot of Classroom Activities, the Read Aloud Profile, the Classroom Literacy Instruction Profile, and the Quality of Instruction in Language and Literacy.

PALS Phonological Awareness Literacy Screening (Invernizzi, Sullivan, Meier, & Swank, 2004) is an assessment tool useful for measuring the fundamental components of literacy for preschoolers and older children; it can be used as a screening, diagnostic, and progress monitoring tool.

phonological awareness The understanding that spoken language can be broken into smaller components and manipulated; the awareness of the sound structure/phonological structure of a spoken word.

PPVT-III The Peabody Picture Vocabulary Test–III (Dunn & Dunn, 1997) is a nationally standardized assessment tool commonly used to measure receptive verbal ability in Standard American English vocabulary for a variety of age levels (ages 2–90 years).

providers   Individuals who provide care for children in a variety of settings, such as home-based child care settings, center/school/institutional settings, and public and/or private settings.

receptive language   Ability to understand spoken language.

school readiness   Skills associated with successful entry to formal school instruction.

syllable   A unit of spoken language. In English, a syllable can consist of a vowel sound alone or a vowel sound with one or more consonant sounds preceding and following.

syntax   The aspects of language structure related to the ways in which words are put together to form phrases, clauses, and sentences.

TEACH   A scholarship opportunity that ties increased compensation to the attainment of a prescribed number of credit hours. It is designed to not only improve the competencies of individual teachers but also to have an impact on child care programs by addressing the retention of staff in programs.

TEMA   The Test of Early Mathematics Ability (Ginsberg & Baroody, 2003) is an assessment instrument used to measure the mathematic performance of young children (ages 3–8 years). It can be used as a diagnostic instrument or a norm-referenced measure.

TERA-3   The Test of Early Reading Ability-3 (Reid, Hresko, & Hammill, 2001) is an assessment measure used to examine the early reading ability of young children (ages 3–8 years).

trainers   Individuals who provide professional development to those working in the field of early childhood education.

REFERENCES

Dunn, L.M., & Dunn, L.M. (1997). *Peabody Picture Vocabulary Test-III.* Circle Pines, MN: American Guidance Service.

Ginsberg, H., & Baroody, A. (2003). *Test of Early Mathematics Ability.* Austin, TX: PRO-ED.

Goodson, B., Layer, C.J., Smith, W., & Rimdzius, T. (2006). *Observation Measures of Language and Literacy Instruction in Early Childhood (OMLIT).* Cambridge, MA: Abt Associates.

Harms, T., Clifford, R., & Cryer, D. (2005). *Early Childhood Environmental Rating Scale–Revised.* New York: Teachers College Press.

Harms, T., Cryer, D., & Clifford, R. (2003). *Infant/Toddler Environmental Rating Scale–Revised.* New York: Teachers College Press.

Harms, T., Cryer, D., & Clifford, R. (2007). *Family Day Care Rating Scale–Revised.* New York: Teachers College Press.

High/Scope Educational Research Foundation. (2004.). *Early Literacy Skills Assessment (ELSA)*. Ypsilann, MI: Author.

High/Scope Educational Foundation. (2000). *Child Observation Record*. Ypsilanti, MI: Author.

Invernizzi, M., Sullivan, A., Meier, J., & Swank, L. (2004). *Phonological Awareness Literacy Screening PreK (PALS-PreK)*. Charlottesville: University of Virginia.

Neuman, S.B., Dwyer, J., & Koh, S. (2007). *Child/Home Environmental Language and Literacy Observation*. Baltimore: Paul H. Brookes Publishing Co.

Pianta, R., La Paro, K., & Hamre, B. (2008). *Classroom Assessment Scoring System™ (CLASS™)*. Baltimore: Paul H. Brookes Publishing Co.

Reid, D., Hresko, W., & Hammill, D. (2001). *Test of Early Reading Ability-3*. Austin, TX: PRO-ED.

Smith, M.W., Brady, J.P., & Anastasopoulos, L. (2008). *Early Language and Literacy Classroom Observation Tool (ELLCO) Pre-K*. Baltimore: Paul H. Brookes Publishing Co.

Smith, M.W., Brady, J.P., & Clark-Chiarelli, N. (2008). *Early Language and Literacy Classroom Observation Tool (ELLCO) K–3, Research Edition*. Baltimore: Paul H. Brookes Publishing Co.

Index

Information in figures and tables is indicated by *f* and *t*, respectively.

Academic language, 55
Accountability, 228–230
Action, in participatory action research, 124, 126
Action stage, 58*t*–59*t*
Administrator engagement, 160
Administrator mentorship, 166–167
Administrator support, 166
Adult learners, 25–26
Advocacy, in professions, 68
Age
  of children, 164
  of teachers, 163–164
Agenda building, mentorship and, 111
Alignment, 12–13
Alphabet knowledge, 5
Assessment
  content driven by, 77–79
  currently available, 191–192
  in early education, 9–10
  formative, 10
  need for new, 192–193
  research-based professional development content and, 73
Attachment relationships, 49

Balance, in coaching, 224–225
Barriers
  to college education, 139–144
  dispositional, 140
  institutional, 140
  mentorship and, 226–227
  overcoming, 141–144
  situational, 140
Behavior, professional development and, 31–32
Bonding social capital, 124, 127–128
Bridging social capital, 124, 128–129
BUILDING BLOCKS for Literacy, 92

C3 project, 156–159
California Early Childhood Mentor Program, 107, 109, 110

Capital
  human, 20–23
  social, 20–23, 124, 127–129
Caregivers, *see* Teachers and caregivers
CDA, *see* Child Development Associate degree
Certification, qualification and, 222
Challenges, in professional development, 51–53
Challenging Teachers Institute, 115
Change
  as cyclical, 131–132
  mentorship and, 57–59, 58*t*–59*t*
  readiness for, 183
  transtheoretical model of, 111–113
  willingness to, 183
CHELLO, *see* Child/Home Early Language and Literacy Observation
Child care, *see* Early education and care
Child Care Development Block Grant, 107
Child Care Employee Project, 107
Child Care Resource and Referral Agency, 125
Child development, as competency, 69–70
Child Development Associate (CDA) degree, 24, 51, 109
Child/Home Early Language and Literacy Observation (CHELLO), 193, 211
Children's Institute, 53
Classroom Assessment Scoring System (CLASS), 191–192
Closure phase, of mentorship, 56
Coaching
  balance, 224–225
  as bridge, 90–91
  collegial, 153
  consultation model of, 79
  content and, 79–81
  corrective feedback in, 225
  data-driven, 79
  definition of, 88–89
  diagnostic/prescriptive model for, 88

Coaching—*(continued)*
  directive, 88, 153
  in Early SUCCESS program, 94–95
  effectiveness of, 10
  further questions on, 100
  mentoring vs., 106
  one-to-one, 153
  on-site, 153
  performance and, 92–100
  prioritization in, 225
  in Project REEL, 95–97
  reflective, 88
  role of, 10–11
  scaffolding and, 224–225
  state of knowledge on, 89–92
  sustained, 224–225
Collaboration, 124, 136
Collegial coaching, 153
Committee on Early Childhood
      Pedagogy, 138
Community colleges
  assumptions about, 139–140
  barriers to education at, 139–144
  community in, 143
  content knowledge and, 144
  dispositional barriers in, 140
  distance learning at, 142
  enrollment in, 139
  faculty in, 143–144
  impact of, on teacher knowledge and
      practice, 138
  institutional barriers in, 140
  mentoring and, 142–143
  nontraditional students in, 139
  overcoming barriers in, 141–144
  overview of, 137
  professionalization and, 145–147
  questions on, 138
  situational barriers in, 140
  student backgrounds in, 139
Community of learners, 167–168
Competencies, 69–70, 224
Compliance, 68–70, 71*f,* 176, 182–183
Consultation model, of coaching, 79
Contemplation stage, 58*t*
Content
  assessment driving, 77–79
  coaching and, 79–81
  increasing knowledge, 142
  research-based, 68–70, 72–73
  sources, 72–73
  standards driving, 74–77

Corrective feedback, 225
Coursework, 24–25
Creative Curriculum for Preschool Imple-
      mentation Checklist, 79
Cultural connection, 164
Cultural mismatch, 52–53
Cultural traditions, 55
Culturally responsive strategies, 55–56
Curricula
  comprehensive, 32–35
  professional development and, 70, 71*f*
  training aligned with, 227–228

Data-driven coaching, 79
Degree programs, *see* Child Development
      Associate (CDA) degree; Com-
      munity colleges
Diagnostic/prescriptive model, for coach-
      ing, 88
Dialogic reading, 154
Directive coaching, 88, 153
Director support, 166
Dispositions, 140, 228
Distance learning, 142
Diversity
  in age, 163–164
  in educational attainment, 164
  of settings, 164
Dosage
  content and, 39
  definition of, 175–176
  of professional development, 11–12
  threshold, 231

Early Childhood Direction Initiative, 125
Early Childhood Educator Professional
      Development (ECEPD), 13–14,
      53–54, 115, 123, 208
Early Childhood Environment Rating
      Scale (ECERS), 95, 132, 229
Early Childhood Professional Development
      program, 165–170
Early education and care
  assessment in, 9–10
  changes in, 137–138
  curricula, 32–35
  importance of, 2
  literacy instruction in, 3–5
  research, 2, 3*t*
  socioeconomic status and, 2

strengthening overall quality of, 32–37, 33*t*, 34*t*

Early Education Partnership (EEP), 138, 139–147

Early Language and Literacy Classroom Observation (ELLCO), 130, 191–192, 193, 211, 231

Early Language and Literacy Classroom Observation Tool Pre-K (ELLCO Pre-K), 77, 97, 114

Early Literacy Skills Assessment (ELSA), 169

Early Reading First, 2, 109, 115

Early SUCCESS, 94–95, 97–100, 193–200

ECEPD, *see* Early Childhood Educator Professional Development

ECERS, *see* Early Childhood Environment Rating Scale

Education, *see* Early education and care

Educational attainment
diversity of, 164
of teachers, 22

EEP, *see* Early Education Partnership

ELLCO, *see* Early Language and Literacy Classroom Observation

ELLCO Pre-K, *see* Early Language and Literacy Classroom Observation Tool Pre-K

ELSA, *see* Early Literacy Skills Assessment

Emotional development, professional development specific to, 31–32

Enabling phase, of mentorship, 56

Engagement, 182–183

Evaluation
alignment in, 12–13
currently available, 191–192
detailed analysis in, 190
fidelity in, 12
global measures and, 189–190
policy and, 12
satisfaction-based, 189

Evidence-based programs, benefits of, 123

Excellence Boys Charter School, 152

Experimental research, 123

Expert trainers, 154

Facilitation, mentoring and, 110

Faculty, responsive interaction with, 143–144

Family Day Care Rating Scale (FDCRS), 96

Feedback, 78

Fidelity
definition of, 12
in evaluation, 12
of implementation, 176, 183, 207–219
in large-scale interventions, 208–217
measurement tool, 213*f*
program process, 207
to program structure, 207
threshold, 231

Financial resources, of work force, 50

Focus, broad, 178

Formative assessment, 10

Foundation for the Improvement of Education, 110

Frequency, of professional development, 176

From Neurons to Neighborhoods: The Science of Early Childhood Development, 69

Gap, school readiness, 138

Generalist/Early Childhood certificate, 68

Global measures, 189–190

Goals, of teachers, 151

Good Start, Grow Smart, 2, 138, 155, 221

Gradual Release of Responsibility Model, 112

Head Start, 2, 107

Head Start CIRCLE training program, 109

Head Start Quality Initiatives, 115

HeadsUp! Reading, 92

Higher education, quality of, 24

HighScope Literacy Curriculum, 109

Historical context of mentoring, 106–108

Human capital, 20–23

Implementation fidelity, 176, 183, 207

Implementation threshold, 231

Individualized learning, 160

Individualized professional development, 182

Induction, 70, 71*f*

Infant care
academic language in, 55

Infant care—*(continued)*
  adapting academic language in, 55
  attachment relationships and, 49
  book selection in, 54
  culturally responsive strategies in,
    55–56
  education of caregivers in, 49
  mentoring for caregivers in, 54
  professional development for, 53–54
  professionalism in, 54
  professionalization challenges in,
    54–59, 58*t*–59*t*
Infant/Toddler Environment Rating Scale-
    Revised (ITERS-R), 55, 60*f,* 95,
    130
Institute of Education Services, 90
Institute of Medicine, 69
Institutional barriers, 140
Intensity
  importance of, 175
  of professional development, 11–12,
    177–180
International Reading Association, 88–89
ITERS-R, *see* Infant/Toddler Environment
    Rating Scale-Revised

Language
  academic, 55
  stimulation of oral, 78
Language development, professional devel-
    opment specific to, 26–29, 27*t*–29*t*
Large-scale interventions, 208–217
LARS, *see* Literacy Activities Rating Scale
LEEP, *see* Literacy Environment
    Enrichment Program
Life stressors, of teachers, 50
Linn-Benton Community College, 138
Literacy
  in early education, 3–5
  importance of, 3
  principles of instruction, 3–4
  professional development and outcomes
    in, 26–29, 27*t*–29*t*
  professional development on instruction
    in, 5–6
  research on, 4–5
  research-based professional development
    and, 75–76
  socioeconomic status and, 4
  standards, 76
  of teachers, 8, 22–23, 52

Literacy Activities Rating Scale (LARS),
    114
Literacy Environment Enrichment
    Program (LEEP), 92, 223
Local cultural connection, 164

Maintenance stage, 59*t,* 113
Mathematics, professional development
    specific to outcomes in, 29–31,
    30*t*
Mentoring
  administrators and, 166–167
  agenda building and, 111
  barriers and, 226–227
  in California, 107
  coaching vs., 106
  community colleges and, 142–143
  emotional barriers and, 142
  facilitation and, 110
  gradual release of responsibility in, 112
  historical context of, 106–108
  for infant caregivers, 54–59
  maintenance stage of, 113
  mentors in, 108–110
  in multidimensional professional devel-
    opment, 113–116
  Partners in Quality program for,
    114–115
  preparation phase in, 56, 112
  relapse stage in, 113
  relationship building and, 110–111
  training and, 155–156
  transtheoretical model and, 111–113
Mentor-protégé relationship, 110–111
Midwest Child Care Research
    Consortium, 51
Mismatch, cultural, 52–53
Moderators, 182–184
MyTeachingPartner, 225

NAEYC, *see* National Association for the
    Education of Young Children
National Adult Literacy Assessment, 52
National Association for the Education of
    Young Children (NAEYC), 24, 68,
    69, 156
National Board For Teaching Standards,
    68
National Center for the Child Care
    Workforce, 107

National Council for the Accreditation of Teacher Education (NCATE), 24, 156

National Early Literacy Panel (NELP), 5, 75

National Education Association (NEA), 110

National Head Start Association (NHSA), 68

National Institute for Early Childhood Professional Development, 70

National Institute for Early Education Research (NIEER), 2, 3*t*

National Institute for Literacy, 75–76

National Research Council, 69, 73, 192–193

National Staff Development Council, 74, 106

NCATE, *see* National Council for the Accreditation of Teacher Education

NEA, *see* National Education Association

Needs, teacher, 159–160

Negotiation phase, of mentorship, 56

NELP, *see* National Early Literacy Panel

NHSA, *see* National Head Start Association

NIEER, *see* National Institute for Early Education Research

No Child Left Behind Act of 2001 (PL 107-110), 88, 107, 221

Nontraditional students, 52, 139

North Carolina Beginning Teacher Support Program, 78–79

North Carolina Early Learning Standards, 75, 76

North Carolina STAR Rating System, 68

Observation, in participatory action research, 124, 126

Observation Measure of Language and Literacy Instruction (OMLIT), 191–192

One-to-one coaching, 153

Ongoing training, 154

On-site coaching, 153

Oral language stimulation, 78

Orientation, professional, 51

Outcomes
professional development for specific, 26–32

review of, in participatory action research, 127–128

teacher quality and, 8

tracking of, in participatory social action research, 133–135

Pacing, 180

PALS Pre-K, *see* Phonological Awareness Literacy Scale for Prekindergarten

Participatory action research
action in, 126
bonding social capital and, 124, 127–128
bridging social capital and, 128–129
collaboration in, 124
cyclical change and, 131–132
observation in, 126
outcome review in, 127–128
planning in, 125–126
principles of, 123–124
reflection in, 125–126
social capital in, 124
social psychology and, 123–124
tracking outcomes in, 129–131
use of, 125–126

Partners in Quality mentoring program, 114–115

Passion, of teachers, 151

Peabody Picture Vocabulary Test–Third Edition (PPVT-III), 169

Performance, coaching and, 92–100

Periodicity, 181–182

Persistence, 176, 182–183

Personality matches, 183–184

Phonological awareness, 5, 78

Phonological Awareness Literacy Scale for Prekindergarten (PALS-Pre-K), 169

Planning, in participatory action research, 124, 125–126

Policy
early education, 2
evaluation and, 12
professional development and, 1
teacher quality and, 7–8

Poverty, *see* Socioeconomic status

PPVT-III, *see* Peabody Picture Vocabulary Test–Third Edition

Precontemplation stage, 58*t*, 112

Prekindergarten/Kindergarten Teacher Performance Appraisal Instrument, 79

Preparation phase, in mentorship, 56, 112
Preparation stage, 58*t*
Preschool Curriculum Evaluation Research
    grant program, 227
Print concepts, 5
Print knowledge, 5
Process fidelity, 207
Professional, definition of, 67
Professional development
    adult learners and, 25–26
    assessment and content of, 77–79
    challenges associated with, 51–53
    collective participation in, 38
    compliance and, 70, 71*f*, 176, 182–183
    confidence and, 53
    continuity of, 175
    coursework content in, 24–25
    cultural mismatch and, 53
    current conditions in, 70–72
    curriculum development and, 32–35
    curriculum in, 70, 71*f*
    delivery principles, 184–185
    depth of, 177
    dosage of, 11–12, 39, 175–176
    duration of, 176, 177–179
    early development setting quality and,
        32–37, 33*t*, 34*t*
    emotional development outcomes and,
        31–32
    engagement in, 182–183
    formats, 152–153
    frequency of, 176
    general approaches in, 35–37, 36*t*
    higher education quality and, 24
    human capital and, 20–23
    individualized, 182
    induction and, 70, 71*f*
    for infant caregivers, 49, 53–54
    intensity of, 11–12, 177–180
    language development outcomes and,
        26–29, 27*t*–29*t*
    for literacy instruction, 5–6
    literacy outcomes and, 26–29, 27*t*–29*t*
    mathematical skills outcomes and,
        29–31, 30*t*
    mentoring and, integration of, 113–116
    moderators, 183–184
    monitoring effects of, 39
    optimal amount of, 180
    organizational context and, 39
    pacing of, 180
    patterns in, 37–39
    periodicity in, 181–182
    persistence in, 176, 182–183
    policy and, 1
    practice as focus of, 38
    professionalization and, 73
    research-based content in, 72–73
    role of, 70–71
    schools, 152–153
    sequencing in, 180–181
    social capital and, 20–23
    social development outcomes and,
        31–32
    social support and, 70, 71*f*
    specific outcomes and, 26–32
    standards and, 73
    strengthening of providers of, 23–26
    target areas in, 20–37, 21*f*
    technology and, 8–9
    terminology, 175–177
    timing of, 176, 180–182
    web-based, 225–226
    well-being and, 23
    workshops, 152
Professional organizations, 68
Professional orientation, 51
Professionalization challenges, in infant
    care, 54–59, 58*t*–59*t*
Professions
    definition of, 67
    features of, 67–68
    guidelines and, 67
    qualifications in, 67
Program process fidelity, 207
Program structure fidelity, 207
Project Great Start, 208–217
Project REEL, 95–97, 97–100, 193–200
Providers, professional development,
    23–26
Psychological well-being, of teachers, 23, 50
Psychology, social, 123–124

Qualification, certification and, 222
Quality, teacher/caregiver
    educational attainment and, 22
    higher education and, 24
    measurement of, 8
    policy and, 7–8
    student outcomes and, 8
Quality Assist Inc., 114–115

Rapid automatic naming, 5
Readiness for change, 183

Readiness gap, 138
Reading, *see* Literacy
Reading readiness, 5
Ready to Learn curriculum, 178
REEL program, 95–97, 97–100, 193–201
Reflection, in participatory action
    research, 124, 125–126
Reflective coaching, 88
Relapse stage, 113
Relationship building, mentorship and,
    110–111
Relevancy, 74
Research
    current state of, 221–230
    early education, 2, 3*t*
    experimental, 123
    future, 230–234
    literacy, 4–5
    in professional development, 1
    rigor in, 125
    in training, 154–155
    see also Participatory action research
Research-based content, 68–70
Research-based practice, 71, 71*f*
Responsibility, gradual release of, 112
Rigor, in research, 123

Scaffolding, 224–225
Scholarship program, 223
School readiness gap, 138
Secondary education, *see* Community col-
    leges
Self-regulation, 67–68
Sequencing, 180–181
Setting diversity, 164
Settings, *see* Early education and care
Situational barriers, 140
Skills, discrete, 178
Social capital, 20–23
    bonding, 124, 127–128
    bridging, 124, 128–129
Social development, professional develop-
    ment specific to, 31–32
Social psychology, 123–124
Social support, 70, 71*f*
Socioeconomic status
    early education and, 2
    literacy and, 4
    vocabulary and, 4
Sources, content, 72–73
South Texas Early Childhood Professional
    Development Program, 165–171

Specialized training, 224
Stages of change, 58*t*–59*t*
Standards
    content and, 74–77
    language, 76
    literacy, 76
    professional development and, 73
    in training, 154–155
STEP, *see* Strategic Teacher Education
    Program
Stimulation, 78
Strategic Teacher Education Program
    (STEP), 107–108
Strategy Checklists, 193–200, 193*t*
Strengths, teacher, 159–160
Stressors, teacher, 50
Structure fidelity, 207
Structured coursework, 223
SUCCESS program, 94–95, 97–100,
    193–200
Summer prekindergarten academies,
    158–159
Support
    of directors and administrators, 166
    ongoing, 154
Sustainability, 232–233

T.E.A.C.H., *see* Teacher Education and
    Compensation Helps
Teacher Behavior Rating Scale, 77
Teacher Education and Compensation
    Helps (T.E.A.C.H.), 223
Teacher Knowledge Assessment, 228
Teachers and caregivers
    academic skills of, 51
    age of, 163–164
    backgrounds of, 49
    characteristics of, 50–51
    competencies of, 69–70
    cultural mismatch of, 52–53
    financial resources of, 50
    goals of, 151
    literacy of, 8, 22–23, 52
    needs of, 159–160
    as nontraditional students, 52
    passion of, 151
    professional orientation of, 51
    see also Quality, teacher/caregiver
Technology, professional development
    and, 8–9
TEMA, *see* Test of Early Mathematics
    Ability-Third Edition

Terminology, 175–177
Test de Vocabulario en Imagenes Peabody
    (TVIP), 169
Test of Applied Literacy Skills, 52
Test of Early Mathematics Ability-Third
    Edition (TEMA), 169
Threshold levels, 231
Time on task, 90
Timing, 176, 180–182
Title I, 2
Tracking outcomes, 129–131
Traditions, cultural, 55
Training
    administrator engagement and, 160
    C3 project for, 156–159
    competencies and, 224
    completion, 22
    curriculum aligned with, 227–228
    degree programs vs., 151
    educational context and, 155
    experts in, 154
    formats, 152–153

immediate needs of children and, 155
individualized learning and, 160
matching to needs in, 151
mentoring and, 155–156
ongoing, 154
quality components of, 153–156
research in, 154–155
schools, 152–153
specialized, 224
standards in, 154–155
workshops, 152
Transtheoretical Model (TTM), 57,
    111–113
TVIP, see Test de Vocabulario en Imagenes
    Peabody

Web-based programs, 225–226
Willingness to change, 183
Work force characteristics, 50–51
Workplace characteristics, 232
Workshops, 152